6th International Workshop on Computational Terminology (COMPUTERM 2020)

Marseille, France
11 – 16 May 2020

Editors:

Batrice Daille
Kyo Kageura
Ayla Rigouts Terryn

ISBN: 978-1-7138-1259-3

LREC 2020 Workshop
Language Resources and Evaluation Conference
11–16 May 2020

**6th International Workshop on Computational Terminology
(COMPUTERM 2020)**

PROCEEDINGS

Batrice Daille, Kyo Kageura, Ayla Rigouts Terryn (eds.)

Proceedings of the LREC 2020
6th International Workshop on Computational Terminology
(COMPUTERM 2020)

Edited by: Béatrice Daille, Kyo Kageura, and Ayla Rigouts Terryn

For more information:
European Language Resources Association (ELRA)
9 rue des Cordelières
75013, Paris
France
http://www.elra.info
Email: lrec@elda.org

Introduction

The aim of this sixth Computerm workshop is to bring together Natural Language Processing (NLP) and Human Language Technology researchers as well as terminology researchers and practitioners to discuss recent advances in computational terminology and its impact within automatic and human applications. This time we will also host a special session for the shared task TermEval, which uses the large manually annotated ACTER (Annotated Corpora for Term Extraction Research) dataset that covers multiple domains and languages.

Terminology has a unique status in language and communication. Theoretically, it is situated within the tension between the flexibility of natural language and the rigidity of artificial sign systems. Reflecting this theoretical status, terms are treated in a specific way in human language practice. In the technical translation pipeline, terms are not "translated" but relevant target language terms are looked up and used, as "mistranslation" can cause grave consequences. Many organisations, including such public institutions as the EU, WIPO and the NLM, and private LSPs, construct and maintain terminologies. Translation quality assurance schemes identify terminology-related issues as one of the focal checking points. Terminologies also provide important resources for education and knowledge transfer.

Although a substantial number of terms are linguistically categorized as so-called multiword expressions, the requirements and desiderata for handling terms as well as their status in language practice pipelines are different from most other multiword expressions such as idioms.

Computational terminology, if it is to make an *in vivo* contribution to the human communication ecosystem, needs to take into account this uniqueness of terminology at every stage of research, from defining problems to be solved and determining methods to be adopted, to developing evaluation schemes to be used.

In the four years since the 5th Workshop on Computational Terminology (Computerm 2016) was held, advancements in distributional representations and deep learning have changed, at least on the surface, the major NLP scene. What about terminology processing? This issue has yet to be fully explored or discussed. For instance, while Neural Machine Translation (NMT) has greatly improved target language fluency, it is sometimes reported that the quality of NMT is on a par with Statistical Machine Translation when it comes to the translation of terminology. Given the unique status of technical terms in communication and language practice, there is much for computational terminology to examine and explore in the face of the recent development of deep learning based NLP technologies, which may not necessarily be in the same line with most NLP tasks.

This workshop thus aims to investigate what deep learning has brought to computational terminology, its impact within human applications, and the new questions that it raises within the scope of terminology. With this in mind, Prof. Dr. Sabine Schulte im Walde (University of Stuttgart) was invited to highlight the new results achieved in modelling noun compound meaning in general and domain-specific language using such statistical methods.

We received 20 submissions, of which 15 are for the general session (9 long papers, 6 short papers) and 5 are for the shared Task TermEval (3 long papers, 2 short papers). We retained 15 papers: 6 long papers for oral presentation (acceptance rate: 30%), of which 4 belong to the general session and 2 to TermEval, and 9 papers for poster presentation (4 long papers and 5 short papers), of which 7 belong to the general session (4 long papers and 3 short papers) and 2 to TermEval (2 short papers).

The 6 long papers retained for oral presentations are the following:

Automatic Term Extraction from Newspaper Corpora: Making the Most of Specificity and Common Features Authors: Patrick Drouin, Jean-Benoît Morel and Marie-Claude L'Homme

TermPortal: A Workbench for Automatic Term Extraction from Icelandic Texts Authors: Steinþór Steingrímsson, Ágústa Þorbergsdóttir, Hjalti Danielsson and Gunnar Thor Ornolfsson

Translating Knowledge Representations with Monolingual Word Embeddings: the Case of a Thesaurus on Corporate Non-Financial Reporting Authors: Martín Quesada Zaragoza, Lianet Sepúlveda Torres and Jérôme Basdevant

Which Dependency Parser to Use for Distributional Semantics in a Specialized Domain? Authors: Pauline Brunet, Olivier Ferret and Ludovic Tanguy

TermEval 2020: Shared Task on Automatic Term Extraction Using the Annotated Corpora for Term Extraction Research (ACTER) Dataset Authors: Ayla Rigouts Terryn, Veronique Hoste, Patrick Drouin and Els Lefever

TermEval 2020: TALN-LS2N System for Automatic Term Extraction Authors: Amir Hazem, Mérieme Bouhandi, Florian Boudin and Beatrice Daille

While these workshop proceedings have been published as planned, the workshop itself could not take place due to the current global pandemic. It is currently postponed indefinitely and any updates about this situation will be posted on the workshop website: https://sites.google.com/view/computerm2020.

B. Daille, K. Kageura, A. Rigouts Terryn Computerm 2020 organizers

COMPUTERM Workshop Organizers:

    Béatrice Daille, LS2N, University of Nantes, France

    Kyo Kageura, Library and Information Science Laboratory, The University of Tokyo, Japan

    Ayla Rigouts Terryn, LT3 Language and Translation Technology Team, Ghent University, Belgium

TermEval Shared Task Organizers:

    Ayla Rigouts Terryn, LT3 Language and Translation Technology Team, Ghent University, Belgium

    Véronique Hoste, Ghent University, Belgium

    Patrick Drouin, OLST Observatoire de Linguistique Sens-Texte, Université de Montréal, Canada

    Els Lefever, LT3 Language and Translation Technology Team, Ghent University, Belgium

Program Committee:

    Ehsan Amjadian, University of Ottawa, Canada

    Lynne Bowker, University of Ottawa, Canada

    Patrick Drouin, University of Montréal, Canada

    Natalia Grabar, CNRS UMR 8163 STL, France

    Gregory Grefenstette, IHMC, USA

    Thierry Hamon, LIMSI-CNRS I& Université Paris 13, France

    Rejwanul Haque, Dublin City University, Ireland

    Geert Heyman, Nokia Bell Labs, Belgium

    Amir Hazem, LS2N, Université de Nantes, France

    Olga Kanishcheva, Kharkiv Polytechnic Institute, Ukraine

    Koen Kerremans, Vrije Universiteit Brussel, Belgium

    Marie-Claude L'Homme, University of Montréal, Canada

    Philippe Langlais, RALI, University of Montreal, Canada

    Thomas Lavergne, Université Paris-Saclay, CNRS, LIMSI, France

    Els Lefever, Gent University, Belgium

    Lieve Macken, Ghent University, Belgium

    Veronique Malaise, Elsevier BV, the Netherlands

    Ruslan Mitkov, University of Wolverhampton, UK

    Emmanuel Morin, LS2N, Université de Nantes, France

    Fleur Mougin, University Bordeaux, France

    Agnieszka Mykowiecka, IPIPAN, Poland

    Rogelio Nazar, University Pompeu Fabra, Spain

    Goran Nenadic, University of Manchester, UK

Carlos Periñán-Pascual, Universitat Politècnica de València, Spain

Selja Seppälä, University College Cork, Ireland

Min Song, Yonsei University, Korea

Koichi Takeuchi, Okayama University, Japan

Jorge Vivaldi Palatresi, University Pompeu Fabra, Spain

Leo Wanner, University Pompeu Fabra, Spain

Xiangqing Wei, Nanjing University, China

Pierre Zweigenbaum, LIMSI, France

Table of Contents

Proceedings of the 6th International Workshop on Computational Terminology (COMPUTERM 2020), pages 1–7
Language Resources and Evaluation Conference (LREC 2020), Marseille, 11–16 May 2020

Automatic Term Extraction from Newspaper Corpora: Making the Most of Specificity and Common Features

Patrick Drouin, Jean-Benoît Morel, Marie-Claude L'Homme
Observatoire de linguistique Sens-Texte (OLST)
Université de Montréal
C.P. 6128, succ. Centre-ville
Montréal (Québec) H3C 3J7 CANADA
{patrick.drouin, jean-benoit.morel, mc.lhomme}@umontreal.ca

Abstract

The first step of any terminological work is to setup a reliable, specialized corpus composed of documents written by specialists and then to apply automatic term extraction (ATE) methods to this corpus in order to retrieve a first list of potential terms. In this paper, the experiment we describe differs from this usual process. The corpus used for this study was built from newspaper articles retrieved from the Web using a short list of keywords. The general intuition on which this research is based is that ATE based corpus comparison techniques can be used to capture both similarities and dissimilarities between corpora. The former are exploited through a termhood measure and the latter through word embeddings. Our initial results were validated manually and show that combining a traditional ATE method that focuses on dissimilarities between corpora to newer methods that exploit similarities (more specifically distributional features of candidates) leads to promising results.
Keywords: terminology, automatic term extraction, unspecialized corpora

1. Introduction

The first step of any terminological work is to setup a reliable, specialized corpus composed of documents written by specialists. It is usually assumed that only domain-specific corpora compiled according to criteria defined by terminologists can represent good starting points for terminological description. This is especially true when relying on automatic term extraction (ATE) tools as the quality of the output is in direct relation to the quality of the input.

However, these "ideal" requirements are not always met in certain fields of knowledge. This is the case of the domain explored in this work, i.e. problematic behavior in the workplace. Its terminology can be disseminated in various forms of textual genres, including unspecialized corpora.

Extracting terminology from unspecialized corpora raises new challenges for ATE since most tools and methodologies are built around the assumption that the corpora being processed are specialized. Tools and methodologies thus tend to target features specific to this type of corpora. One efficient strategy for spotting domain-specific terms consists in comparing the behavior of the lexicon of a specialized corpus (an analysis corpus, AC) to the behavior of the lexicon in a general language corpus (a reference corpus, RC), thus exploiting the difference between text genres.

Such a technique has proved efficient for extracting relevant and interesting term candidates. One question remains however: Can we expect this comparison method to yield similar results when comparing corpora that belong to the same genre or when using an analysis corpus that is unspecialized? We believe that, although still useful, the method would need to be complemented with further processing.

This paper presents an automatic term extraction experiment carried out on a newspaper corpus that contains texts that address directly or indirectly the topic of discrimination. We first explore the results of a hybrid corpus comparison ATE experiment and propose new techniques in order to increase the precision of the results obtained. We believe that the proposed approach is useful to tackle ATE from unspecialized corpora and that the underlying ideas can be used for ATE in other situations.

2. The task

For the project described in this paper, we have been working with a private company (Valital[1]) whose core business is the real-time online analysis of job candidates behavior and the automated confirmation of their work experience. Their process digs into various sources of information with the aim of defining a textual profile for different kinds of misconduct in the workplace. Among these sources, are newspaper articles dealing with problematic behavior (e.g. violence, discrimination), but most articles do not concern the workplace as such. One of the tasks assigned to our team was to capture the terminological profile for each of these behaviors. This terminological profile was to be implemented in an ontology at a later stage.

From a terminological standpoint, newspaper articles are "atypical" textual sources since they are targeted at the general public. Even if these articles were automatically filtered according to the topic they address based on a short list of keywords, they may or may not concern the workplace as such. In other words, articles can report on a discrimination situation, but this situation could have taken place anywhere. The challenge in this case was to be able to locate relevant terms in an unspecialized corpus.

Our task involved an additional less typical aspect. The terminology related to misconduct includes various types of terms such as verbs (e.g. *discriminate*), adjectives (e.g. *discriminatory*) or single-word predicative nouns (e.g. *discrimination*). The term extraction method needed to be able to identify single-word terms and terms that belong to different parts of speech.

---

[1] https://www.valital.com

3. Related Work

Different methods were devised to identify terminology and such methods are now well-established and used for different applications (Indurkhya and Damerau, 2010). Automatic term extraction (ATE) methods are usually categorized as linguistic, statistical or hybrid. The first techniques rely on linguistic descriptions (grammars, dictionaries, surface patterns), while statistical methods rely on information like frequency and co-occurrence, etc. In the last 20 years, most tools use both statistical and linguistic information and fall into the hybrid category. The tools try to evaluate how interesting items extracted are for terminologists, leading to various methods for calculating *termhood* (Kageura and Umino, 1996). Among the three traditional categories, hybrid methods were evaluated as those that led to better results (Macken et al., 2013). But in the last few years, the research field of ATE has undergone profound changes. Progress in machine learning and more specifically in deep learning has lead to methodologies which cannot be easily described using the three traditional categories (Rigouts-Terryn et al., 2020). In this work, we will explore a traditional hybrid method that compares compora and combine it with more recent techniques such as word embeddings (Mikolov et al., 2013; Amjadian et al., 2016; Kucza et al., 2018; Qasemizadeh and Handschuh, 2014; Pollak et al., 2019). Our work is similar to (Hätty et al., 2019) as far as the method is concerned. However, our aim is to identify terms in unspecialized corpora. Given this, we cannot only target changes in meaning or reduction of number of attested meanings in a specialized corpus when compared to a general one. We take the opposite approach and attempt to spot potential meaning similarities to remove candidates that would be very similar regardless of the corpora.

An efficient method for ATE consists of comparing a domain-specific corpus (an analysis corpus, AC) to a general one (a reference corpus, RC) and computing a specificity score for lemmas. For instance, a corpus of English texts dealing with the topic of climate change can be compared to a general balanced corpus such as the British National Corpus. This method was implemented in TermoStat described in (Drouin, 2003). It was evaluated for the extraction of single-word terms with satisfactory results (Lemay et al., 2005) and supports multiple languages[2]. The concept of "specificity" aims to capture the potential of term candidates to behave like terms (termhood). In most cases, termhood is linked to a higher than expected frequency in a specialized corpus based on a theoretical frequency computed from a general corpus. Various statistical measures can be used to compute specificity.

When comparing corpora of different genres, terms ranking high retrieved from the AC usually correspond to terms. When the analysis corpus is less specialized (even if its content is topic-specific), it is to be expected that the strong opposition between corpora is lost. We can no longer focus on the single assumption that there is a high level of divergence in the way words behave in the AC and the RC as

in (Hätty et al., 2019). This work addresses this problem and suggests a method that could still make the most of the terminological content of the AC even if it belongs to a text genre that is the same or very similar to that of the RC.

4. Hypotheses

In this paper, we are dealing with corpora that belong to the same genre even though one of the corpora covers a broader spectrum of topics. Our hypotheses are:

- A traditional approach to ATE based on frequency comparison can still be used to locate relevant terminology. In other words, **the dissimilarity between the topics of the two corpora can still be exploited by an automatic term extraction method (Hypothesis 1).**

- However, given the fact that textual genres are quite similar, it is likely that a number of tokens will need to be filtered (probably more that usual). One strategy consists in using some of the features shared by both corpora to further refine term extraction. We can exploit the fact that some words have a similar behavior in the two corpora and use this feature to filter out the results obtained by simple corpus comparison. This method is likely to increase precision. However, in order to capture this behavior, we need to go beyond frequency measures and model semantic features in some way, e.g. using distributional information and word embeddings. Thus, **the similarities between the corpora are also useful and can be exploited with distributional analysis and word embeddings (Hypothesis 2).**

The main idea behind (1) is that, since our AC is limited to one topic, specificity can be used to retrieve term candidates (TC). In contrast, since both the AC and the RC are comparable from a text genre point of view, in (2) we want to capture the fact that some items that might be retrieved by the specificity carry *meanings* that do not contrast sharply with the ones they convey in general language corpora. In order to do so, we will compare word embeddings built from our AC and freely available prebuilt embeddings. This comparison will be used to filter out the results obtained based on (1).

5. Methodology

The overall process is illustrated in Figure 1. The regular approach to term extraction when comparing corpora is represented by the stages in light blue. The analysis and reference corpora are preprocessed; term extraction is performed using specificity scores; finally, term candidates are ranked according to the score they obtained. We are adding a layer (steps in light yellow) designed to compare word embeddings in order to re-rank the output produced by steps in blue.

5.1. Corpora

Basic preprocessing is applied to both the AC and the RC. All files from the corpora are tokenized, then tagged and lemmatized using TreeTagger (Schmid, 1994). The Treetagger format is used as a common input for subsequent tasks.

---

[2] `http://termostat.ling.umontreal.ca`, (Drouin, 2020)

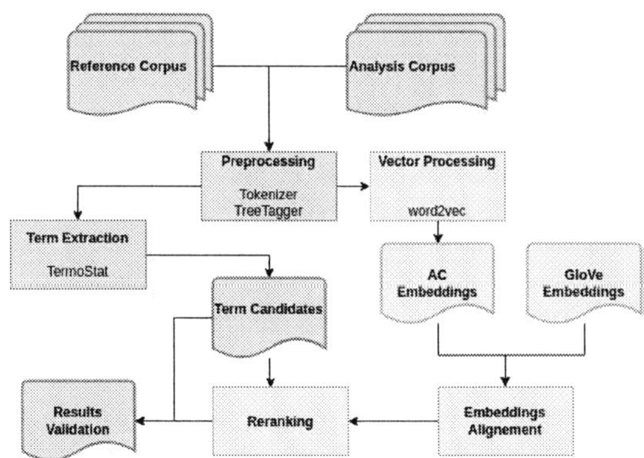

Figure 1: Overview of the process

	Reference Corpus	Specialized Corpus	Total
Freq. term	a	b	a+b
Freq. of other words	c	d	c+d
Total	a+c	b+d	N=a+b+c+d

Table 1: Contingency table of frequencies

5.1.1. Analysis Corpus

The corpus that was built by our partner comprises several text documents dealing with unwanted behavior from potential employees: *Addiction*, *Discrimination*, *Fraud*, *Harassment*, and *Violence*. It is important to mention that all files in the corpus were retrieved automatically from the web based on a short list of keywords related to each of these topics. All files come from online Canadian English newspapers and have been preprocessed to remove HTML markup. Since the crawling process was keyword based, the various corpora are noisy and thus do not lend themselves easily to standard term extraction process. In this work, we will focus solely on the Discrimination corpus as work on this topic is more advanced than for the other topics. The corpus contains 1,541,987 tokens.

5.1.2. Reference Corpus

The reference corpus used was built from subsets of two large corpora: the British National Corpus (BNC) (Consortium, 2007) and the American National Corpus (ANC) (Reppen et al., 2005). We extracted 4M tokens from each of these corpora in order to compile our 8M tokens reference corpus. In both cases, only newpaper texts were retrieved.

5.2. Term Extraction

The extraction process was limited to single-word lexical items including nouns, verbs and adjectives, since, as was mentioned above, important concepts in this field can be expressed with terms that belong to different parts of speech. TermoStat computes a *Specificity* score to represent how far the frequency in the specialized corpus deviates from a theoretical frequency. Its calculation relies on an approximation of the binomial distribution using standard normal distribution. In order to do so, a measure proposed by Lafon (1980) is used.

Using values from Table 1, specificity can be calculated as follows:

$$log\ P(X{=}b) = log\ (a{+}b)!\ +\ log\ (N{-}(a{+}b))!\ +\ log\ (b{+}d)!$$
$$+\ log\ (N{-}(b{+}d))!\ -\ log\ N!\ -\ log\ b!\ -\ log\ ((a{+}b){-}b)!\ -\ log$$
$$((b{+}d){-}b)!\ -\ log\ (N{-}(a{+}b){-}(b{+}d){+}b)!$$

This measure was tested in previous studies (Lemay et al., 2005; Drouin and Langlais, 2006; Drouin, 2006; Drouin

and Doll, 2008; Drouin et al., 2018) and leads to excellent results for the extraction of both single-word and multi-word terms. Specificity can be used to spot items that are both over- and under-represented in a corpus. In the case of terminology, a domain- and genre-oriented lexicon, we are solely interested in positive specificities which highlight items that are over-represented in the AC.

Since the specificity scores cannot be represented on a predefined scale, for the current experiment, we expressed them on a scale ranging from 0 to 1 where the max specificity score is mapped to 1. This mapping, which does not impact the overall distribution of scores, leads to a less granular representation of the scores and a more flexible set of scores to assess. The specificity score is used to test hypothesis 1.

5.3. Embeddings

5.3.1. Computed Word Embeddings

To build embeddings for our AC, we used the word2vec (Mikolov et al., 2013) implementation included in Gensim (Řehůřek and Sojka, 2010). We used default values for the skipgram algorithm with a window of 5 words, a minimum frequency threshold of 5 and 300 dimensions for the vectors.

5.3.2. Pre-trained Word Embeddings

To compare the behavior of tokens in a large unspecialized language corpus, we used the pre-trained word GloVe embeddings (Pennington et al., 2014). More specifically, we used the Common Crawl embeddings built from 42B tokens with a 1.9M vocabulary (uncased) and. The embeddings' vectors have 300 dimensions.

5.3.3. Alignment of Word Embeddings

Since our embeddings and the GloVe embeddings are built from different corpora and we want to be able to compare the vectors for words in both of them, the embeddings must be aligned. In order to do this, we used the technique proposed by (Hamilton et al., 2016) based on the code provided by Tyler Angert and available from his GitHub[3]. Such an approach is been used in (Hätty et al., 2019) to compare vectors between corpora for term extraction. During the alignment process, only the shared vocabulary[4] between embeddings is kept.

---

[3]https://gist.github.com/tangert/106822a0f56f8308db3f1d77be2c7942

[4]By *shared vocaulary*, we mean words that are common to both embeddings.

5.4. DistSpecificity

Words with similar behaviors in a large unspecialized corpus (Glove embeddings in our case) and our AC (our corpus built embeddings) are assumed to carry the same *meanings* based on the distributional features/patterns captured by the embeddings. From this idea we can use a simple cosine distance to compare vectors. Similar vectors will lead to cosine distance closer to 0 and dissimilar vectors to values closer to 1. We represent the distance using a score called GloveDist.

What is of interest to us is to lower the Specificity score for TCs whose distributional behavior is the same in both corpora. The rationale behind this strategy is that even though the Specificity score seems to indicate that TCs are valid terms, their overall *meaning* is the same. We thus factor this information in a new score called DistSpecificity which is used to test our hypothesis 2.

*DistSpecificity = GloveDist*Specificity*

Using this score, the Specificity score of a very specific TC that has almost the same distributional behavior in both corpora will be closer to 0 (since GloveDist will tend towards 0). On the other hand, a dissimilar behavior in both corpora will not impact Specificity as such (since GloveDist will have a value closer to 1).

5.5. Validation

All results were manually validated by a terminologist who has been involved in the project from the start. For the purpose of the current experiment, we are mainly interested in the potential of our score to rank valid terms at the top of the list of term candidates. Our manual validation was limited to the first 250 TCs retrieved using each of our three scores (Specificity, GloveDist and DistSpecificity) ranked from the highest to the lowest value. We thus validated a total of 750 TCs. As can be seen in Table 3, some TCs could appear in two or three lists.

The criteria used for the validation of TC were the following:

1. Terms must appear in contexts that are *meaningful* according to our task;

2. Terms must appear in at least 10 knowledge-rich contexts (KRC) (Meyer, 2001) related to *discrimination*;

3. TCs can also be considered terms if they hold syntagmatic or paradigmatic relations (e.g., as synonymy, antonymy or argumental) with already validated terms. (L'Homme, 2020).

What we define as a *meaningful* context (Criteria 1) is a context in which a misconduct is described. Even though some TCs could appear in an important number of contexts, we selected to base our study on KRCs only (Criteria 2). This methodological decision makes our validation process more challenging but our results more interesting.

The following sentence is a good example of a KRC for TCs such as *race* or *religion*: *In New York State, we have no tolerance for discrimination on the basis of race, religion, sex, national origin, disability, sexual orientation or perceived sexual orientation.* KRCs provide insights on how

TCs can be linked to each other in a specific domain. In this KRC, it shows us how *race* and *religion* can be linked to *discrimination* (also a TC) in our domain.

In addition to meeting the above-mentioned criteria, some TCs were also validated according to Criteria 3. For example, *anti-discriminatory* was labelled as a term on the basis of being an antonym for *discriminatory*; *woman* on the basis of being an argument of verbs such as *discriminate* or predicative nouns such as *discrimination*. Both TCs meet the other criteria as well.

The validation process was challenging due to the fact that often TCs did not convey a very technical meaning in the AC, i.e. a meaning that one could easily distinguish from general usage. Our approach was to consider TCs that were relevant according to the topic of discrimination and this "relevance" was constantly refined as we skimmed through the list of candidates.

TCs that met the previous criteria were labelled as *Term*; TCs that did not meet these criteria as *Non-Term*; and TCs that we had doubts about as *Uncertain* (see Tables 5 to 7).

6. Results and Discussion

As can be seen from the precision values in Table 2, ATE on unspecialized corpora is not a trivial process. We provide two precision measures for each score. Precision[1] is obtained by dividing the total number of valid TCs by 250 (the total in our lists) while Precision[2] corresponds to the number of valid TCs evaluated on the set of TC that we could validate (ignoring the TCs classified as Uncertain from the calculation). Values obtained by both measures are quite low, but not to the point of making the ATE extraction useless. Recall was not evaluated for this experiment since we do not have a gold standard that can be used and a manual evaluation of recall on newspaper corpora does not serve a larger purpose for the time being. The main issue with a task like the one we describe in this paper is still reaching acceptable precision values.

Score	Specificity	GloveDist	DistSpecificity
Term	145	106	135
Non-Term	87	128	97
Uncertain	18	16	18
Total	250	250	250
Precision[1]	0.58	0.42	0.54
Precision[2]	0.63	0.45	0.58

Table 2: Precision values for all 3 scores

Since we are more interested in the potential of each score to rank the valid information at the top of the list presented to the terminologist, we can evaluate precision at each position in the TC lists. This information is provided in Figure 2 which shows the precision values obtained by the three scores (Specificity, GloveDist and DistSpecificity) over the whole list. For these scores, entries identified as Uncertain were considered as errors, we are thus using the Precision[1]. We can easily see that GloveDist does not perform as expected. This means that using solely distributional information from a large unspecialized corpus as captured by GloVe embeddings and comparing them to our local vectors is not sufficient in itself. The distance between the vectors does not allow us to distinguish Terms from Non-Terms. Specificity presents a somewhat stable curve which means that valid TCs are distributed evenly along the list of 250 TCs. These results show that Specificity remains an interesting score to identify potential terms in unspecialized corpora by comparing them to larger unspecialized corpus. On the other hand, Figure 2 shows that it is not the best score to maximize valid TCs at the top of list.

As mentioned earlier, our DistSpecificity score combines both Specificity and GloveDist, the idea being to lower the importance of TCs that have a high Specificity but a similar behavior in both our corpora and the corpus used to build the GloVe embeddings. Figure 2 shows that this seems to be the case as precision values for DistSpecificity are higher for an important part of the list of TCs (until we reach candidate 165).

Spec	Status	DistSpecificity	Status
ms	Non-Term	ms	Non-Term
law	Term	read	Non-Term
woman	Term	employee	Term
newsletter	Non-Term	white	Term
lawsuit	Term	state	Term
story	Non-Term	law	Term
court	Term	file	Term
employee	Term	hide	Non-Term
subscribe	Non-Term	court	Term
photo	Non-Term	bill	Term
read	Non-Term	case	Term
state	Term	lawyer	Term
case	Term	justice	Term
lawyer	Term	complaint	Term
plaintiff	Term	religion	Term

Table 5: Top common TCs

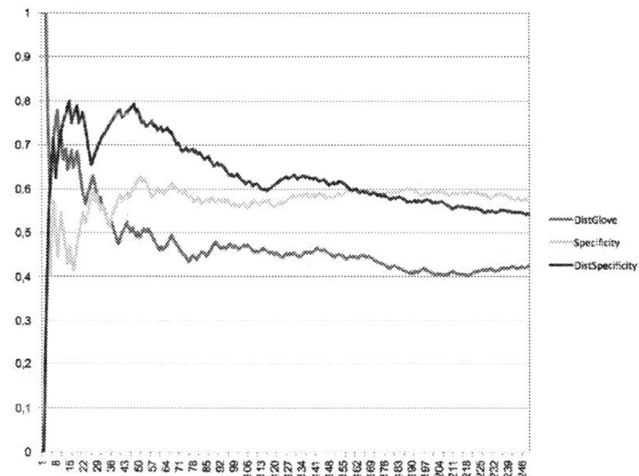

Figure 2: Overall precision of the scores

Table 3 details the contributions of each score. It shows that they share 60 common terms while bringing unique contributions to the overall list of TCs. However, Specificity locates more valid terms than GloveDist.

	Specificity	DistSpecificity
Common	60	60
Unique	84	75
Total	144	135

Table 3: Overall Contribution of Scores for Valid Terms

	Specificity	DistSpecificity
Common	50	50
Unique	47	47
Total	97	97

Table 4: Contribution of Scores for Valid Terms < 165

Nearly a third (30%) of the top 165 candidates are common to both scores, the top 15 can be seen in Table 5. One can clearly see by looking at the *Non-Terms* that the nature of the corpus had an inpact on the results. For example, items such as *ms, newsletter, subscribe, hide* can be attributed to the fact that the corpus was built from Web pages. The results at the top of the list for DistSpecificity are much better and contain terms relevant to the task at hand.

Spec	Status	DistSpecificity	Status
discrimination	Term	dismissal	Term
gender	Term	argument	Term
percent	Non-Term	argue	Term
update	Non-Term	politics	Term
advertisement	Non-Term	contend	Term
transgender	Term	person	uncertain
discriminate	Term	epithet	Term
right	Term	man	uncertain
emails	Non-Term	retaliate	Term
program	Non-Term	advertiser	Non-Term
verify	Non-Term	caste	Term
robot	Non-Term	city	Non-Term
minority	Term	engage	Term
sex	Term	request	Non-Term
disability	Term	resign	Term
hire	Term	asylum	Non-Term
racism	Term	noose	Term
ruling	Term	dissent	Non-Term
view	Non-Term	analyze	Non-Term
neighborhood	uncertain	officer	Non-Term

Table 6: Top unique TCs

Table 6 shows some of the unique contributions of the scores. Once again in this context we can oberve the influence of the nature of the corpus on the TCs retained: *advertisement, robot, view, request, verify, etc.*. Such TCs were again more present in the first TCs proposed by the Specificity score which means that DistSpecificity was, to some extent, succesfull in re-ranking them.

Table 7 contains the TCs that were most positively affected by the re-ranking. Although some results can be explained by the content of the documents that make up the corpus

Term	Status	Delta
flag	Non-Term	+184
buraku	Term	+180
enact	Term	+179
try	Non-Term	+159
be	Non-Term	+155
harass	Term	+149
department	Non-Term	+146
defendant	Term	+144
university	Non-Term	+143
accuse	Term	+142
gap	Term	+135
legislation	Term	+132
allege	Term	+123
ethnicity	Term	+123
remark	Term	+122

Table 7: Top positive re-ranking of Specificity by Dist-Specificity

(*university, department*), some are quite puzzling (*try, be*) and need to be investigated further. Since the AC is made of newspaper articles, academics who study the phenomenon of *discrimination* are often quoted and it explains the strong presence of the former in our corpus. However, it does not explain why their distributional features are so different in the two corpora. This will also be subjected to further investigation.

Term	Status	Delta
advocate	Term	-59
orientation	Term	-63
bias	Term	-71
bar	Term	-73
hate	Term	-73
subscribe	Non-Term	-75
promotion	Non-Term	-76
segregation	Term	-78
newsletter	Non-Term	-78
behavior	Term	-87
administration	Uncertain	-114
lawsuit	Term	-138
housing	Non-Term	-149
suit	Term	-165
click	Non-Term	-189

Table 8: Top negative re-ranking of Specificity by Dist-Specificity

At the other end of the spectrum are the results contained in Table 8 which include the TCs that have been negatively re-ranked by DistSpecificity. As we mentioned earlier, the good news is that this score is able to capture the fact that some TCs that are more closely related to the Web than the subject matter of the corpus and lower their termhood lowered (*click, promotion*, etc.). Nonetheless, some valid terms are being affected quite strongly while they should not be (*advocate, orientation, bias, bar*). In some cases

(*bar, hate, orientation*), it seems that polysemy can be a factor affecting the quality of the results.

7. Future Work

All experiment results were evaluated by a single terminologist and limited to the first 250 TCs provided by each score. Working with a larger sample and a team of validators would allow us to test inter-annotator agreement over a larger sample.

For the current task we limited our investigation to single-word TCs. We believe our findings could be applied to multiword TCs in order to see if we can corroborate the results obtained here. In order to do so, we would need to conduct an experiment using word embeddings that can capture distributional information from multiword TCs. Relying on more recent (and more complex) embeddings algorithms would also help to capture contexts in which TCs are used and perhaps mitigate the effects of polysemy observed in out results.

An interesting extension of the method presented here would be to apply it other genres of unspecialized corpora such as texts retrieved from social media. Some social platforms such as Twitter and Reddit host communities of specialists. These specialists exchange knowledge in informal settings and the terms carrying this knowledge should be described.

Provided that our results can be replicated in larger settings, integrating our method into the compilation process of terminological resources and into our term extraction tool would be beneficial.

8. Conclusion

In this paper we proposed a method for extracting terminology from unspecialized corpora. Our first hypothesis was that traditional corpus comparison techniques could be used in such a task in order to capture the dissimilarity between the topics of the two corpora. We have verified that this is the case and that the results of such a technique could still be used in terminology work although they are noisy. Our second hypothesis was that the similarities between the corpora are also useful and can be exploited with distributional analysis and word embeddings. To test our second hypothesis we devised a new way to re-rank TCs provided by a classic corpus comparison method in an effort to compare distributional features of TCs in our unspecialized corpus to those observed in a general langue corpus. Using this technique leads to very good results, as far as we could tell from the first part of a list of candidate terms. For terminologists, this method would allow them to focus on more relevant terms.

9. Acknowledgements

The authors would like to thank Valital for working with our team on this project and for the corpora they provided as well as IVADO (Institut de valorisation des données) [5] for making this possible through its financial support.

---

[5] https://ivado.ca/

10. Bibliographical References

Amjadian, E., Inkpen, D., Paribakht, T., and Faez, F. (2016). Local-Global Vectors to Improve Unigram Terminology Extraction. In *Proceedings of the 5th International Workshop on Computational Terminology*, pages 2–11, Osaka, Japan.

Drouin, P. and Doll, F. (2008). Quantifying termhood through corpus comparison. In *Terminology and Knowledge Engineering (TKE-2008)*, pages 191–206, Copenhague, Danemark, Août. Copenhagen Business School, Copenhagen, Copenhagen Business School, Copenhagen.

Drouin, P. and Langlais, P. (2006). Évaluation du potentiel terminologique de candidats termes. In *Actes des 8es Journées internationales d'Analyse statistique des Données Textuelles. (JADT 2006)*, pages 389–400, Besançon, France.

Drouin, P., L'Homme, M.-C., and Robichaud, B. (2018). Lexical profiling of environmental corpora. In Nicoletta Calzolari (Conference chair), et al., editors, *Proceedings of the Eleventh International Conference on Language Resources and Evaluation (LREC 2018)*, pages 3419–3425, Paris, France, May. European Language Resources Association (ELRA).

Drouin, P. (2003). Term extraction using non-technical corpora as a point of leverage. *Terminology*, 9(1):99–115.

Drouin, P. (2006). Termhood experiments: quantifying the relevance of candidate terms. *Modern Approaches to Terminological Theories and Applications*, 36:375–391.

Hamilton, W. L., Leskovec, J., and Jurafsky, D. (2016). Diachronic Word Embeddings Reveal Statistical Laws of Semantic Change. In *Proc. Assoc. Comput. Ling. (ACL)*.

Hätty, A., Schlechtweg, D., and Schulte im Walde, S. (2019). SURel: A gold standard for incorporating meaning shifts into term extraction. In *Proceedings of the Eighth Joint Conference on Lexical and Computational Semantics (*SEM 2019)*, pages 1–8, Minneapolis, Minnesota, June. Association for Computational Linguistics.

Indurkhya, N. and Damerau, F. (2010). *Handbook of Natural Language Processing, Second Edition*. Chapman & Hall/CRC machine learning & pattern recognition series. CRC Press.

Kageura, K. and Umino, B. (1996). Methods of automatic term recognition. *Terminology*, 3(2).259–289.

Kucza, M., Niehues, J., Zenkel, T., Waibel, A., and Stüker, S. (2018). Term Extraction via Neural Sequence Labeling a Comparative Evaluation of Strategies Using Recurrent Neural Networks. In *Interspeech 2018*, pages 2072–2076, Hyderabad, India, September. ISCA.

Lemay, C., L'Homme, M.-C., and Drouin, P. (2005). Two methods for extracting specific single-word terms from specialized corpora: Experimentation and evaluation. *International Journal of Corpus Linguistics*, 10(2):227–255.

L'Homme, M.-C. (2020). *Lexical Semantics for Terminology: An introduction*. John Benjamins.

Macken, L., Lefever, E., and Hoste, V. (2013). TExSIS: Bilingual Terminology Extraction from Parallel Corpora Using Chunk-based Alignment. *Terminology*, 19(1):1–30.

Meyer, I. (2001). Extracting knowledge-rich contexts for terminography. In Didier Bourigault, et al., editors, *Recent advances in computational terminology*, page 279. John Benjamins.

Mikolov, T., Sutskever, I., Chen, K., Corrado, G. S., and Dean, J. (2013). Distributed representations of words and phrases and their compositionality. In C. J. C. Burges, et al., editors, *Advances in Neural Information Processing Systems 26*, pages 3111–3119. Curran Associates, Inc.

Pennington, J., Socher, R., and Manning, C. D. (2014). Glove: Global vectors for word representation. In *Empirical Methods in Natural Language Processing (EMNLP)*, pages 1532–1543.

Pollak, S., Repar, A., Martinc, M., and Podpečan, V. (2019). Karst Exploration: Extracting Terms and Definitions from Karst Domain Corpus. In *Proceedings of eLex 2019*, pages 934–956, Sintra, Portugal.

Qasemizadeh, B. and Handschuh, S. (2014). Investigating Context Parameters in Technology Term Recognition. In *Proceedings of SADAATL 2014*, pages 1–10, Dublin, Ireland.

Řehůřek, R. and Sojka, P. (2010). Software Framework for Topic Modelling with Large Corpora. In *Proceedings of the LREC 2010 Workshop on New Challenges for NLP Frameworks*, pages 45–50, Valletta, Malta, May. ELRA. http://is.muni.cz/publication/884893/en.

Rigouts-Terryn, A., Drouin, P., Hoste, V., and Lefever, E. (2020). Termeval 2020: Shared task on automatic term extraction using the annotated corpora for term extraction research (acter) dataset. In *Proceedings of Computerm 2020*.

Schmid, H. (1994). Probabilistic part-of-speech tagging using decision trees. In *International Conference on New Methods in Language Processing*, pages 44–49, Manchester, UK.

11. Language Resource References

BNC Consortium. (2007). *British National Corpus, version 3 BNC XML edition*. British National Corpus Consortium, ISLRN 143-765-223-127-3.

Drouin, Patrick. (2020). *TermoStat 3.0*. http://termostat.ling.umontreal.ca.

Reppen, Randi and Ide, Nancy and Suderman, Keith. (2005). *American National Corpus (ANC) Second Release*. Linguistic Data Consortium, ISLRN 797-978-576-065-6.

Proceedings of the 6th International Workshop on Computational Terminology (COMPUTERM 2020), pages 8–16
Language Resources and Evaluation Conference (LREC 2020), Marseille, 11–16 May 2020

TermPortal: A Workbench for Automatic Term Extraction from Icelandic Texts

Hjalti Daníelsson[1,2], **Ágústa Þorbergsdóttir**[2] **Steinþór Steingrímsson**[2], **Gunnar Thor Örnólfsson**[2]
[1]University of Iceland
[2]The Árni Magnússon Institute for Icelandic Studies
hjaltid@hi.is, agusta.thorbergsdottir@arnastofnun.is,
steinthor.steingrimsson@arnastofnun.is, gunnar.thor.ornolfsson@arnastofnun.is

Abstract

Automatic term extraction (ATE) from texts is critical for effective terminology work in small speech communities. We present TermPortal, a workbench for terminology work in Iceland, featuring the first ATE system for Icelandic. The tool facilitates standardization in terminology work in Iceland, as it exports data in standard formats in order to streamline gathering and distribution of the material. In the project we focus on the domain of finance in order to do be able to fulfill the needs of an important and large field. We present a comprehensive survey amongst the most prominent organizations in that field, the results of which emphasize the need for a good, up-to-date and accessible termbank and the willingness to use terms in Icelandic. Furthermore we present the ATE tool for Icelandic, which uses a variety of methods and shows great potential with a recall rate of up to 95% and a high C-value, indicating that it competently finds term candidates that are important to the input text.

Keywords: terminology extraction, corpora, Icelandic

1. Introduction

Terminology extraction is the task of automatically extracting relevant terms from a given corpus. An up-to-date reliable termbase of systematically collected terms or term candidates from recent texts is of great importance to translators and users of translated texts. Such a tool can be very useful for standardizing vocabulary in specialized fields, which again is crucial for translation work, leading to increased translator productivity and helping to make new texts and translations more coherent and unambiguous.

Until now, terminology databases in Iceland have been constructed manually by experts in their subject fields. Termbases in more than 60 different fields have been created and made available online in Íðorðabankinn[1]. The Translation Centre of the Ministry for Foreign Affairs has also made their terminology database available online[2].

There are several downsides to manual collection of terminology. New terminology often takes a long time to reach publicly accessible termbases. Some of the collected terms may not see widespread use before being supplanted by newer or better-known ones, but nonetheless linger on in the termbase, increasing the risk of ambiguity unbeknownst to the termbase editors. In certain fields there may also be a lack of experts interested in doing the terminology work, making standardization of terminology even harder. Through the adoption of state-of-the-art methods for the automatic extraction of terms, new terminology can be made available much earlier in publicly accessible termbases, where it can facilitate more effective standardization. Editors can also more easily collect statistics about terminology use and cite real-world usage examples.

We present TermPortal, the first build of a workbench for semi-automatic collection of Icelandic terminologies. The workbench includes an automated terminology extraction tool that provides editors of terminologies with lists of new terminology candidates from relevant texts. For our initial version we focus on the acquisition of potential new terms, and the domain of finance. An emphasis on recall over precision allows us to potentially create a corpus with which to conduct future research. Meanwhile, since financial terminology is used in a variety of different texts, there is abundant data on which to try our system – a useful property both for developing our system and for learning about how difficult it is to automatically extract terminology from different texts.

There is also a great need for a continually updated termbase in this active field, as was confirmed in a thorough survey conducted at the start of the project. We describe the methodology for the survey and the results in Section 3, while the emphasis on term acquisition over term filtering is noted in Section 4.

TermPortal consists of two main pieces of software: One is the TermPortal workbench described in Section 4, which includes an automatic pipeline to extract terminology from media and a web platform where users can create, manage and maintain termbases. The other is the Automatic Term Extraction (ATE) system described in Section 5. It is a central component in the TermPortal workbench, but can also be used in isolation.

2. Related Work

TermPortal is not the first termbase management tool to offer ATE, although it is the first to support Icelandic.

2.1. ATE Management

Tilde Terminology[3] is a cloud-based terminology extraction and management tool based on the Terminology as a Service (TaaS) project (Gornostay and Vasiljevs, 2014). It allows users to upload monolingual documents and employs the CollTerm term extraction system (Pinnis et al., 2012) to extract term candidates, as well as offering various methods for automatic identification of translations for the candidates, such as lookup in EuroTermBank (Rirdance, 2006; Gornostaja et al., 2018) and parallel data that

---

[1]`http://idord.arnastofnun.is`
[2]`http://hugtakasafn.utn.stjr.is`

[3]`term.tilde.com`

Tilde have mined from the web. There are also several multilingual terminology workbenches available on the web. Terminologue[4] is an open-source cloud-based terminology management tool developed by Dublin City University. It is quite flexible and enables users to define the languages used in a given termbase, as well as employing a hierarchical structure for terminology domains. It also supports importing and exporting termbases in TBX format. A multitude of commercial solutions is also available. Among the solutions available are SDL MultiTerm, TermWiki and Termbases.eu.

In our work, we sacrifice some of the flexibility provided by workbenches such as Terminologue for the sake of making the process of extracting the terms themselves as straightforward and linear as possible. Much like in Tilde Terminology, we offer ATE as well as lookup in an existing termbank[5], but do not support term alignment between languages in the current version.

2.2. Automatic Extraction

While there are no studies on automatic extraction specifically for Icelandic, much less a particular domain such as finance, terminology extraction from monolingual corpora is a well-established field applying many different approaches. It can be said that there are two general approaches to automated terminology extraction from monolingual texts: statistical and rule-based. The rule-based methods commonly include tokenization, PoS-tagging, lemmatization, stemming and other common Natural Language Programming (NLP) approaches to linguistic analysis. A number of tools support these approaches for Icelandic texts: Some are multifunctional, such as Reynir (Þorsteinsson et al., 2019), and the IceNLP collection (Loftsson and Rögnvaldsson, 2007), while others are specialized in particular tasks: ABLTagger, a new BiLSTM PoS-tagger, has reached 95.17% accuracy for PoS-tagging Icelandic texts with a rich morphosyntactic tagset (Steingrímsson et al., 2019); and a recent lemmatization tool, Nefnir, has shown good results for lemmatizing Icelandic texts (Ingólfsdóttir et al., 2019). Some of these tools are employed in our extraction process.

In terminology extraction, linguistic features specific to an individual language are commonly used, in particular morphosyntactic information and discourse properties that distinguish noun phrases which are technical terms (Justeson and Katz, 1995). The statistical methods range from very basic approaches like counting the number of n-grams in a document to using statistical measures and recently word embeddings in neural networks. The use of statistical measures in automated term extraction can be governed by two aspects of terms, termhood and unithood, introduced by Kageura and Umino (1996). Termhood is considered to be "the degree to which a stable lexical unit is related to some domain-specific concepts", a notion closely related to a standard definition of a term. Meanwhile, unithood is "the degree of strength or stability of syntagmatic combinations and collocations". Certain methods can exploit both unit-

hood and termhood, the C-value introduced by Frantzi et al. (2000) being a common measure. Many successful systems, however, employ a hybrid approach, using linguistic features to limit the search space and then applying statistical filtering. See Vintar (2010) for an example of such an approach. More recently deep learning approaches have been tested, using word embeddings. Zhang et al. (2018) give an example of such a method, using word embeddings to compute 'semantic importance' scores for candidate terms, which are then used to revise the scores of candidate terms computed by a base algorithm using linguistic rules and statistical heuristics. Bilingual extraction is another approach to ATE. In contrast to monolingual extraction which is concerned with identifying terms in a corpus, bilingual extraction primarily deals with aligning terms in different languages. Recently some advances have been made in automatically extracting terms from comparable corpora using deep learning methods (Liu et al., 2018; Heyman et al., 2018). The general idea in these methods is to project word embeddings in both languages to a shared vector space. In our work, however, we focus on monolingual extraction.

3. The Survey

Given the apparent scarcity of up-to-date terminology databases in Iceland, the first part of our project was to examine the views domain specialists hold on terminology. More specifically, we wanted to investigate the perceived value of terminological data, the level of interest in the use, acquisition, and sharing of terminology, the quality of facilities currently employed for storage of term databases, and the level of importance assigned to instant access to current terminological data.

In order to be better able to deliver a useful system, we decided to work on only one domain for the first version of our system, the domain of finance. There were several reasons for the choice of this particular domain. While term collections in any domain require regular updates to prevent their obsolescence, Iceland's financial environment has changed extensively in recent times. The introduction of European directives alone has brought a host of new concepts to the field. Extant Icelandic terminology databases and dictionaries now contain a great number of deprecated, obsolete and superseded terms, making it even more difficult to find the correct Icelandic financial terms in what is already a relatively complex field for terminology.

By narrowing our focus we are also able to get a comprehensive view of the term usage and needs of a specific group. We therefore commissioned a survey on the subject of terminology within this domain, and submitted it to financial institutions, corporations, and translation agencies.

3.1. How the Survey was Formulated

The survey included questions on term-related issues, term cataloging, and opinions on terminology and term-related tasks, including the importance of terms in the workplace and the willingness to share collected terminology.

---

[4] www.terminologue.org

[5] The Icelandic Term Bank: https://idord.is, https://clarin.is/en/resources/termbank/

Question	Very High	High	Neutral	Low	Very Low	None
Importance of term translations	60.9%	21.7%	17.4%	0.0%	0.0%	0.0%
Interest in free access to a trustworthy termbank	69.7%	26.1%	0.0%	4.2%	0.0%	0.0%
Willingness to share terminology with others through a termbank	50.0%	22.7%	22.7%	0.0%	0.0%	4.5%
Willingness to take part in terminology work with others	27.3%	27.3%	36.3%	9.1%	0.0%	0.0%

Table 1: Questions in survey about interest in using and working towards a common termbase.

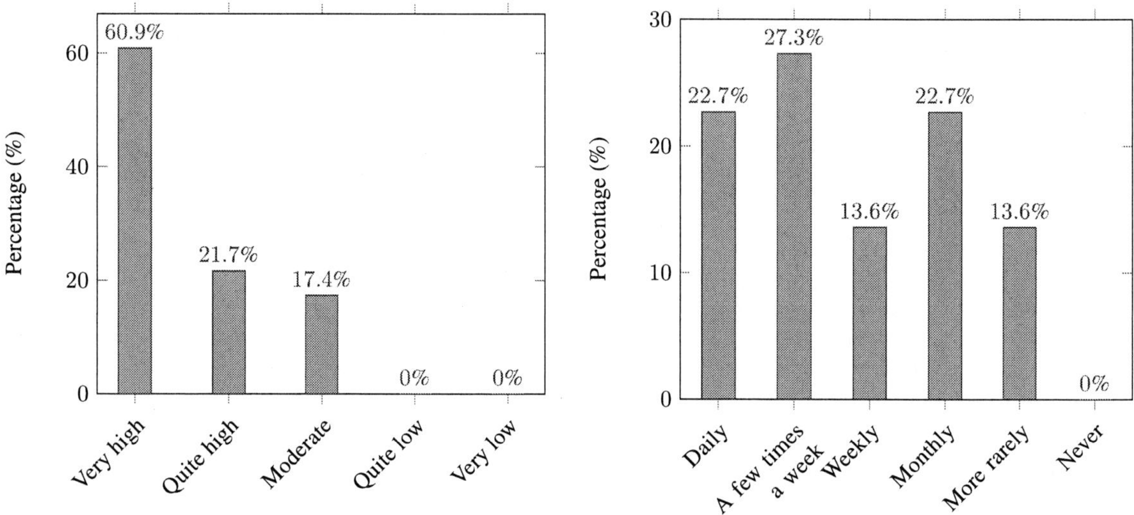

Figure 1: Are term translations of high or low importance?

Figure 3: How often do participants look up domain terms?

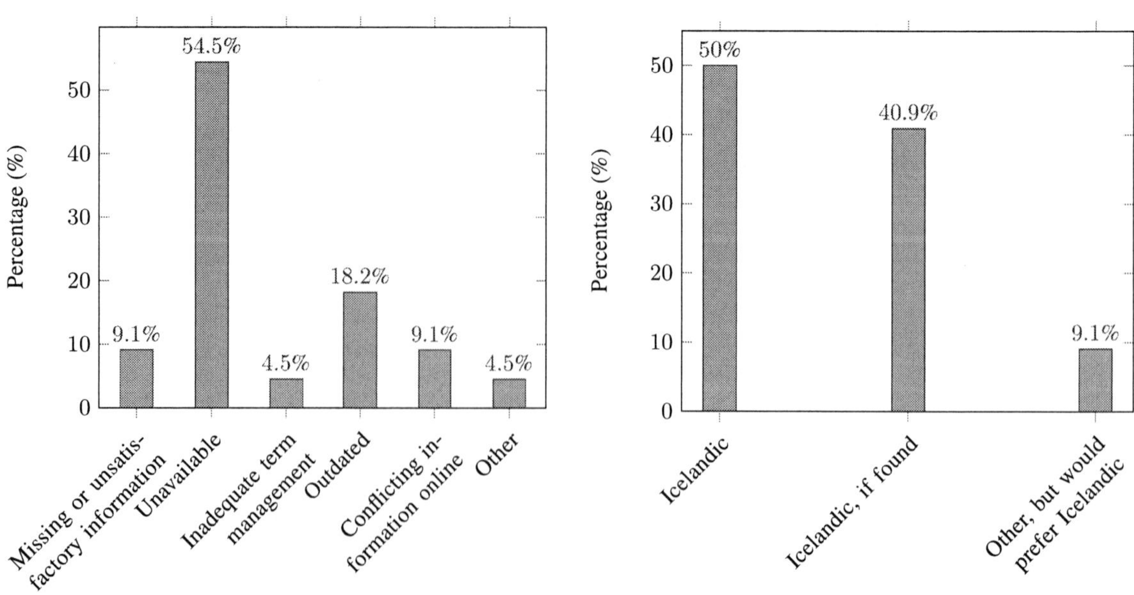

Figure 2: Most pressing issues related to terminology in the workplace.

Figure 4: What is the language of choice for terminology?

3.2. Survey Results

Since the subject matter was so clearly delineated – terminology within a single domain – the survey was only directed at the most prominent organizations in that particular field. For each participating organization, the survey was put to the single representative considered to have the most extensive experience and play the most significant role in that organization's approach to, and policies on, terminology. The number of invited participants was consequently kept fairly low, but was also estimated to represent those organizations that would have the greatest interest in the potential value of terminology within the field, and the most extensive abilities to deploy that terminology in everyday tasks. As a result, their opinions on the subject were considered highly relevant and extremely valuable. Out of the twenty-five invited organizations, twenty-three took part in the survey – a response rate which the survey conductors considered to be quite high and thus likely to result in more reliable survey results. Moreover, the conductors noted that the representatives' extensive experience within their respective organizations was likely to produce informed, thought-out answers that could be trusted to be truthful; even more so since the survey was anonymous and conducted through an intermediary rather than The Árni Magnússon Institute for Icelandic Studies directly. The only overt classification of participants was a grouping of answers into the three categories mentioned earlier: institutions, corporations and translation agencies.

Participants were asked sixteen questions. The results were decisive, and markedly in the terms' favor. Table 1 shows the responses to four of the questions, those concerning interest in using a common termbase and willingness to take part in building one. The survey participants see definite value in domain terminology with almost everyone in favor of free access to a trustworthy termbank and the majority interested or willing to take part in terminology work. Table 1 also displays a notable downward gradient among the percentage of responses in the Very High column: There is clear interest among participants in having access to high-quality terminology, but slightly less so in participating in information sharing with others (including potential competitors), and rather less so in devoting time and manpower of their own to create a terminology collection at all. Of the three types of participating organizations, translation agencies - which tend to have the smallest staff - were the ones with the lowest willingness to share their own data and take on additional work load. This puts The Árni Magnússon Institute for Icelandic Studies at an advantage, being an institute whose domain is separate from the survey participants and whose staff includes experts knowledgeable in this field: It indicates that if we were to lay the terminology groundwork by establishing TermPortal, we would have gotten past any major hurdles of cooperation from these participants, and could likely expect a higher willingness in active participation (such as through user testing) during future stages of the tool's development.

Access to terminology and term databases was deemed both of clear importance (see Figure 1) and, in its current form, severely lacking (see Figure 2). Also, even though the majority of respondents estimated that their staff look up domain terms weekly or more often (see Figure 3), most participants responded that no term registration whatsoever was performed within their organization. At the same time, a majority believed the most pressing issue related to terminology in the workplace was that up-to-date terms had not been collected and made available to all (see Figure 2).

This lack of availability of Icelandic-language collections, both for up-to-date terms and in general, was reinforced when the organizations were asked where their staff would look for assistance with translations of finance terminology. A majority responded that they would ask their coworkers, rather than look to online resources, specialists in the field or any other potential resource.

Attitudes toward Icelandic terminology in particular were predominantly positive. As evident from Figure 4, when asked about their chosen language for terminology, none of the participants explicitly said they preferred non-Icelandic terms and over 90% stated they used Icelandic terminology, either when available or exclusively.

These results clearly indicate the importance of easy and open access to up-to-date data. Indeed, the availability of Icelandic terminology may be seen as a vital precondition for clear and efficient communication in each field.

To be able to meet the needs of this influential user group, and other professional terminology users, exploring new ways of implementing terminology collection and storage was necessary. We need to look beyond the increasingly dated methods of manual termbase construction and try to simplify the process of preparing, storing, and sharing term glossaries. This will enable specialists in the field to focus on more productive endeavors than basic terminology work and make it easier to centralize that work. Our aim was that all potential users of Icelandic terminology, including field specialists and translators, would be able to spend less time hunting down possible term candidates, and instead could simply edit or approve listed candidates, ensuring greater consistency in terminology use, dissemination, standardization, and translation.

4. The TermPortal Workbench

The TermPortal workbench is an online terminology acquisition and management system. Authenticated users can create termbases and upload texts which are subsequently processed by the automatic term extraction (ATE) tool described in Section 5. After candidate terms are extracted, they are displayed alongside the source text. Selecting a term candidate highlights each of its occurrences in the text, allowing the user to quickly see the phrase in context. An example of this is shown in Figure 5. Furthermore, each occurrence's enveloping sentence is stored, for later use as usage examples.

Term candidates have five defined stages:

- Automatically extracted

- Rejected

- Manually entered / Accepted

- Reviewed

- Publishable

sem bendir til þess að samdráttur eftirspurnar hafi beinst í meiri mæli að innfluttri vöru og þjónust en búist var við.
Horfur eru hins vegar á meiri samdrætti á seinni hluta ársins en spáð var í ágúst sem fyrst og fremst má rekja til verulegs samdráttar í vöruútflutningi á þriðja ársfjórðungi. Þá eru vísbendingar um að hægt hafi á vexti einkaneyslu og að fjárfestingarútgjöld fyrirtækja verði minni en áður var talið. Spáð er að landsframleiðslan dragist saman um 0,2% í ár eins og í ágústspánni. Horfur fyrir næsta ár hafa hins vegar versnað. Nú er talið að hagvöxtur verði 1,6% á árinu í stað 1,9% og skýrir breytingin fyrst og fremst af lakari horfum um vöxt innlendrar eftirspurnar.
Samkvæmt vinnumarkaðskönnun Hagstofu Íslands fækkaði störfum um 0,4% milli ára á þriðja fjórðungi ársins – í fyrsta sinn síðan seint á árinu 2011. Atvinnuleysi mældist 3,7% og breyttist lítið milli fjórðunga en það var 0,6 prósentum meira en það var á fyrsta fjórðungi ársins, áður en WOW Air féll. Talið er að starfandi fækki enn frekar á fjórða ársfjórðungi og að atvinnuleysi eigi eftir að aukast og ná hámarki í ríflega 4% áður en það minnkar aftur er líður á næsta ár. Á sama tíma tekur slakinn í þjóðarbúinu sem myndaðist um mitt þetta ár að minnka á ný og spáð er að nýting framleiðsluþátta verði kominn á eðlilegt stig undir lok næsta árs.
Verðbólga var við 2,5% verðbólgumarkmið bankans fram eftir síðasta ári en jókst í kjölfar lækkuna á gengi krónunnar þá um haustið.
Eftir að verðbólga náði hámarki í 3,7% í desember sl. hefur hún smám saman hjaðnað á ný og var

Figure 5: A term candidate highlighted in context in the TermPortal workbench.

At this stage the user can either accept or reject the term candidate. Rejected term candidates will be hidden from future ATE results for that termbase, but can be viewed separately and recovered.

The tool extracts term candidates and makes note of each candidate's occurrences in the source text, highlighting them on command. Users can then choose whether to accept or reject each of the term candidates provided by said tool. Accepted candidates are added to the active termbase, and can be further processed, adding definitions, references to related terms and translations. Lists of fully or partially processed terms can be exported in standard formats such as TBX[6] and CSV[7], enabling easy integration of those termbases into other systems which conform to those standards. In addition to supporting exportation of termbases, users can share them with other users with varying privileges.

- *Owners*, or co-owners have full privileges over the termbase, including giving other users privileges and general termbase administration in addition to managing the terms within the termbase. The user who creates a termbase is by default its owner.

- *Editors* have privileges over terms and texts within the termbase, but not the termbase itself. Their privileges include uploading and processing texts, accepting or rejecting term candidates, and modifying term entries.

- *Reviewers* can supply commentary on terms which have previously been accepted by *editors* or *owners*. They also have rights to mark terms as 'reviewed'.

- *Viewers* have view-only rights to the termbase and no edit privileges.

Until now, no publicly available workbench designed for terminology work in Icelandic has existed, meaning that editors for each domain set their own individual workflows and standards, which can cause difficulty when termbases

are combined and centralized. A standardized work environment for terminology collection will enforce homogeneity in termbase structure between subject areas, facilitating easy termbase compilation. Interactive use of the ATE component turns the complex task of identifying new terms into a sequence of binary questions, greatly simplifying the workflow of termbase editors and potentially increasing productivity.

5. Automatic Term Extraction

The ATE tool lies at the heart of the TermPortal workbench. It accepts input in the form of Icelandic text, processes the text in order to find possible candidates, calculates the candidates' term likelihoods, and outputs a sorted list of those terms it deems most likely to be heretofore unseen terms within a given domain.

As noted, this is the first tool of its kind to support Icelandic, and terminology databases have until now been constructed by hand. As a result, our focus was on maximizing the tool's ability to gather potential new terminology and create a sizable initial database suitable for further computerized work and research. Accordingly, term recall was considered to be of primary importance, and was heavily emphasized over precision during the tool's development. Fine-tuning precision will be part of future work on TermPortal.

5.1. Data Preparation

Although the ultimate goal of the ATE tool is to be capable of handling texts from any domain, we initially focus on the financial sector as we do in other parts of the project. This means that we sourced testing data solely from that particular field. The data came in two forms: Randomly selected texts originating from various sources in the financial sector, primarily laws, regulations, reports, and educational materials; and known finance terms listed in the aforementioned terminology database compiled by the Translation Centre of the Ministry for Foreign Affairs (see Section 1). While the random compilation of the general texts – some of which carry confidentiality clauses – makes it impractical to publish them as datasets, all the known finance terms may be accessed through the Ministry's website, which allows content filtering according to subject area.

---

[6]ISO 30042:2019
[7]RFC 4180

Test Set	Random Clauses	Known Terms	Total
1	250	250	500
2	500	500	1,000
3	1,000	1,000	2,000
4	2,000	2,000	4,000

Table 2: The four test sets.

In order to evaluate the tool, we created four text files that combined these two types of data. Each file contained one sentence or clause per line and had an equal ratio between lines of random clauses and lines of known terms. The smallest file of 500 lines thus contained 250 random clauses and an additional 250 known terms; and with each test set the file size doubled, as shown in Table 2. During each test, one of these files served as the program's main input. Alongside that file, we provided the tool with two others: A unique list of just over 2,000 known finance terms, in lemmatized form, whose contents did not overlap with the terms added to the input file, and a list of 280 grammatical category patterns that corresponded to all known financial terms. Each entry in the pattern list contained an ordered sequence of grammatical tags, such as ('a', 'v', 'n'), corresponding to ('adjective', 'verb', 'noun'). In section 5.3 we describe how these patterns are used to identify potential term candidates in the program's input.

5.2. Methods for term extraction

In choosing our methods, we needed to consider certain constraints while trying to provide maximum coverage. The Icelandic language is morphosyntactically rich, with a relatively free sentence word order, high inflectional complexity, and a high ratio of compound words, all of which affect the linguistic aspects of term extraction (Bjarnadóttir et al., 2019). Moreover, while we focused on the financial sector during development, the ATE tool needed to be domain-agnostic by design and be able to run without any prior training, which already eliminates a host of options. Lastly, certain supplementary data, in the form of known terms and stop-words from that domain, might be available at times but could not be a prerequisite. As a result of these factors, we implemented three methods of term extraction, all of which are applied to input that the tool has already lemmatized.

The first method is C-value (Frantzi et al., 2000), modified to include single-word terms (Barrón-Cedeno et al., 2009). This is likely one of the best-known term search methods in existence. It is language- and domain-independent, does not require any information other than the text input itself, and relies on the kind of linguistic preprocessing (i.e. tagging and category filtering) that would likely always be incorporated by any ATE tool when applied to Icelandic texts. The second method, which we term the 'stem ratio', is one we created specifically for this particular project, and is intended to take advantage of the high number of compound words in Icelandic while remaining unaffected by the issue of multiple potential word orders. When applying this method, the ATE tool employs a separate program called

Kvistur, which decompounds Icelandic words (Daðason and Bjarnadóttir, 2015). Icelandic compounds are morphologically right-headed (Bjarnadóttir, 2017), so through Kvistur the ATE tool analyzes the morphological structure of the words contained within each term candidate, extracts all rightmost stems, and compares them to all rightmost stems found in known candidates. If the total number of all the stems in the words of a given candidate is A, and the total number of those same stems in the entirety of known candidates is B, the stem ratio for that candidate is A/B. (Candidates with no compound words are simply not assigned stem ratios.) Hence, the more common that a candidate's morphological heads are within known terms, the higher its stem ratio will be. A candidate with a high stem ratio shares a great deal of both morphological structure and meaning with existing terms, and is itself thus likely to be a new term. It should be noted that Icelandic is a fairly complex language; as such, we will constrain our discussion of ATE methods to ways in which this particular project was implemented, since any further details would require a separate chapter unto themselves.

The third method is Levenshtein-distance, which in our context is the minimum number of single-character edits required to change one string into another. The Levenshtein algorithm is comparatively straightforward, well supported in Python, and has been used or considered for ATE (Nazarenko and Zargayouna, 2009; Droppo and Acero, 2010) and other term-extraction-type projects in the past (Runkler and Bezdek, 2000). For each candidate, we find the lowest possible Levenshtein-distance between it and any known term. The lower this value is, the more the candidate resembles a known term letter-for-letter, irrespective of factors such as multiple inflections or morphosyntactic structures.

Overall, these three methods cover a wide range of possible terms. The C-value finds those candidates that are clearly important to the input itself, in terms of their unithood and termhood. The stem ratio finds any candidates – generally lengthy and complex ones – whose composition, structure and meaningful parts bear clear resemblance to existing terms, even when the less-meaningful parts may be completely dissimilar. Lastly, Levenshtein-distance takes a much rawer approach and finds those candidates – here generally ones that are short or contain simple words – which simply resemble known ones in terms of spelling, and which might otherwise be overlooked by the stem ratio. It should be noted that since the latter two methods rely on comparisons to the list of known terms, they will not be adversely affected by candidates' low frequencies of occurrence in the input – but they do require an actual list of terms in order to work at all. In addition, variations on all three approaches are certainly possible, but for the most part we decided to refrain from complicating our algorithms until we'd compiled a solid database of terms for further testing; the one exception being a slight change to C-value calculations to account for single-word terms (Barrón-Cedeno et al., 2009).

Linguistic Processing Tool	Set size	C-value	L-distance	S-ratio	Recall (%)
ABLTagger + Nefnir		1.744	7.080	22.746	80.00
Reynir	500	1.820	7.676	23.554	92.80
ABLTagger + Nefnir		1.735	6.903	22.930	83.20
Reynir	1,000	1.773	7.247	23.031	92.40
ABLTagger + Nefnir		2.115	6.883	20.254	84.90
Reynir	2,000	2.238	7.315	20.342	89.60
ABLTagger + Nefnir		2.433	7.101	19.538	89.35
Reynir	4,000	2.501	7.421	20.041	89.00

Table 3: Average values for ATE methods across linguistic processors for all data sets. Threshold values not applied.

5.3. Usage

The tool is divided into the following four sections, which run sequentially: Preprocessing, linguistic processing, statistical processing, and output.

During preprocessing, the tool checks what data is being supplied – the main input and a list of category patterns are mandatory for every activation, while a list of known terms and a separate list of stop words (not used in our tests) are optional – and loads any comparison data into memory. If a list of known terms is included, its contents are expected to be in lemmatized form for comparison purposes, although if need be the ATE tool itself is capable of lemmatizing the list's contents by using the linguistic support programs detailed below. If the tool is provided with such a list it will also, through the aforementioned program Kvistur, compile an additional list containing the compound word heads of all known terms.

In the linguistic section, the tool reviews one line at a time, and tokenizes, tags and lemmatizes it. There are two primary ways in which the tagging and lemmatization may be done, decided on by the tool's administrator: Through the Reynir[8] Python package (Þorsteinsson et al., 2019), or through the tagger ABLTagger[9] (Steingrímsson et al., 2019) and lemmatizer Nefnir[10] (Ingólfsdóttir et al., 2019). For a language as morphologically rich as Icelandic, we felt it necessary to have more than one processing option, although it should be stated that our purpose is not to compare the programs themselves – the primary notable difference is that Reynir automatically performs a more exhaustive and thus more time-consuming analysis. At the end of this section, each line has been converted to a sequence of tuples, where each tuple contains a single, now lemmatized word from the phrase, and a corresponding tag for that word's grammatical category.

One last function serves as a bridge to the statistical section: Before the ATE tool applies any of the three extraction methods, it compares each tuple sequence against every single entry in the list of grammatical category patterns known to represent known terms. Any continuous part of the sequence that matches a known grammatical word pattern is automatically added to the list of term candidates. The extraction methods – C-value, stem ratio and Levenshtein-distance – are then calculated for every entry on that candidate list.

In the output section, the tool prepares the list for use by subsequent parts of TermPortal. The tool also includes threshold values that may be set for each of the three methods, in which case every candidate will have to meet at least one of the thresholds (if applicable, since not all methods are necessarily being applied each time) in order to remain on the candidate list at all. ATE programs generally require specialist input when the final term lists are reviewed. As such, these threshold values help keep the output manageable, particularly while the tool's focus is still on recall.

5.4. Evaluation

In a project of this nature – where the ATE tool will be applied to an input of continuously changing size and content, rather than a predetermined corpus – the primary focus of evaluation is whether the tool demonstrably works against test inputs of, again, varied sizes and content: If it can properly parse the input, compare it against known terms, find the majority of candidates we know to be present, and display sensible statistical values over a spectrum of different inputs. This effectively means we wanted to measure its recall of the candidates we had intentionally inserted. As noted earlier, measuring precision, on the other hand, was not considered a priority at this stage of development. For a similar reason, we do not focus on narrowing the threshold values during this initial run; rather, we expect to continually adjust them once the TermPortal is actively receiving live data and compiling terminology. Instead, we want to see if the values are being applied in a consistent manner during these initial runs.

The results from our four datasets were consistent and promising, as may be seen in Table 3. Therein, we see the results of applying the two linguistic processing methods and subsequently the three statistical processing methods (C-value, Levenshtein-distance and Stem ratio) to the four data sets described in Table 2 (in each case, the terms being measured for recall were removed from the list of known terms that the program used to calculate Levenshtein-distance and Stem ratio). The lowest recall percentage, 80.0%, resulted from the smallest dataset when parsed by ABLTagger and Nefnir, while Reynir had 92.8% on that same dataset. Larger datasets increased overall recall for ABLTagger and Nefnir with both models, reaching 89.35% on the largest set, while Reynir's lowest recall dipped only to 89.0% with that same set. As may be seen, once the amount of input reaches a particular threshold, the

[8]https://pypi.org/project/reynir
[9]https://github.com/steinst/ABLTagger
[10]https://github.com/jonfd/Nefnir

recall rates between the two processing options tend to converge.

Averages for the values calculated by the statistical methods – C-value, Levenshtein-distance and stem ratio – were assigned to every possible candidate, not merely the ones on our recall list, and were highly consistent across both linguistic options for every dataset. The highest difference in averages was 0.123 for C-value in the 2,000-line set, 0.596 for Levenshtein-distance in the 500-line set, and 0.808 for stem ratio in the 500-line set.

Lastly, it should be noted that between them, these linguistic processing tools collectively managed impressive recall. In fact, out of the 2,000 known terms we inserted into the largest dataset, only 100 failed to be acknowledged at all. Given that many of the financial terms contain complex words that may at times be quite dissimilar from most text that the linguistic programs were trained on or programmed to recognize, a collective 95% recall rate – meaning that in at least one of the two processing options, the words were correctly tokenized, tagged, lemmatized, matched to known grammatical category patterns, and passed on for value calculation – is a highly positive result. As noted earlier, the two options offer differing depths of linguistic processing, with the associated increase in workload and processing time. As such, Reynir is likely to be used more often on shorter texts, particularly if a more thorough approach is required, while ABLTagger and Nefnir are the preferred choice for processing greater volumes of incoming text at a reasonable pace.

6.   Availability and licensing

The TermPortal is in closed testing. It will be open for use for all parties interested in undertaking terminological work in Iceland, running on servers at The Árni Magnússon Institute for Icelandic Studies[11]. The ATE tool is available under an open Apache 2.0 license.

7.   Conclusion and Future Work

We have presented TermPortal, a workbench for terminology work using an automated term extraction tool, adapted to Icelandic and the domain of finance. The automatic term extraction tool, built for the workbench, shows promising results with a recall rate of up to 95%. The workbench and the ATE tool show great potential in answering the needs of industry, as manifested in a survey we conducted among the most prominent user group, which shows great interest in improving the state of affairs in Icelandic terminology work within the field of finance.

We have implemented approaches to term extraction suitable to data at hand. As more data accrues we expect to develop a far more robust test set than the one used for our initial tests. This will permit greater granularity of test results, along with variations such as testing other term ratios than 50/50 in the program's input. Other future work may include using deep learning approaches, such as word embeddings and bilingual extraction where parallel data is available. To improve the workbench, prospective users will be involved in testing and the resulting feedback used

to help adapt the system even further to the needs of users. Users are also expected to help test the quality of our term databases, with an eye toward improving the precision with which the ATE tool collects new terms. Furthermore, user testing will yield precision statistics for the ATE tool, enabling us to tweak the parameters of the system to give a good balance of precision and recall.

8.   Bibliographical References

Barrón-Cedeno, A., Sierra, G., Drouin, P., and Ananiadou, S. (2009). An improved automatic term recognition method for Spanish. In *International Conference on Intelligent Text Processing and Computational Linguistics*, pages 125–136. Springer.

Bjarnadóttir, K., Hlynsdóttir, K. I., and Steingrímsson, S. (2019). DIM: The Database of Icelandic Morphology. In *Proceedings of the 22nd Nordic Conference on Computational Linguistics*, NODALIDA 2019, Turku, Finland.

Bjarnadóttir, K. (2017). Phrasal compounds in modern Icelandic with reference to Icelandic word formation in general. In *Further investigations into the nature of phrasal compounding*, pages 13–48. Language Science Press, Berlin.

Daðason, J. F. and Bjarnadóttir, K. (2015). Kvistur: Vélræn stofnhlutagreining samsettra orða. *Orð og tunga*, 17:115–132.

Droppo, J. and Acero, A. (2010). Context dependent phonetic string edit distance for automatic speech recognition. In *2010 IEEE International Conference on Acoustics, Speech and Signal Processing*, pages 4358–4361. IEEE.

Frantzi, K. T., Ananiadou, S., and Mima, H. (2000). Automatic recognition of multi-word terms:. the C-value/NC-value method. *International Journal on Digital Libraries*, 3:115–130.

Gornostaja, T., Auksoriūtė, A., Dahlberg, S., Domeij, R., van Dorrestein, M., Hallberg, K., Henriksen, L., Kallas, J., Krek, S., Lagzdiņš, A., et al. (2018). eTranslation TermBank: stimulating the collection of terminological resources for automated translation. In *Proceedings of the XVIII EURALEX International Congress*, EURALEX 2018, Ljubljana, Slovenia.

Gornostay, T. and Vasiljevs, A. (2014). Terminology resources and terminology work benefit from cloud services. In *Proceedings of the Ninth International Conference on Language Resources and Evaluation*, LREC 2014, Reykjavik, Iceland.

Heyman, G., Vulic, I., and Moens, M.-F. (2018). A deep learning approach to bilingual lexicon induction in the biomedical domain. In *BMC Bioinformatics*.

Ingólfsdóttir, S. L., Loftsson, H., Daðason, J. F., and Bjarnadóttir, K. (2019). Nefnir: A high accuracy lemmatizer for Icelandic. In *Proceedings of the 22nd Nordic Conference on Computational Linguistics*, NODALIDA 2019, Turku, Finland.

Justeson, J. S. and Katz, S. M. (1995). Technical terminology: some linguistic properties and an algorithm for identification in text. *Natural Language Engineering*, 1:9–27.

Kageura, K. and Umino, B. (1996). Methods of automatic term recognition: A review.

Liu, J., Morin, E., and Saldarriaga, S. P. (2018). Towards a unified framework for bilingual terminology extraction of single-word and multi-word terms. In *Proceedings of the 27th International Conference on Computational Linguistics*, COLING 2018, Santa Fe, New Mexico.

Loftsson, H. and Rögnvaldsson, E. (2007). IceNLP: A Natural Language Processing Toolkit for Icelandic. In *Proceedings of Interspeech – Speech and language technology for less-resourced languages*, Interspeech 2007, Antwerp, Belgium.

Nazarenko, A. and Zargayouna, H. (2009). Evaluating term extraction.

Þorsteinsson, V., Óladóttir, H., and Loftsson, H. (2019). A wide-coverage context-free grammar for Icelandic and an accompanying parsing system. In *Proceedings of the International Conference on Recent Advances in Natural Language Processing (RANLP 2019)*, pages 1397–1404.

Pinnis, M., Ljubešic, N., Stefanescu, D., Skadina, I., Tadic, M., and Gornostay, T. (2012). Term extraction, tagging, and mapping tools for under-resourced languages. In *Proceedings of the 10th Conference on Terminology and Knowledge Engineering*, TKE 2012, Madrid, Spain.

Rirdance, S. (2006). *Towards Consolidation of European Terminology Resources: Experience and Recommendations from EuroTermBank Project*. Tilde.

Runkler, T. A. and Bezdek, J. C. (2000). Automatic keyword extraction with relational clustering and Levenshtein distances. In *Ninth IEEE International Conference on Fuzzy Systems. FUZZ-IEEE 2000 (Cat. No. 00CH37063)*, volume 2, pages 636–640. IEEE.

Steingrímsson, S., Kárason, Ö., and Loftsson, H. (2019). Augmenting a BiLSTM tagger with a morphological lexicon and a lexical category identification step. In *Proceedings of Recent Advances in Natural Language Processing*, RANLP 2019, Varna, Bulgaria.

Vintar, S. (2010). Bilingual term recognition revisited: the bag-of-equivalents term alignment approach and its evaluation. *Terminology*, 16:141–158.

Zhang, Z., Gao, J., and Ciravegna, F. (2018). SemRe-Rank: Improving automatic term extraction by incorporating semantic relatedness with personalised PageRank. *TKDD*, 12:57:1–57:41.

Proceedings of the 6th International Workshop on Computational Terminology (COMPUTERM 2020), pages 17–25
Language Resources and Evaluation Conference (LREC 2020), Marseille, 11–16 May 2020

Translating Knowledge Representations with Monolingual Word Embeddings: the Case of a Thesaurus on Corporate Non-Financial Reporting

Martín Quesada Zaragoza, Lianet Sepúlveda Torres, Jérôme Basdevant
Datamaran
Valencia, Spain
{martin, lianet, jerome}@datamaran.com

Abstract

A common method of structuring information extracted from textual data is using a knowledge model (e.g. a thesaurus) to organise the information semantically. Creating and managing a knowledge model is already a costly task in terms of human effort, not to mention making it multilingual. Multilingual knowledge modelling is a common problem for both transnational organisations and organisations providing text analytics that want to analyse information in more than one language. Many organisations tend to develop their language resources first in one language (often English). When it comes to analysing data sources in other languages, either a lot of effort has to be invested in recreating the same knowledge base in a different language or the data itself has to be translated into the language of the knowledge model. In this paper, we propose an unsupervised method to automatically induce a given thesaurus into another language using only comparable monolingual corpora. The aim of this proposal is to employ cross-lingual word embeddings to map the set of topics in an already-existing English thesaurus into Spanish. With this in mind, we describe different approaches to generate the Spanish thesaurus terms and offer an extrinsic evaluation by using the obtained thesaurus, which covers non-financial topics in a multi-label document classification task, and we compare the results across these approaches.
Keywords: thesaurus, cross-lingual word embeddings, bilingual lexicon induction, English, Spanish

1. Introduction

Corporate Social Responsibility (CSR) is a concept that aims to understand, categorise, monitor and regulate the actions of corporations regarding environmental, social, governance (ESG) and technological issues. Following Fontaine (Fontaine, 2013), one of the primary goals of CSR is to encourage corporations to engage in responsible behaviour when it comes to these issues (amongst others). CSR has become extremely relevant in the past decade. Customers, stakeholders and investors have increasingly begun to demand a robust integration of sustainable development practices into the wider business model - making sustainability a financially material issue. A growing number of policies and regulations, both voluntary and otherwise, have pushed companies towards public disclosure of non-financial (i.e. ESG) information in annual reports or stand-alone documents. The latest KPMG Survey of Corporate Responsibility Reporting (KPMG, 2017) indicates that 93% of the 250 largest companies by revenue (based on the Fortune Global 500 2016 index) have adopted non-financial reporting (NFR).

These corporate-derived disclosures are not the only factor to consider. The media, which informs about corporations and how they tackle ESG issues, is also a player when it comes to shaping discourse. Individuals, too, share on social media networks their views about organisations and sustainability. All these sources are relatively unstructured (i.e., they are only organised as natural language) textual data. As data scientists, we need to know what information we want to extract and how to organise it in a meaningful way if we want to gain insights and provide evidence for a data-driven decision making process. The sources that we are working with in this paper are courtesy of Datamaran, an ESG focused machine learning platform designed for material analysis of these issues. Datamaran already has an English-language thesaurus built to classify and structure data, which has been manually created and maintained by experts in sustainability matters. It covers over 100 topics and amounts to more than 6000 terms in an ongoing effort that has so far spanned over five years. However, analysing sources in English is only a part of the picture. If we really want to know what is happening in Spain or Latin America, we will need to be able to analyse texts in Spanish.

There are basically two options when it comes to annotating Spanish-language data:

1. to translate all the texts in Spanish into English and use our English thesaurus and pipeline to annotate the information in English, or

2. to create a thesaurus in Spanish so we can analyse texts in Spanish.

The first option seems at a glance to be the easiest and fastest solution. However, using a third-party translation API at scale is very expensive. Training your own Machine Translation (MT) model is not trivial, especially if you aim to translate from low-resource languages. The crux of the issue is to obtain appropriate machine-training data.

Manually creating a thesaurus in Spanish (or in any other language) would allow us to avoid the challenge of accurately translating large amounts of data. However, it would require finding experts in the field with command of the target language, or human translators with extensive ESG knowledge, and going through the process of terminology management and validation. This would be quite costly and slow. However, there is a valid option here if by substituting the thesaurus into our system, we can use the same automatic procedure to analyse text.

Our approach is based on using word embedding and cross-lingual mapping techniques in order to obtain seeds of terms for the Spanish thesaurus that correspond to the English thesaurus terms. Bearing this in mind, we evaluate the Artetxe et al. (2019) proposal, excluding the exposed unsupervised tuning procedure over the bilingual phrase table extracted from the cross-lingual mapping. Our primary objective is to obtain a mapping between the topics mentioned in English and Spanish. For that, we propose a set of heuristics to generate more terms in Spanish using the initial terms extracted from the cross-lingual mapping. The novelties of this proposal are: (i) an extrinsic evaluation of the Artetxe et al. (2019) approach on a multi-label document classification task and (ii) the creation of metrics to validate the quality of our results.

In Section 2. we provide an overview of the different approaches to solve the problem of analysing texts in a target language using a thesaurus in a different language. Next, we present the datasets used, we describe the experiments and the proposed heuristics in Section 3. The evaluation methodology is presented in Section 4.1. Later, we examine the results of the experiments and comment them in Section 5. Finally, we conclude with a summary of what we have learnt and remarks on future work in Section 6.

2. Related Work

Cross-lingual word embedding (CLE) techniques have raised and experienced rapid growth over the past few years, aided by the developments around neural word embeddings such as Word2vec (Mikolov et al., 2013a). Word embeddings are already a popular tool to induce bilingual lexicon, as continuous word embedding spaces exhibit similar structures across languages, even when considering distant language pairs (Mikolov et al., 2013b). Cross-lingual word embedding methods exploit these similarities to generate a common representation space that allows transferring information between two languages. Although early CLE techniques relied on partial parallel data, mapping-based CLE approaches only require seed translation dictionaries (Mikolov et al., 2013b; Faruqui and Dyer, 2014; Gardner et al., 2015) or no bilingual information at all (Artetxe et al., 2018a; Lample et al., 2018). The latter are especially effective in low-resource languages (Ruder et al., 2017) or specific domains. CLE facilitates a number of tasks that can benefit greatly from this unsupervised approach, one of which is bilingual lexicon induction (BLI).

Traditional BLI techniques extract word translations from monolingual corpora through a variety of monolingual distributional similarity metrics, such as orthographic, contextual and temporal similarity metrics to discover equivalent words in different languages (Haghighi et al., 2008; Knight, 2002). The popularity of CLE has encouraged research in applying both techniques together in order to induce a bilingual dictionary capable of obtaining successful results (Zhou et al., 2019; Søgaard et al., 2018a).

In this proposal we intend to use this latter BLI approach to generate a new thesaurus in a target language from a preexisting thesaurus in a different source language. We already possess an English thesaurus that groups a set of related lexical terms into topics or labels. For example, *acid rain, air contamination, air emission, air pollutant, air quality* are some of the terms grouped under the topic *Air Emissions*. Our main objective is to induce the English groups of terms that constitute each topic into Spanish, thus maintaining a topic alignment for both languages, but not necessarily a direct term equivalence.

Previous work on multilingual thesaurus alignment has already taken advantage of the structural correspondence between word embeddings in different languages and the semantic information that they offer to outperform alignment methods based on string similarity metrics (Gromann and Declerck, 2018). Our proposal further exploits these characteristics through the CLE mapping method VecMap (Artetxe et al., 2018a). VecMap is currently one of the most effective unsupervised CLE approaches, both in terms of BLI and cross-lingual document classification performance (Glavas et al., 2019). We chose this cross-lingual word embedding mapping method because of its performance and ease of use, as all of its code is publicly available and it works over the very common Word2vec toolkits. The method allows us to generate a new thesaurus in the Spanish language from a preexisting English thesaurus whilst avoiding any need for bilingual parallel data. To map the different labels or topics of our original thesaurus into another language, we translate each of their terms using a bilingual dictionary induced from a common representation space, according to the procedure described in Artetxe et al. (2018b). This cross-lingual space was previously generated from two monolingual word embeddings, following Artetxe et al. (2018a). We employ fastText (Bojanowski et al., 2016) to train the monolingual word embeddings. FastText is a Word2vec implementation that also captures sub-word information (Mikolov et al., 2013a). Unlike Word2vec, which trains the embedding considering the word as the smallest unit in a corpus, fastText learns word vectors at the character level of each word, which has a higher memory and time cost when compared to Word2vec. However, it is generally accepted that fastText performs better than Word2vec with out of vocabulary words, as it considers terms that do not appear in the training corpus.

Although more recent work introduces synthetic Statistical Machine Translation (SMT) and Neural Machine Translation (NMT) models in order to generate sensible multi-word translation from a common representation space (Artetxe et al., 2019), we instead introduce some heuristics that perform adequately in the described thesaurus translation task and simplify the overall application of the method.

Unsupervised CLE tasks often prove to be hard to evaluate, especially when no manual standard exists for the downstream task at hand. In this proposal, we also offer a multi-label document classification evaluation method based on the annotation of a given parallel corpus that can be generalised to different thesauri.

3. Methodology

Our main objective is to use a cross-lingual word embedding and a thesaurus in a source language to generate a thesaurus in a target language without relying on parallel data. The source embeddings can be trained exclusively with data extracted from our ongoing analysis tasks, which is already available, easy to obtain and closely matches the characteristics of the information that will be analysed in the actual downstream use of the translated thesaurus. In this section we will describe the particular features of the knowledge base used in the application of this method, as well as characterise the bilingual lexicon induction techniques applied and our evaluation strategies. Finally, we propose an optimisation strategy for manual validation applied to the translated thesaurus.

3.1. Thesaurus

In order to structure the non-financial information, a thesaurus in English has been manually created by experts in sustainability matters. The thesaurus is a formal specification of concepts related to 100 NFR disclosure topics. For example, *air pollutant, air pollution, dust emission* are some of the concepts covering the topic *Air Emissions*. Our terms are both words or multi-word expressions and there are a significant quantity of noun phrases.

The thesaurus groups into topics more than 6000 terms in an ongoing effort that spans over five years. The terms of the thesaurus are expressed as lexical patterns to build a knowledge base of a matching algorithm responsible to automatically detect the mention of topics in different textual resources.

The patterns were created using the spaCy NLP library (Honnibal and Johnson, 2015). spaCy provides a rule-based matching feature that scans the text at token level according to some predefined patterns. These patterns are built considering some word-level features such as lemmatization, parts-of-speech, dependency parser and others. The matching algorithm compares the token attributes, specified by the pattern, with the attribute of the token in the input text to match or not the sequence. See below examples of the patterns we used.

```
[
{"LOWER" : "dust"}, {"LOWER" : "emission"},
{"LOWER" : "diesel"}, { "LOWER" : "emissions"},
{"LOWER" : "air"}, {"LOWER" : "pollutant"}
]
```

In the above patterns, each element inside the square brackets represents one or more words that should appear consecutively. Each element inside the curly brackets represents a token. The *LOWER: diesel* means that we want to match a word whose lower form is *diesel*. For example, any of the following sequences will be annotated with the second pattern: *diesel emissions or DIESEL Emissions or Diesel emissions*.

Due to a lack of a Spanish thesaurus, we initially considered different alternatives to extract topics from Spanish texts: (1) maintaining a parallel thesaurus between source and target languages, which is a non-scalable process and required experts in target language; (2) using a Commercial Machine Translation System to translate the Spanish text into English. Although using a translation service seems a technically sound solution with adequate quality results, it is not financially feasible; or (3) training our own MT model, which requires too much effort and is also very costly. As a result, we moved on to BLI techniques to derive a Spanish thesaurus.

3.2. Building monolingual embeddings

To generate embeddings that can be used in the CLE method that we have selected for our translation purpose, we need two monolingual datasets: one in the source language in which our original thesaurus was built and another in the target language to which we want to migrate the said thesaurus. We apply lowercase and tokenization to both datasets, with which we then train two fastText embeddings with default hyperparameters and limiting the vocabulary to the 200,000 most frequent tokens as per Artetxe et al. (2019), although any Word2vec-based toolkit should suffice. The English and Spanish spaCy models were used to apply lowercase and to tokenize the datasets in both languages.

3.3. CLE method

To obtain an inducted bilingual dictionary from monolingual data, we recreated the VecMap projection-based CLE method (Artetxe et al., 2018a) using the word embeddings mentioned in the previous section and mapped them into a shared space. We then extracted a source-to-target and target-to-source-phrase table using the technique described in Artetxe et al. (2018b).

A bilingual dictionary is directly induced from the source-to-target phrase-table by ranking the entries of a given term according to their corresponding likelihood in the phrase-table, thus transforming the quantitative ranking of the phrase-table into a bilingual dictionary with positional ranking. Figure 1 shows a fragment of the phrase-table obtained for the English term *market* and its Spanish candidate translations. Terms with higher likelihood will appear first in the entry for *market* in the induced bilingual dictionary dictionary.

This dictionary is used to translate the terms that make up our thesaurus. This approach maintains equivalence between source and target at the token level. However, many of the thesaurus terms are multi-word expressions. To cover this limitation and in order to build sensible combinations using the translated words, some heuristics are considered. As a result, token-level equivalence is often ignored.

3.4. Heuristics to generate terms in the target language

Using the cross-mapping embeddings we obtain a bilingual dictionary containing exclusively unigrams, which means that some techniques have to be applied in order to translate multi-word terms. In this section, we will outline several heuristic techniques that are applied to increase the coverage of the first bilingual dictionary. These heuristics use the phrase-table to generate new terms.

Literal translation Multi-word expressions are translated term by term, maintaining their original structure. The chosen translation for each word is the first-ranked one in the bilingual dictionary, or a special symbol if there is no possible translation for that term. This is the crudest possible form of translation using a bilingual unigram dictionary, and

```
              English-Spanish phrase-table: market
market ||| mercado |||  1.3001774277654476e-05 1.6413794583059916e-05 0.001 0.001
market ||| cotizadas |||  1.1253831871727016e-05 1.4111649761616718e-05 0.001 0.001
market ||| segmento |||  1.1057323717977852e-05 1.3955321264802478e-05 0.001 0.001
market ||| volatilidades |||  1.0948665476462338e-05 1.3841265172231942e-05 0.001 0.001
market ||| alzas |||  1.0891376405197661e-05 1.3713594853470568e-05 0.001 0.001
market ||| repuntan |||  1.0761069461295847e-05 1.3223184396338183e-05 0.001 0.001
market ||| múltiplo |||  1.0691576790122781e-05 1.3163543371774722e-05 0.001 0.001
...
market bilingual dictionary: {market:
                mercado, cotizadas, segmento, volatilidades, alzas ...
                }
```

Figure 1: Fragment of market phrase-table and its candidate translations

19

Source language corpus	Target language corpus	Mean reciprocal rank
108,000 English news	84,000 Spanish news	0.093
220,000 English news	260,000 Spanish news	0.107

Table 1: Mean Reciprocal Rank that evaluates a bilingual dictionary against the full English to Spanish bilingual dictionary found in MUSE (Lample et al., 2018).

it serves as the baseline for all other heuristic approaches to building expressions. For example, for the English term **diesel emissions**, the literal translation that is obtained is *diesel emisiones*, which can be represented as the following pattern:

[{"LOWER" : "emisiones"},{ "LOWER" : "diésel"}]

Permutations Expressions are first translated term by term, after which all of their possible permutations are added into the thesaurus. In languages that do not share a very similar grammatical structure, translating the expressions maintaining their original order may produce incorrect sentences. Moreover, this technique may help capture all possible variations in languages that present a flexible word order, such as Romance languages, Hungarian, etc. See below an example of the pattern obtained for the English term **diesel emissions** after obtaining its literal translation in Spanish and applying the permutation heuristic explained in this paragraph.

[{ "LOWER" : "diésel"},{"LOWER" : "emisiones"}]

Lemmatized terms with permutations All terms are translated in their original order, then lemmatized. Finally, like in the previous case, every possible permutation is considered. We lemmatize all terms in an attempt to reduce the variability that morphologically rich languages (that commonly also have a rather flexible word order) might bring, which is often a source of problems for unsupervised bilingual dictionary induction methods, as per Søgaard et al. (2018b). The following example shows the patterns generated using the current heuristic.

[
{"LEMMA" : "emisión"},{ "LEMMA" : "diésel"},
{ "LEMMA" : "diésel"},{"LEMMA" : "emisión"}
]

Lemmatized terms with permutations and wildcard inclusion We use the same setup as in the aforementioned approach, but adding a wildcard match before and after every word with the intent of boosting the coverage of the annotation. The longest possible match for each wildcard is selected, where the match can contain multiple tokens, and its sequence within the analysed text is no longer eligible for new matches. That is, we avoid overlap between different term matches. This logic might reduce the overall precision of the system, since overlap between the terms belonging to different labels is possible. We chose to operate in this manner to preserve the structure of our original thesaurus, as it does not present any overlaps between the terms of different labels. See below an example of one of the patterns generated adding the wildcard heuristic.

[
{"LEMMA" : "emisión"}, { "OP" : "*", "IS_ALPHA" : true}, {"LEMMA" : "diésel"}
]

Figure 2: Topic Workforce changes (WFChges) mentioned in an English Europarl sentence

4. Experimental settings

4.1. Data

The corpora necessary to build the initial monolingual word embeddings were generated using a preexisting collection of news articles from different online sources that are used in the Datamaran platform[1]. We chose to build these embeddings from news corpora because the English thesaurus that we intend to translate is used within Datamaran to analyse the content of online news, which would also be the purpose of this new translated Spanish thesaurus. Therefore, the domain of the corpora from which the monolingual word embeddings are built matches that of the text analysed in the downstream application of our system. The contents of the employed corpora are detailed below:

- Source language corpus, which contains 220,000 English news published during 2019, and more than 137,000,000 tokens.

- Target language corpus, composed by 260,000 Spanish news that appeared in online press during 2018-2019, containing around 118,000,000 tokens.

To validate the quality of the generated Spanish thesaurus we proposed a multi-label document classification task, that will be explained in Section 4.2.2. For that purpose, Version 7 of the English-Spanish Europarl corpus (Koehn, 2005) was used, as it contains a sufficient amount of terminology included in our particular thesaurus (datasets with very sparse annotation would not be very informative). Figure 2 shows an English sentence extracted form the Europarl corpus that mentioned the topic Workforce changes[2] (WFChges).

The Europarl corpus contains documents published on the European Parliament's official website, therefore it does not belong to the same domain as the corpus used to build the embeddings, which is a corpus of the news domain. This ensures that the performance obtained in the evaluation task

---

[1] https://www.datamaran.com/

[2] References to variation in number of people employed by an entity. Includes changes due to restructuring. E.g. reorganisations, turnover rates, outsourcing.

Translation Method	Phrase composition heuristic	Precision	Recall	KLD
VecMac (Artetxe et al., 2018a)	Literal translation	0.3871	0.2505	5.1149
VecMac (Artetxe et al., 2018a)	Permutations	0.5295	0.4590	1.6293
VecMac (Artetxe et al., 2018a)	Permutations and lemmatization	0.4236	0.5045	1.2235
VecMac (Artetxe et al., 2018a)	Permutations, lemmatization and wildcards	0.4580	0.6976	0.8027
Commercial Machine Translation System	None (the whole document is translated)	0.8209	0.8005	0.0233

Table 2: Multi-label document classification comparison over the parallel corpus Europarl for the English-Spanish pair. The embeddings used for the CLE approach (VecMap) were built from the corpora detailed in 4.1. Validation metrics at thesaurus level.

never surpasses what would be achieved when operating over a dataset that closely matched the information used to generate the embeddings, thus providing a pessimistic estimation for the effectiveness of the evaluated translated thesaurus. We find this property desirable, as it allows us to estimate the quality of the translation in the worst cases with a higher confidence level. Additionally, it can reveal faulty translations that could go undetected in a corpus of the same domain because of context similarities. For instance, the term "typhoons" is translated as "aviones" ("airplanes") in the bilingual dictionary generated with the techniques detailed in 3.3. using the aforementioned datasets. This could be because in news about typhoons it is usually mentioned that there will be delays or cancellations in commercial flights that operate in the affected region. However, airplanes are not necessarily mentioned next to typhoons in the Europarl corpus nearly as often, which means that when performing a multi-label document classification task it will be possible to appreciate that articles that only discuss the effects of reducing commercial flights in pandemics or passenger rights issues are getting labelled as if they were related to natural disasters.

4.2. Evaluation tasks

Even though CLE models are commonly evaluated considering only BLI tasks, their performance is heavily dependent on their actual application (Glavas et al., 2019), which highlights the need of using downstream performance evaluation tasks alongside BLI metrics.

4.2.1. BLI evaluation over a bilingual dictionary

A bilingual lexicon induction task is used to assess the quality of the bilingual dictionary generated as detailed in 3.3. This dictionary is compared against a ground-truth translation dictionary over the same language pair. The score of each term is obtained as the position of the first suggested translation for a term in the ground-truth bilingual dictionary within the list of possible translations for the same term of our induced bilingual dictionary, or zero if said translation is not included as an option in the generated dictionary. This scoring method is known as mean reciprocal ranking (MRR). MRR is equivalent to mean average precision (MAP) if only one valid translation per query is considered, in this case the top result. We chose this metric rather than the more common precision at rank k ($P@k$), which instead scores a term translation with one point if its position in the induced bilingual dictionary is equal or above k. This decision was made because MRR provides a more detailed evaluation, as it does not treat all models that rank the cor-

rect translation below k equally Glavas et al. (2019). In the evaluation, only terms from the ground-truth dictionary that had one or more of their possible translations appear in the induced translation dictionary were considered.

4.2.2. Multi-label document classification

Although BLI evaluation is a decent indicator our cross-lingual embedding quality along with the bilingual dictionary induce from it and can help the developer fine-tune this particular piece of the translation system, it does not directly correlate with the downstream performance of the system at hand, which in this particular use case corresponds to document classification. We propose a multi-label document classification task that directly matches the intended use of a translated thesaurus (where the classes of the task directly correspond to the topics of said thesaurus) and can be easily applied to other similar setups because of the simplicity of its logic.

The parallel bilingual corpus (i.e. the Europarl corpus referenced in section 4.1.) is considered, divided in different documents using an arbitrary window and one of the monolingual sections is annotated with the preexisting source language thesaurus (for our application, the source language in which the original thesaurus was written was English, so we would score the English section of the parallel corpus). This process will yield a score per document, which may have a different representation depending on the specific analysis criteria, be it mentions of a certain topic or the frequency of the terms with which it is related (i.e. combined incidences for all the terms that belong to a certain topic in a text). The source language thesaurus is then translated using a bilingual dictionary induced from two monolingual embeddings mapped into a common space, which are represented by two source-to-target and target-to-source cross-lingual embeddings, as seen in section 3.3.. This new thesaurus is used to annotate the section of the parallel corpus written in the target language (the Spanish section of the corpus in our case), thus obtaining a new list of document-score tuples. To get a better idea of how this parallel scoring would look in our case, we can see Figure 3, which shows two fragments of English and Spanish news extracted from https://elpais.com in which the topic Renewables alternatives[3] (Renew) was mentioned. Next to each highlighted term in Figure 3 we can see a label that indicates the topic

---

[3] References to energy from natural processes and/or non-traditional sources that are replenished on a human timescale. E.g. alternative energy sources, photovoltaic, biomass.

Topic code	Source frequency	Target frequency	Precision	Recall	Log-ratio	Priority
AEmiss	0.0112	0.0045	0.3269	0.2602	1.3067	0.1664
AltAccnt	0.0015	0.0012	0.5476	0.8214	0.2971	0.0006
AltFuel	0.0019	0.0103	0.0507	0.5625	-2.4477	0.2637
AntUse	0.0008	0.0046	0.1320	0.84	-2.4465	0.0528
AntiCorr	0.0314	0.0177	0.8649	0.8913	0.8272	0.8204
Biod	0.0075	0.0073	0.4701	0.8939	0.0398	0.0022
BrdComp	0	0.0002	0	0	-12.9659	0.0007
BuildAct	0	0.00005	0	0	-10.9665	0.00003
CChg	0.0234	0.0304	0.1633	0.4899	-0.3740	0.3465

Table 3: Multi-label document classification comparison over the parallel corpus Europarl for the English-Spanish pair. Validation metrics at topic level

to which it belongs (for instance "photovoltaic" is a term included in the topic Renew in our English thesaurus, and it appears in the English version of the article).

We now have two different scores per document, one obtained using the original thesaurus over the source language version of the article, and the other extracted with the induced thesaurus to rank the target language version of this same article. Based on the difference in label scoring per document we can obtain recall and precision at label (only scoring related to a specific topic is considered, i.e. hits from terms that belong to a specific topic) and thesaurus level (all topics are taken into consideration). We use micro averaging for both metrics, as the labels or topics of our thesaurus can present differences in the number of terms that they contain and how common those are. Furthermore, extracting the relative frequency of each label allows us to calculate the binary log of the ratio of relative frequencies (log-ratio) at label level and Kullback–Leibler divergence (KLD) (Kullback and Leibler, 1951) at thesaurus level.

Equation 1 is used to estimate the KLD, which quantifies how much a probability distribution diverges from another one in terms of the amount of additional information needed, where $P(x)$ and $Q(x)$ are the relative frequency of a category x in each corpora P or Q with respect to the categories in the same corpora. The higher the KLD value, the greater the divergence. If the value is 0, it means that both distributions are identical.

$$KLD(P\|Q) = \sum P(x)log(\frac{P(x)}{Q(x)}) \quad (1)$$

Log-ratio (LR) is a metric commonly used for the task of keyword extraction, as it tells us how relevant the difference between two probability distributions is. It is estimated using Equation 2. We used the binary logarithm to better represent the dissimilitude pointed by the log-ratio measure.

$$LR(P\|Q) = log(\frac{P(x)}{Q(x)}) \quad (2)$$

In our case, KLD compares the source and target language thesauri as a distribution of probabilities, where the relative frequency of each topic acts as the dependent variable, and the labels themselves are a qualitative factor (that is, the frequency is a topic or label-level metric, so its value will be different depending on the chosen topic). This comparison yields the expectation of the log difference between

the probability of a topic in the original thesaurus distribution with the generated thesaurus distribution, which is the amount of information that is lost when we approximate the source language thesaurus with the target language one. The log-ratio is also given per topic and its estimation is based on the ratio of the relative frequency of a topic in the source and target corpora, providing a measure of how many times a topic is more frequent in one corpus compared with the other.

4.3. Optimising manual validation

No matter the performance of the technique in charge of translating a knowledge base, subsequent human validation will need to be applied in order to ensure the quality of the final product. This usually means that the thesaurus goes through a number of iterations before reaching its final state. However, knowledge bases can contain a tremendous volume of information, which complicates obtaining a complete human validation. With the objective of achieving an optimal partial validation, we establish a priority for each label or topic in our thesaurus and work over them in the resulting descending order. This priority metric guides the manual validation of the topic in the sense that topics with higher values should be the first to be reviewed manually, as they have a more significant impact over the quality of the translated thesaurus when compared with topics with lower priority. We achieve this by multiplying the absolute value of the log-likelihood ratio detailed in 4.2.2. with the source or target language frequency of the topic, depending on the sign of said log-ratio. For example, if the log-ratio is positive there are instances of the topic in the source language that are not being registered when analysing the text with the translated thesaurus in the target language. We multiply frequency of the topic in the original language with the absolute value of this positive log-ratio in order to get an idea of the negative impact of the translation of the aforementioned topic over the quality of our translated thesaurus.

$$Prio_i = |lr_i| * (of_i * (lr_i >= 0) + tf_i * (lr_i < 0)) \quad (3)$$

Where $Prio_i$ corresponds to the priority given to topic i, lr_i is the log-ratio obtained for topic i and of_i and tf_i are the original and target frequency for topic i respectively.

One of the side effects of using this formula is that topics that have close to no frequency at source and target will be classified as having low priority, even if their recall and

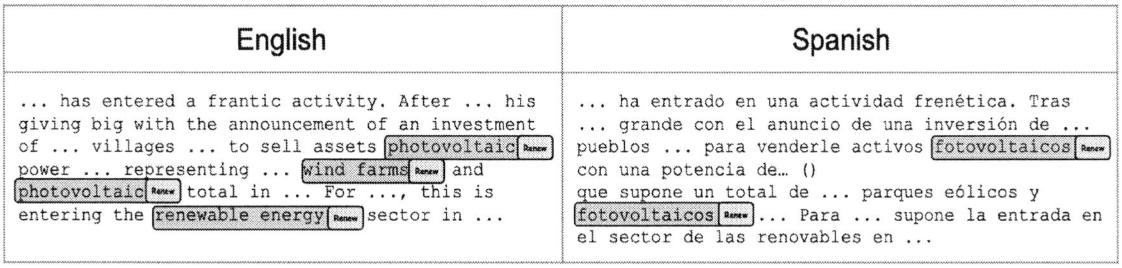

English	Spanish
... has entered a frantic activity. After ... his giving big with the announcement of an investment of ... villages ... to sell assets [photovoltaic][Renew] power ... representing ... [wind farms][Renew] and [photovoltaic][Renew] total in ... For ..., this is entering the [renewable energy][Renew] sector in ...	... ha entrado en una actividad frenética. Tras ... grande con el anuncio de una inversión de ... pueblos ... para venderle activos [fotovoltaicos][Renew] con una potencia de... () que supone un total de ... parques eólicos y [fotovoltaicos][Renew] ... Para ... supone la entrada en el sector de las renovables en ...

Figure 3: Multi-level classification for English and Spanish news using the thesauri in both languages

priority are zero or close to zero. We considered that, although recall and priority can be very low for a topic, if the source and target frequency are too low it becomes hard to assess the quality of the translation for the group of terms grouped under this topic, so human validation is not as useful as in other cases. Additionally, we can consider that uncommon terms will have a lower impact over the quality of the translated thesaurus even if their translations are not very good.

5. Results and discussion

Table 1 shows the MRR obtained from evaluating the bilingual dictionary generated from the base corpus described in the previous section (as well as a similar, smaller dataset) against the full English to Spanish bilingual dictionary provided in the MUSE specification (Lample et al., 2018). The bilingual dictionary evaluated is obtained according to the procedure described in 3.3. We compare a smaller corpus of online news against another dataset with a bigger volume that contains news from the same sources, the latter one being our main experimental corpus. Mean reciprocal rank for the generated bilingual dictionary does not always correlate directly with the actual downstream performance of the system, and some authors use it as a threshold of quality of the BLI procedure, like in Glavas et al. (2019), where 0.05 was established as a minimal value to consider a language pair translation run as acceptable. During our experiments, we have only considered MRR when measuring the impact of the size of the monolingual datasets with which our word embeddings are generated over the induced CLE-phrase table. It is displayed here to show how it can help developers evaluate certain pieces of the translation system individually (in this case our induced bilingual dictionary), and as a reference for future CLE-related tasks.

Conversely, our multi-label document classification evaluation (Table 2) yields much more informative results about the performance of both the source-to-target language alignment and the heuristic used to build terms from the induced unigram bilingual dictionary. As expected, literal translation returns low precision and recall scores, paired with a high KLD value, which indicates that most of the information contained in the original thesaurus is being lost. Part of the reason for this outcome can be attributed to the grammatical differences between Spanish and English, which are not properly accounted for when translating token by token.

Providing all possible permutations for each term has a notable impact for all metrics, but especially over the Kullback–Leibler divergence. Because KLD is a measure of information loss between two probability distributions (in this case modelled after the frequency of the topics in each thesaurus), we can infer that, although precision and recall are still relative low, this information loss is distributed more evenly across all the labels of the thesaurus. That is, the probability distributions that are modelled after topic annotation in the source and target language present a more similar shape.

Lemmatization seems to increase recall, which is expected, especially when working with a highly-inflectional language such as Spanish. However, it might introduce some noise, because it amplifies the coverage of all terms. This means that terms that were originally meaningful but that have been translated into common expressions will have a noticeable negative impact in the quality of the translated thesaurus. For instance, the term "unionized" that belongs to the topic "Union" is translated into Spanish as "trabajadores" (workers) in the bilingual English-Spanish dictionary obtained using the procedures detailed in 3.3. with the experimental settings mentioned in 4.1. "Trabajadores" is a much more common word that does not only appear in news articles concerning unionisation issues. This faulty translation already caused a loss in precision when using literal translation and permutation heuristics, but only in instances where the exact word appeared in the text. Moreover, the translation procedure depends on the actual contents of the used monolingual word embeddings, so it is possible that "trabajadores" often appears in a similar context to "unionized" and the precision is not affected excessively. However, after applying lemmatization, all possible forms of this term ("trabajadoras", "trabajador", "trabajadora") will produce a hit for the topic "Union".

Lastly, the addition of wildcards on top of the previous heuristics provides the best overall scores save for precision, which is still improved over using only permutations and lemmatization heuristics. The remarkable improvement of the recall is to be expected when applying this kind of "loose matching" (multiple tokens can appear in between the word that make up a multi-word term) over the Spanish language, which presents a flexible phrase structure. Even so, precision and KLD are still relatively far from the results obtained with the commercial machine translation system. In terms of precision, we have observed that our resulting bilingual dictionary has a tendency to place common terms as the most likely translation over more scarce expressions that may match the original term better. This phenomenon is likely related to the noise that results from the word embeddings cross-mapping procedure (Artetxe et al., 2018a). Further refinements in such processes and integration of the CLE-generated phrase-table into statistical or neural machine translation models may mitigate the issue, among other possibilities that we will briefly explore at the end of this section.

The results of our experiments show that the proposal does not perform equally for all the topics. This could be due to some topics being more or less specific, or due to factors that affect the number of occurrences of each topic in the training corpus. In Table 3 it is possible to see the frequency of each topic at source and target languages. For example, in the Europarl corpus we did not find mentions for any of the terms grouped under the topics BrdComp and BuildAct in the original English thesaurus, so the source frequency for both of these topics is 0. As a result, their precision and recall are zero independently of whether there are incidences for the same terms when translated with the method in our proposal (that is, their target frequency). However, this value for precision and recall does not imply that the translation of these two terms is necessarily bad. Instead, in cases where the source frequency for a topic is relatively low when compared to other topics, our confidence about the recall and precision values obtained will be lower. To reflect this, source and target frequency of the terms grouped under a topic contributes to the estimation of the priority of said topic, and the priority metric guides the manual validation of the topic in the sense that topics with higher values should be the first to review manually because they have worse results. For instance, the topic AntiCorr has a higher priority value, although it presents better precision and recall. In this case the priority metric is telling us that, even though this topic has been translated better than others, it appears very frequently in the analysed text, which means that it has a big impact over the quality of the translated thesaurus and should be reviewed before other topics. We can get to this conclusion because the priority is a function of the absolute value of the log-ratio and the frequency, which itself affects this calculation of the log-ratio the most. Consequentially, some topics have similar precision and recall values (i.e. Biod and AltAccnt), but the priority of one of them is lower (AltAccnt) because its terms are not very frequent. For cases where a topic has low values of precision and recall but its priority is still low, recommending additional terms for this topic could be useful.

Future improvements could include refining the phrase-table obtained from cross-lingual embeddings so as to obtain a better bilingual dictionary, as it has already been proposed in Artetxe et al. (2019), which also reduces the need for heuristics that build multi-word expressions. Term matching overlap can be tuned in order to maximise performance, although it would mean that the logic behind some of the terms of the original thesaurus might be compromised, which in some cases might be a better fit for the target language. It could also be of interest to evaluate terms that are found commonly as false positives according to their relevance (i.e. relying on tf–idf), discarding those that are too general by establishing a threshold and speeding up manual validation without losing meaningful terms.

6. Conclusion

In this work we offer a practical application of a bilingual lexicon induction (BLI) method based on cross lingual embeddings (CLE) (Artetxe et al., 2018a; Artetxe et al., 2018b) that allows us to induce a domain specific Spanish thesaurus from a preexisting English thesaurus used for multi-label document classification within Non-Financial Reporting. We include some possible heuristics that may help build sensible expressions from a unigram translation dictionary, which is itself induced from the aforementioned CLE procedure, and compare their performance against each other and a commercial machine translation system. To this end, we also offer some evaluation metrics that measure the performance of the proposed multi-label document classification task, along with a term prioritisation strategy for manual annotation. We hope that some of the strategies proposed here pave the way for an easier application of CLE-based BLI techniques, especially for tasks that rely on transferring information across multilingual knowledge representations, and help understand better the behaviour of these methods for similar use cases.

7. Acknowledgements

This paper was developed by a research team at Datamaran, Ltd. Datamaran is a company that develops AI-driven software for identifying and monitoring external risks and opportunities tied to ESG issues. We are thankful to our colleagues who provided expertise that greatly assisted the research.

8. Bibliographical References

Artetxe, M., Labaka, G., and Agirre, E. (2018a). A robust self-learning method for fully unsupervised cross-lingual mappings of word embeddings. In Proceedings of the 56th Annual Meeting of the Association for Computational Linguistics (Volume 1: Long Papers), pages 789–798, Melbourne, Australia, July. Association for Computational Linguistics.

Artetxe, M., Labaka, G., and Agirre, E. (2018b). Unsupervised Statistical Machine Translation. Technical report.

Artetxe, M., Labaka, G., and Agirre, E. (2019). Bilingual Lexicon Induction through Unsupervised Machine Translation. In Proceedings of the 57th Annual Meeting of the Association for Computational Linguistics, pages 5002–5007, Stroudsburg, PA, USA. Association for Computational Linguistics.

Bojanowski, P., Grave, E., Joulin, A., and Mikolov, T. (2016). Enriching Word Vectors with Subword Information. 7.

Faruqui, M. and Dyer, C. (2014). Improving vector space word representations using multilingual correlation. In Proceedings of the 14th Conference of the European Chapter of the Association for Computational Linguistics, pages 462–471, Gothenburg, Sweden, April. Association for Computational Linguistics.

Fontaine, M. (2013). Corporate social responsibility and sustainability: the new bottom line? *International Journal of Business and Social Science*, 4(4).

Gardner, M., Huang, K., Papalexakis, E., Fu, X., Taluk-dar, P., Faloutsos, C., Sidiropoulos, N., and Mitchell, T. (2015). Translation Invariant Word Embeddings. Technical report.

Glavas, G., Litschko, R., Ruder, S., and Vulic, I. (2019). How to (Properly) Evaluate Cross-Lingual Word Embeddings: On Strong Baselines, Comparative Analyses, and Some Misconceptions. 2.

Gromann, D. and Declerck, T. (2018). Comparing pre-trained multilingual word embeddings on an ontology alignment task. In Proceedings of the Eleventh International Conference on Language Resources and Evaluation (LREC 2018), Miyazaki, Japan, May. European Language Resources Association (ELRA).

Haghighi, A., Liang, P., Berg-Kirkpatrick, T., and Klein, D. (2008). Learning bilingual lexicons from monolingual corpora. pages 771–779, 01.

Honnibal, M. and Johnson, M. (2015). An improved non-monotonic transition system for dependency parsing. In Proceedings of the 2015 Conference on Empirical Methods in Natural Language Processing, pages 1373–1378, Lisbon, Portugal, September. Association for Computational Linguistics.

Knight, K. (2002). Learning a translation lexicon from monolingual corpora. 05.

Koehn, P. (2005). Europarl: A Parallel Corpus for Statistical Machine Translation. Technical report.

KPMG. (2017). The KPMG Survey of Corporate Responsibility Reporting 2017. Technical report.

Kullback, S. and Leibler, R. A. (1951). On information and sufficiency. *Ann. Math. Statist.*, 22(1):79–86, 03.

Lample, G., Conneau, A., Ranzato, A., Denoyer, L., and Jégou, H. (2018). Word translation without parallel data. Technical report.

Mikolov, T., Chen, K., Corrado, G., and Dean, J. (2013a). Efficient Estimation of Word Representations in Vector Space. 1.

Mikolov, T., Le, Q. V., and Sutskever, I. (2013b). Exploiting Similarities among Languages for Machine Translation. 9.

Ruder, S., Vulić, I., and Søgaard, A. (2017). A Survey Of Cross-lingual Word Embedding Models. 6.

Søgaard, A., Ruder, S., and Vulić, I. (2018a). On the limitations of unsupervised bilingual dictionary induction. In Proceedings of the 56th Annual Meeting of the Association for Computational Linguistics (Volume 1: Long Papers), pages 778–788, Melbourne, Australia, jul. Association for Computational Linguistics.

Søgaard, A., Ruder, S., and Vulić, I. (2018b). On the Limitations of Unsupervised Bilingual Dictionary Induction. 5.

Zhou, C., Ma, X., Wang, D., and Neubig, G. (2019). Density matching for bilingual word embedding. In NAACL-HLT.

Proceedings of the 6th International Workshop on Computational Terminology (COMPUTERM 2020), pages 26–36
Language Resources and Evaluation Conference (LREC 2020), Marseille, 11–16 May 2020
© European Language Resources Association (ELRA), licensed under CC-BY-NC

Which Dependency Parser to Use for Distributional Semantics in a Specialized Domain?

Pauline Brunet[1], Olivier Ferret[1], Ludovic Tanguy[2]
1. CEA, LIST, F-91191 Gif-sur-Yvette, France
2. CLLE: CNRS & University of Toulouse, France
{pauline.brunet,olivier.ferret}@cea.fr
ludovic.tanguy@univ-tlse2.fr

Abstract

We present a study whose objective is to compare several dependency parsers for English applied to a specialized corpus for building distributional count-based models from syntactic dependencies. One of the particularities of this study is to focus on the concepts of the target domain, which mainly occur in documents as multi-terms and must be aligned with the outputs of the parsers. We compare a set of ten parsers in terms of syntactic triplets but also in terms of distributional neighbors extracted from the models built from these triplets, both with and without an external reference concerning the semantic relations between concepts. We show more particularly that some patterns of proximity between these parsers can be observed across our different evaluations, which could give insights for anticipating the performance of a parser for building distributional models from a given corpus.

Keywords: Dependency parsing, distributional semantics, specialized corpus, biomedical domain

1. Introduction

This work takes place in the broader context of studying distributional semantic analysis methods for specialized corpora. This type of corpora are usually small-sized (a few million words or less), which poses a challenge for distributional methods, and contain specific, highly technical vocabulary, meaning that adapting methods based on large generic corpora might be difficult. We make the hypothesis, supported by the work of (Tanguy et al., 2015), that the small amount of data may be circumvented by a method based on syntactic contexts. Such methods have already been investigated by a large body of work. The largest part of it is dedicated to count-based approaches (Grefenstette, 1994; Habert et al., 1996; Lin, 1998; Curran and Moens, 2002; Padó and Lapata, 2007; Baroni and Lenci, 2010) but it also includes work adding dimensionality reduction methods (Lapesa and Evert, 2017) or more recently, work about word embeddings (Levy and Goldberg, 2014). One of our focuses is to select the best-suited tools for semantic analysis of specialized corpora. In particular, given that syntactic contexts will be a building block for the task, which syntactic parser should be used to extract these contexts? The goal of this article is, thus, to study the impact of the choice of parser on the construction of a distributional model with a frequency-based method. Our work is not the first work on comparing different parsers. Several evaluation campaigns were previously organized for various languages: the Easy (Paroubek et al., 2008), Passage (De La Clergerie et al., 2008), SPMRL (Seddah et al., 2013) and CoNLL (Zeman et al., 2018) campaigns as well as more focused studies like (Candito et al., 2010) or (De La Clergerie, 2014). However, the benchmarks used in these studies, adopting the kind of diverse, generic corpora on which the tools have been trained, might not be the most relevant option for specialized corpus parsing. Moreover, even though some of these campaigns are recent, the main tools available have not been compared on the same evaluation sets. We previously performed a first study (Tanguy et al., 2020), comparing 11 different versions of parsers on a small specialized corpus made up of Natural Language Processing papers for French. However, we lacked a reliable external reference to measure the results of the parsers against. So our evaluation was only a qualitative comparison.

2. Overview

To go beyond the limitation in (Tanguy et al., 2020), we have chosen, in the work we present in this article, to run a new evaluation on a small, specialized biomedical corpus, whose building is described in Section 3.1 and for which we may compare the relations implied by the extracted syntactic contexts against an external resource, the Unified Medical Language System (UMLS) (Bodenreider, 2004), which contains relations between medical and biomedical concepts (see Section 3.3).

More precisely, we defined the following process: we applied each of the 10 studied parsers we present in Section 3.2 to the corpus, outputting morphological, syntactic and grammatical information. In parallel, we ran MetaMap (Aronson and Lang, 2010), a biomedical entity linker, to identify biomedical concepts as defined and recorded in the UMLS. Then, we aligned these concepts with the tokens outputted by the parsers (see Section 4.1). From this alignment, we were able to extract grammatical relations between concept-mapped tokens and other tokens, which gave us syntactic contexts for concept-mapped tokens, and, therefore, for biomedical concepts themselves (see Section 4.2). We then built distributional thesauri for each of the parsers (see Section 5.1), leading to a large set of distributional similarity relations between biomedical concepts. Finally, we compared these similarity relations to the relations between biomedical concepts given by the UMLS (see Section 5.3) and used this comparison for characterizing our studied parsers.

3. Experiment Framework

3.1. Corpus

For this experiment, we used a small part of the Open Access subset of the PubMed Central corpus (PMC)[1], a collection of more than 5 million full-text articles from thousands of biomedical and life science journals. This corpus, originally in a very rich XML format, was cleaned up by removing a lot of non-parsable content like tables, formulas, links, then converted to raw text for parsing. We chose a subset based on a specialty domain centered on stem cells. Articles in PMC OA are indexed by the MeSH index, which tags each article with their themes (or subject headings), with an indication of whether the theme is a main theme of the article or not. To obtain a corpus that was the right size for our purposes, we chose to include any article that was tagged with a heading containing the words "Stem Cells", which includes headings such as "Stem Cells", "Adult Stem Cells", "Totipotent Stem Cells", "Mouse Embryonic Stem Cells", and others. This was done regardless of whether the heading was indicated as a main theme of the article or not. The resulting corpus is comprised of 23,094 articles, and 104 million words.

3.2. Syntactic Parsers

We selected 5 tools able to perform dependency parsing in English, focusing on easily available and ready-to-use parsers, i.e. those that take in charge the whole processing chain, from raw text to dependencies. These tools were applied with their default options.

All these tools use statistical models trained on annotated corpora. Their differences concern implementation choices like parsing techniques (graph- or transition-based, for instance), learning models (SVM, maximal entropy or more recently, recurrent neural networks), and upstream or side processing (segmentation, lemmatization). There is much less choice among the training corpora, given the high cost of the annotation and validation processes.

CoreNLP (Manning et al., 2014), the main tool of the Stanford team, implements a maximum entropy tagger, which uses the Penn Treebank tagset (Marcus et al., 1993), and a transition-based parser.

StanfordNLP (Qi et al., 2018) is a tool that, on top of giving access to the CoreNLP chain in Python, implements an entirely different parsing chain. Its graph-based parser relies on a LSTM neural network. StanfordNLP offers 3 English models, trained on the UD **EWT** (Silveira et al., 2014), **LinES** (Ahrenberg, 2015) and **ParTUT** (Bosco et al., 2012) corpora. We used all three of these models.

Spacy is an industry-targeting tool whose main characteristic is its speed compared to most other parsers. The tagger is based on a perceptron, with attributes based on Brown clusters, following (Koo et al., 2008). It implements a non-monotonous transition-based parser which can revise previous decisions (Honnibal and Johnson, 2015). The default model we used was

trained on OntoNotes (Hovy et al., 2006) and uses the ClearNLP dependency labels[2].

UDPipe (Straka and Straková, 2017) uses a neural network with a Gated Recurrent Unit mechanism to do both tokenization and segmentation at once. For PoS tagging, it generates possible tags for words from their suffix and performs disambiguation with a perceptron. The transition-based parsing relies on a simple one-layer neural network. UDPipe includes four English models. We used all of them, trained on the UD **GUM** (Zeldes, 2017), **EWT**, **LinES** and **ParTUT** corpora.

Talismane (Urieli and Tanguy, 2013) uses a mix of statistic models and language-specific features and rules incorporating linguistic knowledge. It was trained on the Penn Treebank.

We are fully aware that these parsers can only be compared on a practical level since the technologies used, their goals, their training data, and even the times at which they were created can scarcely be compared.

3.3. Terminological Reference Resource

The UMLS is a set of knowledge sources related to biomedical sciences. The main part of the system is the UMLS Metathesaurus, which aggregates nearly 200 biomedical controlled vocabularies in an attempt to provide a reference frame for medical and biomedical concepts and links the different names under which they are known in different vocabularies as synonyms. The Metathesaurus is organized around these concepts, which, in theory, have only one meaning, and are unique in the Metathesaurus. Each concept has a unique identifier called CUI and is linked to one or more names, in specific vocabularies, for this concept, which have identifiers called AUI.

For example, the concept "Headache" (CUI: C0018681) can be found as the following variations (among others): in vocabulary SNOMED, "Headache" (AUI: A2882187), in vocabulary MeSH, "Headache" (AUI: A0066000) and "Cranial Pain" (AUI: A1641293), and in vocabulary DxP, "HEAD PAIN CEPHALGIA" (AUI: A0418053).

On top of these concepts, the Metathesaurus provides some relations between concepts[3]. Most of these relations come from individual source vocabularies; some of these are added by the Metathesaurus maintainers and the others by the users.

All relations have general REL labels, which specify the type of relations: synonym, parent, child, sibling, broader, narrower, qualifier, qualified by, or unspecified (several degrees). There are 14 possible REL labels.

Around one-fourth of relations also have a RELA label, which further specifies the relation, like is_a, has_ingredient, property_of... These labels come from the source vocabularies. As such, they are more diversified

---

[1] http://www.ncbi.nlm.nih.gov/pmc

[2] https://github.com/clir/
clearnlp-guidelines/blob/master/md/
specifications/dependency_labels.md

[3] https://www.ncbi.nlm.nih.gov/books/
NBK9684/#_ch02_sec2_4_

than the REL labels, with nearly 900 different labels in total, and we cannot assume that they are coherently used throughout the Metathesaurus.

We observed that the distribution of relations among concepts (CUI) is not very well balanced:

	number of relations / CUI
mean	23.7
standard deviation	160.0
median	6.0
max	14,112
min	1

Some concepts have a very large number of relations but most of them are only linked to a restricted number of other concepts. As a consequence, since our objective in this study is to characterize the distributional neighborhood of the largest number of concepts as possible, we chose to keep for our evaluation as many reference relations as possible and not to select them according to their type in the UMLS Metathesaurus.

The only selection was performed in relation to our target domain. We had no indication in the Metathesaurus for selecting the relations specifically tied to the domain of stem cells. Hence, this selection was done indirectly by keeping only the relations between the concepts identified in our corpus for this domain. In practice, starting from an initial set of 112,790 concepts linked by 2,845,112 relations for the whole Metathesaurus, we obtained a set of 45,762 concepts linked by 1,272,224 relations. The selection rate is quite comparable for concepts and relations – 40.6% for concepts and 44.7% for relations – and the distribution of the number of relations by concept after this selection is close to that for the whole Metathesaurus:

	number of relations / CUI
mean	24.6
standard deviation	135.9
median	7.0
max	8,338
min	1

4. From Corpus to Dependency Triples

4.1. Concept Identification

The first step in our study is to match tokens, as segmented by various parsers, to biomedical concepts, as recognized by a biomedical entity linking tool. This task was greatly impeded by various alignment issues.

There are some available tools for biomedical UMLS concepts extraction from text. After testing several of them, among which cTakes (Savova et al., 2010) and QuickUMLS (Soldaini and Goharian, 2016), we decided to use MetaMap (Aronson, 2001), the reference tool for this task, because it had the clear advantage of providing disambiguation between possible candidate concepts for a phrase.

MetaMap splits the input documents into sentences, which are further split into phrases. It analyzes these phrases individually and outputs candidate mappings of UMLS concepts to the phrase. These mappings are given an evaluation score based on 4 metrics: centrality, variation, coverage, and cohesiveness. The mapping with the highest score may be selected as the most likely to be correct but MetaMap also provides a disambiguation module based on context. We exploited the possibility of MetaMap to output only the most likely mapping based on score and context disambiguation.

For instance, the phrase "Generation of single-copy transgenic mouse embryos" is linked to UMLS concepts "Generations" (C0079411), "Singular" (C0205171), "Copy" (C1948062), "Mice, Transgenic" (C0025936) and "Embryo" (C0013935).

The linguistic analysis performed by MetaMap for identifying concepts in documents is, of course, different from the analysis performed by our target parsers. More precisely, the tokenization step is particularly important for aligning the concepts it identifies with the tokens issued from the various tokenizations of our parsers. MetaMap gives two position data for each match. The first one gathers the character offset in the phrase and the length of the matched words. This information is highly difficult to match with parsers' offsets because of imprecisions and different counting conventions from both MetaMap and the various parsers.

The second position information is the rank of the matched words in the phrase. For instance, in the above example, the concept "Generations" has both a *TextMatchStart* and *TextMatchEnd* attributes equal to 1 while "Mice, Transgenic" has a *TextMatchStart* attribute of 5 and a *TextMatchEnd* attribute of 6. However, this information cannot be directly matched with the tokenization of a parser since it depends on both the tokenization and MetaMap's phrase splitting.

The first step is then to associate each concept identified by MetaMap with its own tokenization, which we later align with each parser's tokenization.

4.1.1. Matching MetaMap's tokens with MetaMap's concepts

This first step is not trivial as the tokenization performed by MetaMap is not directly accessible in its output. However, each phrase in this output is segmented into syntactic units and each of these units is associated with a list of tokens. For example, "single-copy" is a syntactic unit associated with the token list ["single", "copy"]. From these syntactic units, we can collect the associated tokens and number them according to their order, which gives us something close to the behind-the-scene MetaMap tokenization. This numbering can be used to match the tokens with the biomedical concepts, but with the necessity to take two additional problems into account. First, the punctuation is not considered in MetaMap's numbering, but must obviously be recorded for the later alignment with the parsers' tokenization. Second, MetaMap's numbering sometimes skips the first or the first few tokens in a phrase if they are not associated with a concept, which is more troublesome. For example, in the phrase "from cells", MetaMap may declare that the "Cells" concept starts from 1 or 2. We were not able to determine the cause of this behavior but we found a workaround for the problem by comparing the offset of the matched starting position to the offset of the phrase starting position. If a discrepancy was found, the character count of each word was added until the discrepancy was filled to compute the number of skipped words.

With this process, we were able to match MetaMap's concepts to its tokenization with very good accuracy.

4.1.2. Matching MetaMap's tokens with parsers' tokens

The next step matches MetaMap's tokenization with each parser's tokenization. Another solution could have consisted in feeding MetaMap's tokenization to the parsers, as most of them are modular enough to allow it. We rejected the idea for two reasons. First, the tokens we retrieved from MetaMap could be different from the initial text: for example, by modifying some punctuations, destroying case information and even expanding acronyms. Second, we wanted to use the parsers out of the box, with their own tokenization suited to their own tagging and parsing processes.

The algorithm for matching these different tokenizations is based on the fact that the tokenizations are essentially similar. The majority of words are tokenized similarly by MetaMap and the parsers. Thus, for each document, we can align the outputs of MetaMap and the considered parser by relying on their common tokens and use a small set of heuristics to deal with discrepancies. The discrepancies we handle are of several types. They may come from parser-specific issues, such as Spacy inserting "SPACE" tokens when confronted with large breaks in the text. One of the two tokenizations may have inserted a sentence break while the other may not, in which case the sentence break is skipped. One of the tokenizations may have split a token while the other may not, such as "single-copy" on one side and "single" followed by "copy" on the other side. In such cases, we add the next tokens on the shorter side, separating them with both spaces and "-" until they stop matching the longer side or the whole split token is covered. If the process has been successful, the longer token is matched with all the smaller ones. If it has failed, we skip tokens on both sides and see if the next ones match. This is especially useful for cases where MetaMap or the parser modifies the tokens in some way, like "99%" becoming "99". Failing that, we are only concerned with finding some part of the text where the tokens match again, ideally as close as possible to the failure point. We implement this strategy by recording, from the failure point, the list of tokens from both MetaMap and the target parser and checking at each step if the last two tokens seen on one side can be found in the list of the other side[4]. If so, we skip up to this part and start matching from there.

This algorithm works fairly well and a very large percentage of tokens are matched.

4.2. Dependency Triple Extraction

The next step is to extract dependency relations between words to build the contexts that will be used for distributional analysis. This follows a similar process to the work

of (Lin, 1998) and produces, from the dependency relations outputted by syntactic parsers, typically illustrated by Figure 1, the representation of the contexts of a word in a corpus under the form of syntactic triplets (dependent, relation, governor).

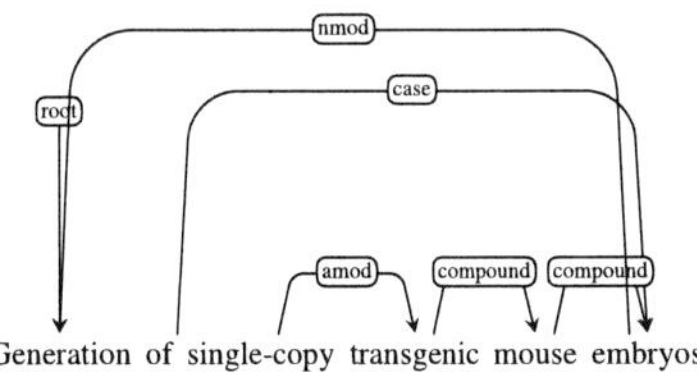

Figure 1: Dependencies identified by the Stanford NLP parser trained on the LinES corpus for the phrase "Generation of single-copy transgenic mouse embryos".

Not all relations provide useful context information. Generally, relations including closed-class words (determiners, conjunctions, pronouns, etc.) are not considered for building distributional contexts. For this study, we performed our selection not on the PoS tag of the governor and dependent, but on the dependency relation itself, choosing to exclude some of them.

For parsers following the Universal Dependency scheme, the excluded relations were `root`, `cc`, `cc:preconj`, `punct`, `case`, `mark`, `det`, `det:predet`, `cop`, `neg`, `aux`, and `nmod:poss`. Typically, relations such as `neg`, `aux` or `det` include negation markers (*not...*), auxiliary verbs (*have*, *be*, *can.*.) or determiners (*the*, *a...*) that we don't want to see in distributional contexts. For Spacy, it was `root`, `ccc`, `case`, `prep`, `det`, `neg`, `expl`, `predet`, `aux`, `auxpass`, and `mark`. For Talismane, given its specific dependency scheme, we had to rely on PoS tags for achieving the same kind of filtering, excluding IN, DT, MD, CC, EX, PDT, PRP, PRP$, TO and, RP.

Relations with prepositions had to be modified to link the actual related words and include the preposition in the relation. We illustrate the different ways this kind of grammatical constructions are parsed with the phrase "region within the cluster". Figure 2 shows the output produced by UD dependency scheme-following parsers.

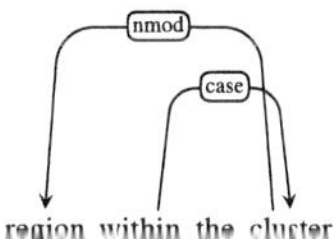

Figure 2: Dependencies identified by Universal Dependencies scheme-type parsers for the phrase "region within the cluster".

Figure 3 gives the result of the parsing by Spacy.

Finally, Figure 3 presents the output of Talismane for this phrase.

These three cases are the three basic patterns of how prepositions are managed in each scheme. We normalize all these

---

[4] We tested the use of one token instead of two but found better results with two tokens.

[6] http://www.mathcs.emory.edu/~choi/doc/ cu-2012-choi.pdf

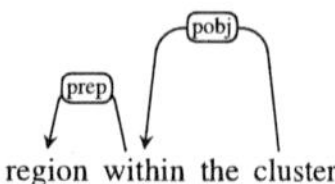

Figure 3: Dependencies identified by SpaCy (Clear Style dependencies)[6] for the phrase "region within the cluster".

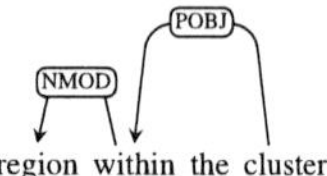

Figure 4: Dependencies identified by Talismane (Penn Treebank dependencies) for the phrase "region within the cluster".

variants with a `prep/within` dependency relation, as illustrated in Figure 5.

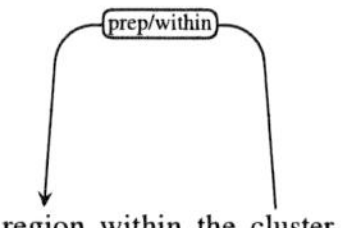

Figure 5: Dependency constructed from the existing dependencies for the phrase "region within the cluster".

For the example of Figure 1, the resulting list of triplets is:

> (embryos, prep/of, generation)
> (generation, prep/of-1, embryos)
> (single-copy, amod, transgenic)
> (transgenic, amod-1, single-copy)
> (transgenic, compound, mouse)
> (mouse, compound-1, transgenic)
> (mouse, compound, embryo)
> (embryos, compound-1, mouse)

However, we need to adapt this representation of context to our task, which is specifically to extract the contexts of biomedical concepts. Thus, we only extract the relations where at least one side, the dependent or the governor, is a token that is part of a concept and the other side is not part of the same concept. Moreover, we only consider nominal concepts, which we define here as concepts where at least one word was tagged as a noun by the MetaMap tagger. Furthermore, for each side of a triplet, we include the following data:

- CUI: the unique UMLS id if it is a concept, _ otherwise;

- PREF: the preferred form of the concept in the UMLS if it is a concept, _ otherwise;

- NORM: the normalized form of the concept as it occurs in the text if it is a concept, _ otherwise. Concretely, it corresponds to the concatenation of all the lemmas of the concept;

- LEMMA of the token actually part of the relation;

- PoS of the token actually part of the relation.

In the above phrase, five concepts were recognized by MetaMap: "Generation" (noun), "Singular" (adj), "Copy (object)" (adj), "Mice, Transgenic" (noun), and "Embryo" (noun). The corresponding triplets are given in Table 1.

4.3. Comparison of Parsers in Terms of Dependency Triples

Several previous studies (starting with (Grefenstette, 1994) and (Lin, 1998)) have considered subsets of syntactic relations for distributional models. More recent works (Padó and Lapata, 2007; Baroni and Lenci, 2010) have selected a short list of core relations, and we decided to limit our experiment to these, which we regrouped in the categories described below. They follow the main syntactic relations identified by dependency parsers and correspond to the minimal configuration of (Padó and Lapata, 2007), to which we added the last one from (Baroni and Lenci, 2010), that consider the prepositions themselves as relations between a head and a dependent word, as described in section 4.2.

N suj V: nominal subject of a verb;

N obj V: nominal direct object of a verb;

ADJ mod N: adjective modifying a noun;

ADV mod ADJ/V: adverb modifying an adjective or a verb;

X coord X: coordination between two nouns, adjectives, adverbs, or verbs (note: the conjunction itself is not considered);

X prep_P X: prepositional binding between nouns, adjectives, or verbs.

This brings down the number of triplets (occurrences) extracted from each parser from around 60M to around 40M, with SpaCy having the least (38.3M) and the version of UDPipe trained on ParTUT having the most (52.4M, far ahead of the others).

We compare the triplets' coverage between parsers but first, we reduce the triplets to some core elements: the CUI of the left-hand side, the CUI or lemma (depending on whether it is a concept or not) and the PoS tag of the right-hand side, and the relation between the two.

Our triplets now look like the following:

    C0040648   N:C0237753_prep/of
    C1883221   ADJ:distinct_mod-1

We also limit ourselves to triplets in which the left-hand side (CUI) appears at least 10 times in each parser's output, and in which the right-hand side (CUI/lemma and PoS) appears at least twice in each parser's output. This results in 39M unique triplets, of which 21M appear for at least two parsers and 3.5M appear for all parsers. Among these 39M triplets, each parser has found around 13M of them, with the least being CoreNLP with 12.2M and SpaCy with 12.5M. The parser with the highest number of common triplets is the ParTUT version of UDPipe, with 16.8M triplets.

Dependent					Relation	Governor				
CUI_1	$PREF_1$	$NORM_1$	$LEMMA_1$	PoS_1		CUI_2	$PREF_2$	$NORM_2$	$LEMMA_2$	PoS_2
C0013935	Embryos	embryo	embryo	NOUN	prep/of	C0079411	Generations	generation	generation	NOUN
C0079411	Generations	generation	generation	NOUN	prep/of-1	C0013935	Embryos	embryo	embryo	NOUN
C0025936	Mice,Transgenic	transgenic_mouse	transgenic	NOUN	amod-1	_	_	_	single-copy	ADJ
C0025936	Mice,Transgenic	transgenic_mouse	mouse	NOUN	compound	C0013935	Embryos	embryo	embryo	NOUN
C0013935	Embryos	embryo	embryo	NOUN	compound-1	C0025936	Mice,Transgenic	transgenic_mouse	mouse	NOUN

Table 1: Syntactic triplets with concepts identified by MetaMap

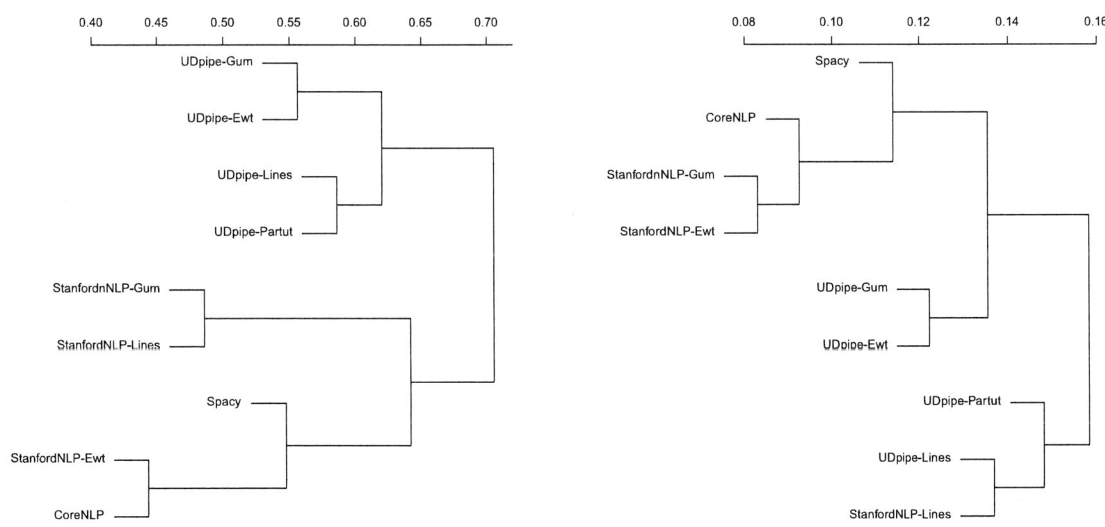

Figure 6: Hierarchical clustering of parsers according to their correlation on the triplets found by at least two parsers (right side) and all parsers (left side).

We computed the agreement of the parsers about the triplets they produced by computing Spearman's correlation coefficient (ρ) both for the 21M triplets shared by at least two parsers and the 3.5M triplets common to all parsers. The first measure focuses on the differences between parsers in terms of diversity of triplets while the second measure looks more precisely at their differences in terms of frequency for the common triplets. We did not include Tallsmane as it was difficult to adapt its PoS tags and dependency labels to our normalization, as was done for CoreNLP and SpaCy. Figure 6 shows the hierarchical clustering of the parsers according to these correlations (more precisely, 1 - ρ for having a distance).

Globally, we can observe that the type of parser has a significant impact on the triplets, which is not a surprise: the UDPipe parsers are particularly close to each other but most of the StanfordNLP models are also grouped. However, the training corpus can also have an impact when we consider the triplets shared by all parsers, with StanfordNLP-Lines much closer to UDpipe-Lines than to the two other StanfordNLP models. This is why the clusterings built for the two sets of triplets are a little bit different, even if they also share some patterns: for instance, SpaCy is close to CoreNLP, which is close to StanfordNLP-Ewt while UDpipe-Gum and UDpipe-Ewt form a group for the two sets.

5. Distributional Models

5.1. Building of Distributional Models

Following the distinction made in Baroni et al. (2014), we built our distributional models according to a count-based approach, such as in (Lin, 1998), rather than according to a predictive approach such as in (Mikolov et al., 2013). The first justification of this choice is that, except for (Levy and Goldberg, 2014), the number of studies relying on dependency relations is very limited among predictive approaches. More importantly, some recent studies (Pierrejean and Tanguy, 2018) have shown that predictive approaches are unstable to some extent concerning the search of the nearest distributional neighbors of a word. Since we want specifically to concentrate on the effects resulting from the use of different syntactic parsers, we adopted a count-based approach.

We implemented this approach by building on the findings of recent studies in the field (Kiela and Clark, 2014; Baroni et al., 2014; Levy et al., 2015) and more particularly took up two main options from (Ferret, 2010): the use of Positive Pointwise Mutual Information (PPMI) for weighting the context elements and the application of very loose filtering that removes the elements of these contexts with only one occurrence. The second choice is justified by both the fairly small size of our target corpus and the experiments of (Ferret, 2010) with linear co-occurrents. The main particularity of our work is the fact that the entries of our distri-

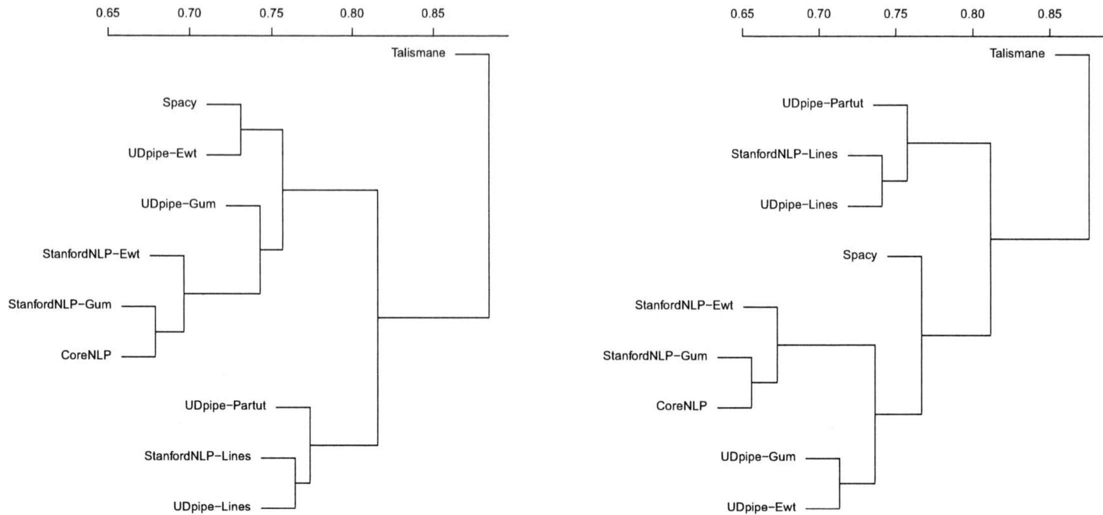

Figure 7: Hierarchical clustering of models according to their agreement on the first nearest neighbor (left side) and according to the RBO measure (right side).

butional models are not words but UMLS concepts. More precisely, each entry is made of the triple (CUI, PREF, PoS) under the form PREF_CUI#PoS. The elements of contexts can be either words or concepts since dependency triples can include concepts or words.

However, this particularity did not influence on the way we built our distributional models and we classically computed the similarity of two concepts by measuring the Cosine similarity score between their contexts vectors. For a given model, this computation was done for each pair of concepts with contexts sharing at least one element. The results of this process can also be viewed as a distributional thesaurus in which each entry corresponds to a concept of the considered vocabulary and is associated with the list of all other concepts of this vocabulary, sorted in descending order of their similarity value with the entry. In practice, only the nearest 100 distributional neighbors are kept, which is a fairly large number compared to the average number of relations by concept – 24.6 – but is justified by the fact that some concepts may have a much higher number of relations.

5.2. Comparison of Distributional Models

The first step for comparing our distributional models, and more indirectly the parsers used for extracting the distributional data they rely on, was to compute their agreement of our models on the nearest neighbors retrieved for each word. Among the concepts shared by all models, 47,647 concepts had at least one distributional neighbor. For each pair of models, the agreement on the nearest neighbor retrieved for each concept was computed[7] and used for building a similarity matrix. Hierarchical clustering was performed from this matrix, which leads to the left side of Figure 7. First, we can observe that the model built from Tal-

---

[7] Ratio of the number of words sharing the same nearest neighbor to the size of the considered vocabulary.

ismane is clearly aside from the others. The second main trend is that the training corpus of the parsers can be more important than the type of parser. For instance, the StanfordNLP and UDPipe parsers trained on the LinES corpus are grouped together and fairly distant from the same parsers trained on the GUM and EWT corpora. However, among the parsers trained on these two corpora, which are fairly heterogeneous compared to the LinES corpus, the proximity between the models they contributed to build is guided by the type of parser.

Even if the overall aspect of the dendrogram is a little bit different due to the position of the model built from Spacy, these trends are globally confirmed by comparing the neighbors of concepts by the means of the *Rank-Biased Overlap* measure (Webber et al., 2010), as illustrated by the right side of Figure 7. This measure is applied to all neighbors of our thesaurus' entries (100 neighbors in practice) and extends the notion of average overlap – the average of the overlap between two lists at different ranks – by decreasing the importance of overlap as the rank of the considered neighbors increases. As a consequence, nearest neighbors are given greater importance. This importance is defined by the p parameter, which can be interpreted as the probability, starting from the beginning of the list of neighbors, to continue to consider the following neighbors in the list. The value $p = 0.98$ used in our case means that the first 50 nearest neighbors of an entry account for around 85% of the evaluation. Figure 7 is based on the distance $1 - RBO$, which can be considered as a metric.

The clusterings of Figure 7 can also be compared to those of Figure 6: Talismane is absent from Figure 6 but has a very limited impact in Figure 7 since it is clearly distant from the other parsers. This comparison shows that the clustering based on the distributional neighbors is much closer to the clustering based on the triplets shared by all parsers than to the clustering based on the triplets shared by only two parsers. This suggests that the triplets of the first set are

Model	#concepts	#eval. concepts	#rel./ concept	Recall	R_{prec}	MAP	P@1	P@5	P@10	P@100
StanfordNLP-Ewt	49,002	42,340	25.4	4.9	3.5	3.0	9.4	5.4	3.9	1.3
CoreNLP	49,022	42,360	25.3	4.7	3.4	2.9	9.2	5.2	3.8	1.2
StanfordNLP-Gum	48,524	41,998	25.4	4.5	3.1	2.6	8.7	4.9	3.6	1.1
StanfordNLP-Lines	47,671	41,275	25.7	4.5	3.1	2.6	8.6	4.8	3.6	1.1
UDpipe-Ewt	47,883	41,366	25.6	4.5	3.1	2.6	8.5	4.8	3.5	1.1
Spacy	49,895	43,112	25.2	4.1	3.1	2.5	8.4	4.6	3.4	1.0
UDpipe-Gum	47,133	40,832	25.7	4.3	3.0	2.5	8.4	4.6	3.4	1.1
UDpipe-Partut	47,233	40,859	25.8	4.3	3.0	2.5	8.3	4.7	3.4	1.1
UDpipe-Lines	46,645	40,408	25.8	4.0	2.7	2.3	7.6	4.2	3.1	1.0
Talismane	48,411	41,812	25.3	3.2	2.2	1.9	6.1	3.3	2.4	0.8

Table 2: Evaluation of our distributional models with UMLS relations as reference (measures x 100).

globally more frequent than the triplets of the second set and can be used for having a first indication of the proximity of the distributional models built from them.

5.3. Evaluation of Distributional Models

The comparison of our distributional models according to the neighbors of their entries gives some insights about their proximity but no information about their relevance for representing the semantic relations in the target domain. This second type of evaluation has to rely on a reference resource accounting for these relations, which can be done in our case by exploiting the UMLS relations we have presented in Section 3.3.

More precisely, we adopted the evaluation framework proposed in (Ferret, 2010), based on the Information Retrieval paradigm: each entry of our models is considered as a query and the sorted list of its distributional neighbors as the list of retrieved documents. In this context, a neighbor is considered as relevant if the pair (entry, neighbor) corresponds to a UMLS relation[8]. As mentioned in Section 3.3, no restrictions are applied to the type of these reference relations for two main reasons. First, we wanted to have a large enough set of relations for making our evaluation as reliable as possible. Second, even at the first level, with the REL labels, the relation types are fairly fuzzy in their definition, which makes the selection of a specific type of relations difficult in practice.

For measuring the relevance of the neighbors of an entry according to the UMLS relations, we adopted the classical measures used in the Information Retrieval field. R-precision, MAP (Mean Average Precision) and precision at various ranks (P@i). R-precision (R_{prec}) is the precision after the first R neighbors were retrieved, R being the number of reference relations while Mean Average Precision (MAP) is the average of the precision values calculated each time a reference relation is found. All these measures are given for each of our distributional models with a scaling factor equal to 100 by the six last columns of Table 2. The second column of this table corresponds to the number of concepts in each model while the third column is the number of these concepts with at least one UMLS

relation. The fourth column gives the average number of UMLS relations for a concept in a model and the fifth column provides the average percentage of these relations that are present in the first 100 neighbors of each concept.

The results of this evaluation lead to several observations. First, their overall level seems to be fairly low. However, this is not abnormal given the size of our corpus. For instance, Ferret (2010) reports a value of 7.7 for R_{prec} with his most complete reference (38.7 reference relations by entry on average) but with a corpus nearly four times the size of ours. We can also observe from the second column that using different syntactic parsers has a limited but not negligible influence on the number of concepts extracted from the corpus: the model based on UDpipe-Lines has 5% fewer concepts than the model based on StanfordNLP-Ewt. In terms of global trends, the first two models, StanfordNLP-Ewt and CoreNLP, are slightly better than a group of seven models with fairly close results while the last model is more clearly distant in terms of performance. This last observation is fully consistent with the separate position of the corresponding model in the dendrograms of Figure 7. More globally, similarities between models in Table 2 are consistent with their similarities in Figure 7, which suggests that even without an external reference, the distributional models can be compared in terms of semantic relevance by focusing on the neighbors retrieved for their entries. For instance, StanfordNLP-Ewt, CoreNLP, and StanfordNLP-Gum are close to each other in the two evaluations. This is also the case for UDpipe-Ewt, Spacy, and UDpipe-Gum. The main difference between the two evaluations concerns the relative importance of the training corpus and the type of the parser: in Table 2, the type of the parser seems to be the main factor while in Figure 7, the two factors are more intertwined.

Figure 8 gives a more global view of similarities between models according to the UMLS relations they retrieve by reporting the same type of analysis as Figure 7 but restricted to neighbors having a UMLS relation with their entry. This view confirms the main observations resulting from the analysis of Table 2. The model built with Talismane is significantly different from the others and the main patterns in terms of clustering are present, with a group made up of CoreNLP, StanfordNLP-Gum, and StanfordNLP-Ewt and a group with UDpipe-Gum and UDpipe-Ewt. As a con-

---

[8]More precisely, it means that the neighbor is part of a UMLS relation including both the entry and the neighbor.

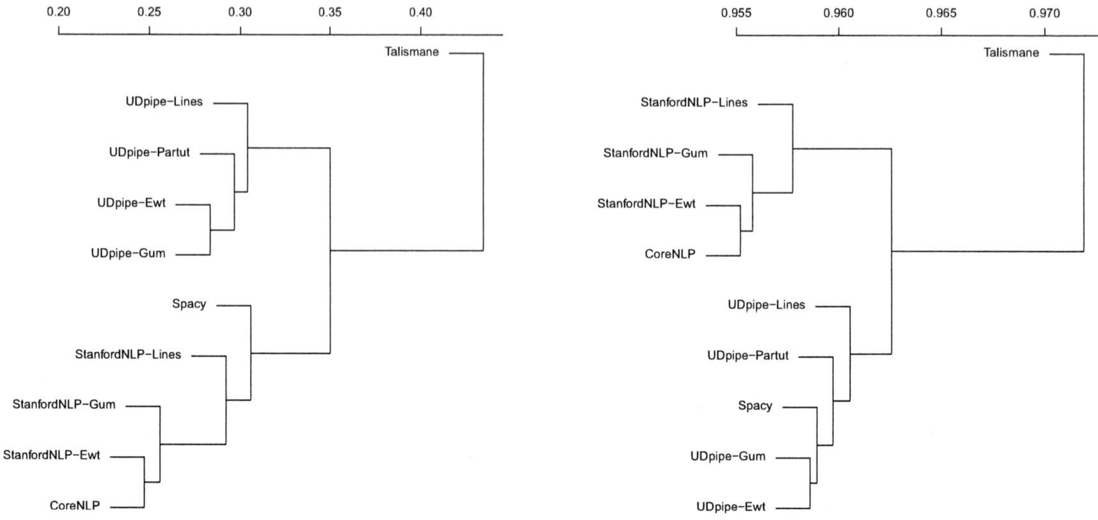

Figure 8: Hierarchical clustering of models according to their agreement on the first nearest neighbor with an UMLS relation with its entry (left side) and according to the RBO measure for all the neighbors having a UMLS relation with their entry (right side).

sequence, this evaluation emphasizes that the type of the parser used for extracting dependency triplets is the first criterion in terms of impact on the distributional models built from them but it also shows that in this context, the corpora used for training these parsers also have an influence and that heterogeneous corpora such as GUM and EWT are probably better for this training than a much more homogeneous corpus such as LinES.

6. Conclusion and Perspectives

In this article, we have investigated the influence of syntactic parsers on the distributional count-based models built from syntactic dependencies. More precisely, we have performed this study in the context of a specialized domain in the biomedical area with a moderate-size corpus made of scientific articles. One particularity of this study is to focus on the concepts of a reference ontology in the medical and biomedical areas. These concepts are mainly present in documents through multi-terms and identified by a reference tool, MetaMap, which requires aligning MetaMap's results with the results of the considered parsers. We have investigated the differences between parsers in terms of syntactic triplets but also in terms of distributional neighbors extracted from the models built from these triplets, both with and without an external reference concerning the semantic relations between concepts. We have more particularly shown the influence of the type of parser in these different evaluations but also the impact of the corpus used for training the parsers. Finally, we have found that some patterns of proximity between parsers are stable across our evaluations, which means that some measures applied to the output of syntactic parsers may perhaps be used to anticipate the performance of a parser for building distributional models from a given corpus. This will be the focus of our future work.

7. Acknowledgments

This work has been funded by French National Research Agency (ANR) under project ADDICTE (ANR-17-CE23-0001).

8. Bibliographical References

Ahrenberg, L. (2015). Converting an english-swedish parallel treebank to universal dependencies. In *Third International Conference on Dependency Linguistics (DepLing 2015), Uppsala, Sweden, August 24-26, 2015*, pages 10–19. Association for Computational Linguistics.

Aronson, A. R. and Lang, F.-M. (2010). An overview of metamap: historical perspective and recent advances. *Journal of the American Medical Informatics Association (JAMIA)*, 17(3):229–236.

Aronson, A. R. (2001). Effective mapping of biomedical text to the umls metathesaurus: the metamap program. In *Proceedings of the AMIA Symposium*, page 17. American Medical Informatics Association.

Baroni, M. and Lenci, A. (2010). Distributional memory: A general framework for corpus-based semantics. *Computational Linguistics*, 36(4):673–721.

Baroni, M., Dinu, G., and Kruszewski, G. (2014). Don't count, predict! A systematic comparison of context-counting vs. context-predicting semantic vectors. In *52nd Annual Meeting of the Association for Computational Linguistics (ACL 2014)*, pages 238–247, Baltimore, Maryland.

Bodenreider, O. (2004). The Unified Medical Language System (UMLS): integrating biomedical terminology. *Nucleic acids research*, 32(suppl 1):D267–D270.

Bosco, C., Sanguinetti, M., and Lesmo, L. (2012). The parallel-TUT: a multilingual and multiformat treebank. In *Proceedings of LREC*, pages 1932–1938. European Language Resources Association (ELRA).

Candito, M., Nivre, J., Denis, P., and Anguiano, E. H. (2010). Benchmarking of statistical dependency parsers for French. In *Proceedings of the 23rd International Conference on Computational Linguistics: Posters*, pages 108–116. Association for Computational Linguistics.

Curran, J. R. and Moens, M. (2002). Improvements in automatic thesaurus extraction. In *Workshop of the ACL Special Interest Group on the Lexicon (SIGLEX)*, pages 59–66, Philadelphia, USA.

De La Clergerie, E. V., Hamon, O., Mostefa, D., Ayache, C., Paroubek, P., and Vilnat, A. (2008). Passage: from French parser evaluation to large sized treebank. In *Proceedings of LREC*.

De La Clergerie, É. V. (2014). Jouer avec des analyseurs syntaxiques. In *Actes de TALN*.

Ferret, O. (2010). Testing semantic similarity measures for extracting synonyms from a corpus. In 7th *International Conference on Language Resources and Evaluation (LREC'10)*, pages 3338–3343, Valletta, Malta

Grefenstette, G. (1994). *Explorations in automatic thesaurus discovery*. Kluwer.

Habert, B., Naulleau, E., and Nazarenko, A. (1996). Symbolic word clustering for medium-size corpora. In *16th International Conference on Computational Linguistics (COLING 1996)*, pages 490–495, Copenhagen, Denmark.

Honnibal, M. and Johnson, M. (2015). An Improved Non-monotonic Transition System for Dependency Parsing. In *Proceedings of the 2015 Conference on Empirical Methods in Natural Language Processing*, pages 1373–1378, Lisbon, Portugal, September. Association for Computational Linguistics.

Hovy, E., Marcus, M., Palmer, M., Ramshaw, L., and Weischedel, R. (2006). Ontonotes: The 90% solution. In *Proceedings of the Human Language Technology Conference of the NAACL (HLT-NAACL 2006), Short Papers*, page 57–60, USA. Association for Computational Linguistics.

Kiela, D. and Clark, S. (2014). A Systematic Study of Semantic Vector Space Model Parameters. In *2nd Workshop on Continuous Vector Space Models and their Compositionality (CVSC)*, pages 21–30, Gothenburg, Sweden.

Koo, T., Carreras, X., and Collins, M. (2008). Simple semi-supervised dependency parsing. *Proceedings of ACL-08: HLT*, pages 595–603.

Lapesa, G. and Evert, S. (2017). Large-scale evaluation of dependency-based DSMs: Are they worth the effort? In *Proceedings of the 15th Conference of the European Chapter of the Association for Computational Linguistics (EACL 2017), Short Papers*, volume 2, pages 394–400.

Levy, O. and Goldberg, Y. (2014). Dependency-Based Word Embeddings. In *52nd Annual Meeting of the Association for Computational Linguistics (ACL 2014)*, pages 302–308, Baltimore, Maryland, June.

Levy, O., Goldberg, Y., and Dagan, I. (2015). Improving Distributional Similarity with Lessons Learned from Word Embeddings. *Transactions of the Association for Computational Linguistics*, 3:211–225.

Lin, D. (1998). Automatic retrieval and clustering of similar words. In *Proceedings of the 17th international conference on Computational linguistics*, pages 768–774. Association for Computational Linguistics.

Manning, C. D., Surdeanu, M., Bauer, J., Finkel, J., Bethard, S. J., and McClosky, D. (2014). The Stanford CoreNLP natural language processing toolkit. In *Proceedings of the 52nd Annual Meeting of the Association for Computational Linguistics: System Demonstrations*, pages 55–60.

Marcus, M., Santorini, B., and Marcinkiewicz, M. A. (1993). Building a large annotated corpus of English: The Penn Treebank.

Mikolov, T., Chen, K., Corrado, G., and Dean, J. (2013). Efficient estimation of word representations in vector space. In *ICLR 2013, workshop track*.

Padó, S. and Lapata, M. (2007). Dependency-based construction of semantic space models. *Computational Linguistics*, 33(2):161–199.

Paroubek, P., Robba, I., Vilnat, A., and Ayache, C. (2008). EASY, Evaluation of Parsers of French: what are the results? In *Proceedings of LREC*.

Pierrejean, B. and Tanguy, L. (2018). Towards qualitative word embeddings evaluation: Measuring neighbors variation. In *Conference of the North American Chapter of the Association for Computational Linguistics: Student Research Workshop*, pages 32–39.

Qi, P., Dozat, T., Zhang, Y., and Manning, C. D. (2018). Universal Dependency Parsing from Scratch. In *Proceedings of the CoNLL 2018 Shared Task: Multilingual Parsing from Raw Text to Universal Dependencies*, pages 160–170, Brussels, Belgium, October. Association for Computational Linguistics.

Savova, G. K., Masanz, J. J., Ogren, P. V., Zheng, J., Sohn, S., Kipper-Schuler, K. C., and Chute, C. G. (2010). Mayo clinical Text Analysis and Knowledge Extraction System (cTAKES): architecture, component evaluation and applications. *Journal of the American Medical Informatics Association*, 17(5):507–513.

Seddah, D., Tsarfaty, R., Kübler, S., Candito, M., Choi, J. D., Farkas, R., Foster, J., Goenaga, I., Gojenola Galletebeitia, K., Goldberg, Y., Green, S., Habash, N., Kuhlmann, M., Maier, W., Nivre, J., Przepiórkowski, A., Roth, R., Seeker, W., Versley, Y., Vincze, V., Woliński, M., Wróblewska, A., and Villemonte de la Clergerie, E. (2013). Overview of the SPMRL 2013 shared task: A cross-framework evaluation of parsing morphologically rich languages. In *Proceedings of the Fourth Workshop on Statistical Parsing of Morphologically-Rich Languages*, pages 146–182, Seattle, Washington, USA, October. Association for Computational Linguistics.

Silveira, N., Dozat, T., de Marneffe, M.-C., Bowman, S., Connor, M., Bauer, J., and Manning, C. D. (2014). A gold standard dependency corpus for English. In *Proceedings of the Ninth International Conference on Language Resources and Evaluation (LREC-2014)*.

Soldaini, L. and Goharian, N. (2016). Quickumls: a fast, unsupervised approach for medical concept extraction. In *MedIR workshop, sigir*, pages 1–4.

Straka, M. and Straková, J. (2017). Tokenizing, POS tagging, lemmatizing and parsing UD 2.0 with UDPipe. In *Proceedings of the CoNLL 2017 Shared Task: Multilingual Parsing from Raw Text to Universal Dependencies*, pages 88–99, Vancouver, Canada, August. Association for Computational Linguistics.

Tanguy, L., Sajous, F., and Hathout, N. (2015). Évaluation sur mesure de modèles distributionnels sur un corpus spécialisé: comparaison des approches par contextes syntaxiques et par fenêtres graphiques. *Traitement automatique des langues*, 56(2).

Tanguy, L., Brunet, P., and Ferret, O. (2020). Extrinsic evaluation of french dependency parsers on a specialised corpus: comparison of distributional thesauri. In *12th International Conference on Language Resources and Evaluation (LREC 2020)*, Marseille, France.

Urieli, A. and Tanguy, L. (2013). L'apport du faisceau dans l'analyse syntaxique en dépendances par transitions : études de cas avec l'analyseur Talismane. In *Actes de TALN*, pages 188–201, Les Sables d'Olonne, France.

Webber, W., Moffat, A., and Zobel, J. (2010). A similarity measure for indefinite rankings. *ACM Transactions on Information Systems (TOIS)*, 28(4):1–38, November.

Zeldes, A. (2017). The GUM corpus: Creating multilayer resources in the classroom. *Language Resources and Evaluation*, 51(3):581–612.

Zeman, D., Haji, J., Popel, M., Potthast, M., Straka, M., Ginter, F., Nivre, J., and Petrov, S. (2018). CoNLL 2018 shared task: Multilingual parsing from raw text to universal dependencies. *Proceedings of the CoNLL 2018 Shared Task: Multilingual Parsing from Raw Text to Universal Dependencies*, pages 1–21.

Proceedings of the 6th International Workshop on Computational Terminology (COMPUTERM 2020), pages 37–42
Language Resources and Evaluation Conference (LREC 2020), Marseille, 11–16 May 2020
© European Language Resources Association (ELRA), licensed under CC-BY-NC

Leveraging the Inherent Hierarchy of Vacancy Titles
for Automated Job Ontology Expansion

Jeroen Van Hautte, Vincent Schelstraete, Mikaël Wornoo
TechWolf, Belgium
{jeroen,vincent,mikael}@techwolf.be

Abstract

Machine learning plays an ever-bigger part in online recruitment, powering intelligent matchmaking and job recommendations across many of the world's largest job platforms. However, the main text is rarely enough to fully understand a job posting: more often than not, much of the required information is condensed into the job title. Several organised efforts have been made to map job titles onto a hand-made knowledge base as to provide this information, but these only cover around 60% of online vacancies. We introduce a novel, purely data-driven approach towards the detection of new job titles. Our method is conceptually simple, extremely efficient and competitive with traditional NER-based approaches. Although the standalone application of our method does not outperform a finetuned BERT model, it can be applied as a preprocessing step as well, substantially boosting accuracy across several architectures.

Keywords: job titles, emerging entity detection, automatic term recognition

1. Introduction

Following the advent of online recruitment, the job market is evolving increasingly towards AI-driven personalised treatment of job seekers (le Vrang et al., 2014). This personalisation is typically powered through the combination of machine learning models with extensive knowledge bases, developed both in the private (Zhao et al., 2015; Neculoiu et al., 2016) and public (le Vrang et al., 2014; De Smedt et al., 2015) sector. In this setup, ontologies serve an important function: just like real-life job seekers start with a rough estimate of a given vacancy based on its title, job ontologies provide a similar estimate for thousands of job titles. As vacancies often do not describe the full job contents, but rather provide details on top of the background information contained in this estimate, this allows for a richer and more complete view of the job posting at hand.

Many of the taxonomies in use today are curated by hand, as opposed to being data driven this allows for overall high quality and carefully considered structure. However, even with great effort their coverage of the job market is still limited. For example, the ESCO taxonomy (ESCO, 2017) only covers around 60% of all job postings available in English, with coverage for other languages often being substantially lower. This disadvantage is typically remedied with machine learning based approaches: an embedding is calculated for any given vacancy title, after which the nearest neighbour among the titles in the knowledge base is selected (Neculoiu et al., 2016). While this technique generally works well, it has a crucial weakness: if the job title at hand is conceptually new (or unknown), it can never be mapped onto the knowledge base correctly. As such, any blind spot of the curators can be the direct cause of errors made by the system. With occupations and skills changing faster than ever, such a setup cannot be kept up to date by hand, even with extensive resources.

Instead of building knowledge bases by hand, it is also pos-

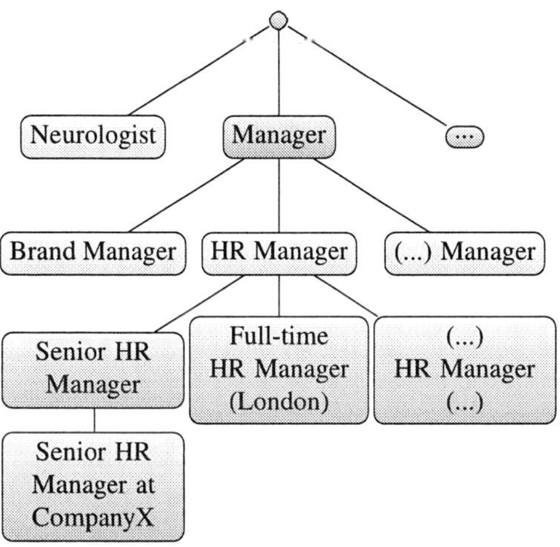

Figure 1: Job titles (green) and vacancy titles (red) tend to follow an intuitive hierarchy based on lexical inclusion.

sible to leverage the massive amount of data produced by online recruitment. More precisely, new job titles can be detected from the stream of vacancy titles.[1] This problem translates to a typical named entity recognition (NER) setup. While this purely NLP-based approach is often effective, it also largely ignores the underlying structure that holds for job titles. In this paper, we introduce a novel data-driven approach that, using only a large set of vacancy titles, is competitive with conventional neural network-based NER methods. Furthermore, our method can be combined both with these models to gain a substantial performance boost. Our approach is intuitive, lightweight and orders of magnitude faster than competitive models.

---

[1]Throughout this paper, 'job title' is used for the name of a function, while a 'vacancy title' is the title of a vacancy page – for example, 'digital marketeer' is a job title, while 'digital marketeer at Google, London' is a vacancy title.

human resources manager

English (en)

Discuss this topic in the Online Forum

Description

Human resources managers plan, design and implement processes related to
the human capital of companies. They develop programs for recruiting,
interviewing, and selecting employees based on a previous assessment of the
profile and skills required in the company. Moreover, they manage
compensation and development programs for the company's employees
comprising trainings, skill assessment and yearly evaluations, promotion,
expat programs, and general assurance of the well-being of the employees in
the workplace.

Alternative label

human resources specialist

career advice office manager

employee benefits manager

staffing manager

recruitment manager

Figure 2: An example of an occupation profile from ESCO. Each occupation has a preferred and alternative labels, a description and a list of optional and essential skills, competences and knowledge.

2. Related Work

2.1. Job & Skill Ontologies

The European Skills, Competences, Qualifications and Occupations taxonomy (ESCO, 2017) is a handcrafted ontology connecting jobs and skills. It is available in 27 languages and covers close to 3000 distinct occupations, as well as more than 13000 skills. ESCO is funded by the European Commission and is under continuous, active development by its Directorate-General for Employment, Social Affairs and Inclusion. This paper uses version 1.0.3 of the ESCO Classification. Figure 2 shows an example of an occupation profile – our setup makes use of the preferred label and alternative labels for each occupation.

While ESCO seeks to model occupations and competences at a European level, there are also many alternatives. Each of these has a similar underlying idea, but a different scope or execution strategy. For example, the United States has its O*NET classification (Peterson et al., 2001), while France has the ROME standard and the Flemish employment agency VDAB has its own, ROME-based competency standard Competent. Although the experts composing these ontologies leverage data to compose their standards, none of them is data-driven: instead, occupation profiles are typically determined per sector by relevant experts.

2.2. NER Models

We compare and combine our novel method with two Named Entity Recognition models: an Iterated Dilated Convolutional Neural Network (ID-CNN) (Strubell et al., 2017) as implemented in SpaCy (Honnibal and Montani, 2017) and a fine-tuned BERT model (Devlin et al., 2019) based on the popular transformers library (Wolf et al., 2019). In both cases, we make use of an IOB named entity tagging scheme.

2.3. Automatic Term Recognition

Finding new job titles in a stream of vacancy titles is a form of automatic term recognition. However, typically this field focuses on finding terminology inside long, grammatical documents rather than titles. Frantzi et al. (1998) use statistical properties of domain-specific language to detect terms in a corpus using their C-value technique. An important principle leveraged in their work is the occurrence of nested terms: terms tend to occur in other, longer terms (as a substring). A useful term is then characterised by its 'independence' from longer terms: if something can be used as a term independently, it typically occurs in a larger number of different longer phrases. Since its publication, the C-value/NC-value technique has been applied broadly for detection of multiword expressions, as well as ontology population and expansion based on free text (Petasis et al., 2011). Lexical inclusion relations have also been found to account for a substantial part of hierarchical relations among medical concepts (Grabar and Zweigenbaum, 2002), showing that these principles can be leveraged to construct an accurate hierarchy at a relatively low computational cost.

2.4. Job Title Detection & Classification

Detecting new job titles and assigning job titles to existing classes are two closely related problems. However, as ontologies have largely been composed manually, the focus of most relevant research has been on the latter: instead of using machine learning to build a structure, the techniques are leveraged to position new samples inside the existing hierarchy. For example, Javed et al. (2016) use a hierarchical classification system to link job titles to the O*NET classification, using the Lingo algorithm (Osinski and Weiss, 2005) to generate a title hierarchy, after which the formed clusters are assigned to different O*NET concepts. Building upon this work, Wang et al. (2019) use a single end-to-end multistream CNN architecture to classify titles, leveraging both vacancy titles and descriptions. Neculoiu et al. (2016), using a different approach, train a siamese neural network to specifically embed vacancy titles in such a way that relevant job title information is prioritised. This network is then used to map titles onto a proprietary ontology. As related work is generally closed-source, only has a high-level description or does not include an evaluation dataset, we are unable to compare our work with it directly.

3. Method

3.1. Job Titles

For this inquiry, we define a job title for a vacancy to be the minimal subspan of the vacancy title that is needed to determine to which occupation inside ESCO it can be linked. For example, for a vacancy titled "Senior HR Manager at CompanyX", the job title would be "HR Manager". Modifiers to the job title that concern seniority, practical details or other information are not needed to classify a job within ESCO, as opposed to the words selected. We assume that a job title is always a single, connected span.

3.2. Title Trees

An important assumption in treating the problem of labelling vacancies with job titles as a NER problem is that inside each vacancy title, a correct job title is present as a subspan. In practice, a vacancy title might not contain a job title (or could contain multiple), but this assumption holds for an overwhelming majority of online job postings, with exceptions typically being poorly composed titles. For example, many of these nonconforming titles are made up of a single, often nonsensical word, most likely provided as a way to fill in a required field, rather than with the intent of informing job seekers. Looking beyond these exceptions, we find a simple, yet interesting hierarchy among job and vacancy titles, as shown in Figure 1. In this structure, the parent-child relationship is that of lexical inclusion: a parent is always a substring of each of its children.[2] As we move deeper into the tree from the root node, the titles encountered grow increasingly specific, as the addition of more information to a title narrows its scope. Following such a path, there are three types of nodes encountered, following a set order:

1. **Pre-title nodes**: these nodes are parts of job or vacancy titles, but are not valid titles themselves. For example, "Manager" or "Junior" are part of this category.

2. **Job title nodes**: these nodes are both valid job and vacancy titles. Some cases, such as "Neurologist", have no parents other than the root node, while others, such as "HR Manager", do.

3. **Vacancy title nodes**: these nodes are valid vacancy titles, but not valid job titles. They are almost[3] always inside a subtree that has a job title node at its root.

Given a set of unlabelled vacancy titles, we can construct this tree structure easily by checking which titles contain which other titles. The problem of finding a job title within a given vacancy title is then reduced to finding the right ancestor for this vacancy title (or possibly the title itself). The tree can be implemented efficiently as a trie. In this structure, each node is represented by an ordered sequence of words, with the root being the empty sequence. To insert a new title starting at a given node, its sequence is compared to that of each child. If a child sequence is contained in the current title, the process is continued starting from this child. When no such child can be found, the title is added as a new child to this node. The construction of this trie has a complexity of $Mlog(N)$, where M is the maximal number of words per title and N is the number of unique titles inside the data structure. By inserting the titles in the order of their number of tokens, each title can be inserted as a leaf node, reducing the implementation complexity substantially.

---

[2]For simplicity, the figure shows a single parent for each title – in practice, multiple copies of the same title can exist for different parents.

[3]Looking at large numbers of online vacancies, we observe that job titles that are frequent enough always occur as standalone vacancy titles.

3.3. Title Occurrence Ratio (TOR)

With this title tree, we have now created a setup very similar to the one used by Frantzi et al. (1998) for their C-Value/NC-Value method. However, while the latter uses a collection of n-grams generated from a longer text, this situation involves a large number of much shorter documents. This exposes an essential incompatibility of the C-value method with vacancy titles: while the C-Value is very suitable to distinguish between pre-title and job/vacancy title nodes, the difference between the latter two is much harder to assess, as both job titles and long vacancy titles get very high C-Values. Using a minimum count and maximum length can provide some relief but does not remove the problem entirely. Using the same principles as Frantzi et al. (1998), we therefore introduce the Title Occurrence Ratio (TOR), which reflects the ratio between how often a title occurs as a standalone vacancy title, and how often it occurs in general (including appearances as a substring of a vacancy title). Unlike the C-Value method, our approach does not treat stop words or certain part-of-speech tags differently, as this was found to make no difference for our use case. The *GetRatio* function in the algorithm below shows how to calculate the ratio for a given title, leveraging the trie data structure described in the previous subsection. Note that for efficiency, the different calls to *BuildTrie* can be replaced by a single, pre-built trie structure.

Input: $T_1 \ldots T_N$ (normalised vacancy titles)
Input: $Counts$ (a dictionary with the count for each title)
Input: $VacTitle$ (the vacancy title at hand)
Output: $JobTitle$ (the predicted job title subspan)

```
 1: function GETPARENTS(Title, T[ ])
 2:     Trie ← BuildTrie(T[ ]) // Build a trie with all titles.
 3:     Anc ← Trie.extract(Title) // Find all ancestors.
 4:     PN ← {} // Initialise parent nodes as empty.
 5:     for X in sort(Anc, key=λX → −X.length) do
 6:         PN.add(X)
 7:         PN ← PN − GetParents(X, Trie)
 8:     end for
 9:     return PN
10:
11: function GETRATIO(Title, T[ ])
12:     C_0 ← Counts[Title]
13:     C_1 ← 0
14:     for X in GetParents(Title, T[ ]) do
15:         C_1 ← C_1 + Counts[X]
16:     end for
17:     return C_0 / (C_0 + C_1)
18:
19: function GETJOBTITLE(VacTitle, T[ ])
20:     Trie ← BuildTrie(T[ ])
21:     Cand ← Trie.extract(VacTitle) + {VacTitle}
22:     Cand.filter(λX → R_min < GetRatio(X) < R_max)
23:     return max(Cand, λX → GetRatio(X))
```

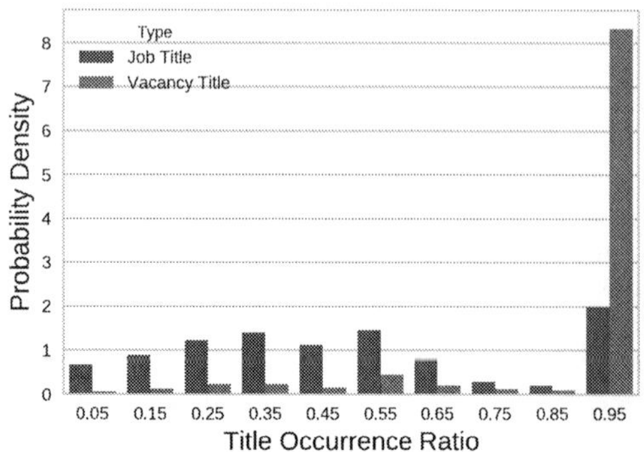

Figure 3: The probability distribution of both job and vacancy titles over their Title Occurrence Ratio.

3.4. The TOR Method

We now propose our novel job title extraction method based on this ratio. As figure 3 shows, the general distribution of vacancy title ratios (in green) differs greatly from that of job titles (in blue). While it is not possible to separate the two based on this number alone, vacancy titles tend to have a ratio close to one, while job titles have a much softer distribution centred around 0.45. It should be noted that the vacancy title distribution contains a component that looks much like the job title distribution – this is potentially linked to job titles not included in the ESCO dataset. Similarly, there are job titles with a very high TOR, which are most likely to be rare job titles that do not occur more than a handful of times within our dataset.

As described in Section 3.2., a path from root to leaf can be seen as having up to three phases, with the job title phase (which we want to select) lodged in the middle. As the title ratio typically increases steadily from root to leaf, we aim to build a very simple selection system by placing an upper and lower bound on the ratio. Both of these boundaries are optimised using a labelled training dataset, after the construction of the title tree using the combined training and test set. With these selection boundaries in place, the job title for a given vacancy title is now predicted to be its closest ancestor that does not violate the upper and lower bound. Our method is applied as a standalone technique, as well as to preprocess titles before feeding them to the CNN and BERT models.

4. Evaluation

The goal of our system is to find new or unknown job titles within a stream of vacancy titles. We measure the success of each approach by evaluating how well it manages to extract job titles from their respective vacancy titles. We make use of two separate types of metrics:

- **Title level metrics**: the main metric is the **title level accuracy**, which measures how often a fully correct title for a vacancy was extracted. This is the most direct representative for the actual value of a system in practice, as high accuracy is required to be able to contribute to an ontology.

- **Token level metrics**: while the title level accuracy allows for the best performance ranking, insights on the token-level predictions for each method can prove valuable as well. By measuring how well each system predicts whether a token in the vacancy title is part of the corresponding job title, we can gain a better understanding of its behaviour. For example, a system might have low title level accuracy due to a bias towards longer titles, which can be easily read from the token level precision and recall.

For each metric, we calculate both the micro and macro average (grouped by the job title label), as to be able to compare performance for frequent and rare job titles. Our main metric, title level prediction accuracy, corresponds directly to a large part of the value of our system in a practical context, as it is only possible to gain useful information about new and unknown titles if they are extracted from vacancies correctly. As to mimic this scenario for our evaluation setup, we separate ESCO into a training set (the set of known titles) and a test set (the set of new/unknown titles). We make sure to avoid these sets influencing each other directly, by ensuring there are no lexical inclusion relations between members of different sets. Using a sample of 1 million scraped vacancy titles[4], we now select the vacancies containing each of these titles, using the contained job title as the gold standard.[5] We find that in 57.4% of all vacancies, an ESCO title is included in the title – vacancies where no match could be found are kept separately in the background set. While this background set is not a part of the training or test set, we include it for the training phase of the TOR method, as to make sure that the evaluation task does not have a bias towards methods based on lexical inclusion properties. In our final dataset, the training set contains 124 108 unique vacancy titles, while the test set contains 45 647 vacancy titles.

We evaluate two separate versions of the TOR method: TOR_{1M}, which is trained on the original set of 1 million vacancy titles (including the training, test and background set) and TOR_{100M}, which is trained on a much larger set of 100 million vacancy titles. Optimising on the training set, we find optimal ratio boundaries of 0.03 and 0.69. TOR_{100M} is only applied as a standalone model, to reflect performance changes when more data is added. For the NER methods, only the longest continuous span of tokens marked as a job title by the model is used as a prediction, as a fragmented prediction would always be counted as an error due to the construction of our dataset. We also include two baselines: the identity baseline, which predicts the entire vacancy title to be part of the job title, and the C-Value method by Frantzi et al. (1998), using an optimal minimum count of 5 and C-Value threshold of 0.

---

[4]From company websites and job boards in the UK.

[5]While this annotation can cause errors in some cases, it resolves the problem of collecting sufficient annotated data.

	Micro Average				**Macro Average**			
Method	Precision	Recall	F_1	Title Acc.	Precision	Recall	F_1	Title Acc.
Identity Baseline	0.33	**1.00***	0.20	0.02	0.53	**1.00***	0.70	0.25
CValue	0.78	0.90	0.83	0.59	0.77	0.56	0.65	0.30
CNN	0.89	0.82	0.85	0.67	0.89	0.79	0.84	0.61
BERT	0.93	0.94	0.93	0.81	0.94	0.89	0.92	0.71
TOR_{1M}	0.88	0.91	0.90	0.72	0.81	0.50	0.62	0.18
TOR_{100M}	0.85	0.93	0.89	0.68	0.86	0.79	0.82	0.59
TOR_{1M} + CNN	0.85	0.93	0.89	0.73	0.88	0.84	0.86	0.64
TOR_{1M} + BERT	**0.94**	0.95	**0.94**	**0.84**	**0.95**	0.90	**0.93**	**0.74**

Table 1: Evaluation results on the constructed task – the best result in each column is marked in bold. (*) Recall of the identity baseline is 1 by construction.

5. Results

The results for the job title extraction task are shown in Table 1. Consistent with earlier work (Devlin et al., 2019), the BERT model substantially outperforms the CNN both in terms of micro and macro average. While the C-Value method outperforms the identity baseline, it generally lags behind other methods across the board. Our novel TOR method is competitive with the neural methods, with both TOR_{1M} and TOR_{100M} outperforming the CNN in terms of micro-average. TOR_{1M} exhibits a clear performance decrease for rare titles, as shown by its low macro averaged scores. However, feeding the same algorithm with 100 million vacancy titles instead, scores show a substantial boost. The TOR method is over 100 times faster than both BERT and the convolutional model, as well as having a smaller memory footprint. This makes our method especially interesting for applications with strict timing requirements or massive amounts of data. For applications where timing is of lesser importance, the TOR method can still be beneficial: the hybrid models, combining TOR with a more typical NER model, show consistent performance improvements across the board. This is especially clear in the improved title-level accuracy, showing that the inherent hierarchical structure of job and vacancy titles can be leveraged to improve general-purpose models. Our method is extremely efficient, compatible with any NER method and easy to implement, making for an easy way to improve job matching systems. By construction, the evaluation setup reflects the discovery of previously fully unknown job titles, showing that these methods are of particular interest for the (semi-)automated expansion of job market ontologies, leveraging data-driven insights to keep standards up to date in a job market that is changing faster than ever. During the review phase for this paper, we applied our method at the behest of VDAB, the Flemish employment agency. In this project, our technique was used to suggest new titles for its Competent standard. As Competent is written in Dutch, we used the RobBERT model introduced by Delobelle et al. (2020). We found results to be comparable to those obtained in English on the ESCO ontology, with the main difference being a higher macro averaged score, likely to be the consequence of the different methodology used to construct Competent. These results show that our method generalises across multiple languages and occupational taxonomies.

6. Conclusion

While the current trend of ever-bigger NLP models does result in the promised performance gains, we have shown that a simple technique incorporating domain knowledge can provide a further boost to the task of extracting job titles from vacancy titles. Our method is conceptually simple, over two orders of magnitude faster than competing models and can be applied in tandem with more general NER models. While our technique struggles with rare job titles when trained on a small dataset, this issue disappears when more data is added, with the TOR method achieving performance comparable to a CNN. Aside from using our method as a standalone model, it can also be leveraged as a preprocessing step, consistently resulting in improved accuracy. Future work will explore the application of our method in different fields, as well as more advanced ways to leverage the title tree used in this paper.

Acknowledgements

We thank the anonymous reviewers for their valuable feedback. This publication uses the ESCO classification of the European Commission. The application of the techniques described in this paper to the Competent standard is part of a project funded by VDAB.

Bibliographical References

De Smedt, J., le Vrang, M., and Papantoniou, A. (2015). Esco: Towards a semantic web for the european labor market. In *LDOW@ WWW*.

Delobelle, P., Winters, T., and Berendt, B. (2020). Robbert: a dutch roberta-based language model. *arXiv preprint arXiv:2001.06286.*

Devlin, J., Chang, M.-W., Lee, K., and Toutanova, K. (2019). Bert: Pre-training of deep bidirectional transformers for language understanding. In *Proceedings of the 2019 Conference of the North American Chapter of the Association for Computational Linguistics: Human Language Technologies, Volume 1 (Long and Short Papers)*, pages 4171–4186.

Frantzi, K. T., Ananiadou, S., and Tsujii, J.-i. (1998). The C-value/NC-value method of automatic recognition for multi-word terms. In *Proceedings of the Second European Conference on Research and Advanced Technology for Digital Libraries*, ECDL '98, pages 585–604, London, UK, UK. Springer-Verlag.

Grabar, N. and Zweigenbaum, P. (2002). Lexically-based terminology structuring: Some inherent limits. In Lee-Feng Chien, et al., editors, *Second International Workshop on Computational Terminology (COMPUTERM 2002)*, pages 36–42, Taipei, Taiwan. ACLCLP.

Honnibal, M. and Montani, I. (2017). spacy 2: Natural language understanding with bloom embeddings, convolutional neural networks and incremental parsing.

Javed, F., McNair, M., Jacob, F., and Zhao, M. (2016). Towards a job title classification system. *arXiv preprint arXiv:1606.00917*.

le Vrang, M., Papantoniou, A., Pauwels, E., Fannes, P., Vandensteen, D., and De Smedt, J. (2014). Esco: Boosting job matching in europe with semantic interoperability. volume 47, pages 57–64. IEEE.

Neculoiu, P., Versteegh, M., and Rotaru, M. (2016). Learning text similarity with siamese recurrent networks. In *Proceedings of the 1st Workshop on Representation Learning for NLP*, pages 148–157.

Osinski, S. and Weiss, D. (2005). A concept-driven algorithm for clustering search results. *IEEE Intelligent Systems*, 20(3):48–54.

Petasis, G., Karkaletsis, V., Paliouras, G., Krithara, A., and Zavitsanos, E. (2011). Ontology population and enrichment: State of the art. In *Knowledge-driven multimedia information extraction and ontology evolution*, pages 134–166. Springer.

Peterson, N. G., Mumford, M. D., Borman, W. C., Jeanneret, P. R., Fleishman, E. A., Levin, K. Y., Campion, M. A., Mayfield, M. S., Morgeson, F. P., Pearlman, K., et al. (2001). Understanding work using the occupational information network (o* net): Implications for practice and research. *Personnel Psychology*, 54(2):451–492.

Strubell, E., Verga, P., Belanger, D., and McCallum, A. (2017). Fast and accurate entity recognition with iterated dilated convolutions. *Proceedings of the 2017 Conference on Empirical Methods in Natural Language Processing*.

Wang, J., Abdelfatah, K., Korayem, M., and Balaji, J. (2019). Deepcarotene-job title classification with multistream convolutional neural network. In *2019 IEEE International Conference on Big Data (Big Data)*, pages 1953–1961. IEEE.

Wolf, T., Debut, L., Sanh, V., Chaumond, J., Delangue, C., Moi, A., Cistac, P., Rault, T., Louf, R., Funtowicz, M., et al. (2019). Transformers: State-of-the-art natural language processing. *arXiv preprint arXiv:1910.03771*.

Zhao, M., Javed, F., Jacob, F., and McNair, M. (2015). Skill: A system for skill identification and normalization. In *Twenty-Seventh IAAI Conference*.

Language Resource References

ESCO. (2017). *European Skills, Competences, Qualifications and Occupations*.

Proceedings of the 6th International Workshop on Computational Terminology (COMPUTERM 2020), pages 43–49
Language Resources and Evaluation Conference (LREC 2020), Marseille, 11–16 May 2020
© European Language Resources Association (ELRA), licensed under CC-BY-NC

Terminology in Written Medical Reports: A Proposal of Text Enrichment to Favour its Comprehension by the Patient

Rosa Estopà, Alejandra López-Fuentes, Jorge M. Porras-Garzón
IULA (Universitat Pompeu Fabra)
{rosa.estopa, alejandra.lopez, jorgemario.porras}@upf.edu

Abstract

The empowerment of the population and the democratisation of information regarding healthcare have revealed that there is a communication gap between health professionals and patients. The latter are constantly receiving more and more written information about their healthcare visits and treatments, but that does not mean they understand it. In this paper we focus on the patient's lack of comprehension of medical reports. After linguistically characterising the medical report, we present the results of a survey that showed that patients have serious comprehension difficulties concerning the medical reports they receive, specifically problems regarding the medical terminology used in these texts, specifically in Spanish and Catalan. To favour the understanding of medical reports, we propose an automatic text enrichment strategy that generates linguistically and cognitively enriched medical reports which are more comprehensible to the patient, and which focus on the parts of the medical report that most interest the patient: the diagnosis and treatment sections.

Keywords: medical terminology, medical report, terminology, automatic text enrichment, text comprehension, doctor-patient communication.

1. Introduction

When we talk about written communication between doctor-patient, we refer to all the written information handed over during a person's healthcare practice and which is included in his or her clinical history. Within all this written information, the medical report constitutes a key element for the patient, since it contains the diagnosis and the prescribed treatment (Delàs, 2005; Falcón and Basagoti, 2012). A medical report is a written document issued by a medical professional regarding a specific healthcare procedure undergone by a patient —for example, a visit to the accident and emergency department or a hospital admission.

Starting from a linguistic analysis of a corpus of 50 medical reports of patients affected by a rare disease in Spanish and Catalan (CORPUS-ER)[1], we have established a set of linguistic parameters which characterise this type of texts and which might interfere, if not used properly, the reader's full comprehension of the medical report. These parameters, of different linguistic nature, have been grouped in different categories: (a) pragmatic-semantic; (b) syntactic; (c) **lexical**[2]; and (d) orthotypographical. Each one of these major categories has been broken down into several specific parameters. For example, within the lexicon parameter, we have considered the use of acronyms, terms with Greco-Latin formants and symbols, among others.

Moreover, lexically speaking, medical reports have a high number of terms, an excessive use of **non-expanded acronyms**, **abbreviations** and **symbols**, and a high occurrence of **semantically non-transparent terms**.

2. What is a Medical Term?

Terminological units or terms are lexical units of a given language which in a determined communicative context activate a very precise specialised property (Cabré, 1999). Words with specialised content in the medical context (e.g. traditionally referred to as medical terms) activate a precise, concise and appropriate specialised sense that enables us to talk about health and illness related topics in a proper way.

Some of these terms are well known, for example the ones we experience first-hand (e.g. *lung, eye, flu, menstruation, muscle*); others, although not strange and apparently semantically transparent, are not easy to define without previous biomedical knowledge since the can be more abstract or polysemous (e.g. *gene, symptom, treatment, cholesterol, cancer, stem cell*); while many others are extremely opaque for a non-expert from the point of view of their meaning (e.g. *acromegaly, Lowe's syndrome, CT scan, PET scan, ALS, perimetrosalpingitis, lobectomy*).

Traditionally, terms used in medical texts in Spanish and Catalan are mostly formed by lexical bases from ancient Greek and Latin (Bonavalot, 1978; López Piñero and Terrada Ferrandis, 1990; Bernabeu-Mestre et al., 1995; Gutiérrez Rodilla, 1998; Wulff, 2004; Anderson, 2016); but at present, medical terminology is also influenced by languages such as German or French, but mainly by English. Thus, words like, *buffer, bypass, core, distress, doping, feed-flush, flapping tremor, follow-up, handicap, lumping, mapping, odds ratio, output, patch test, pool, relax, scanner, score*, or *screening* (Navarro, 2001; García Palacios, 2004) are just a small sample of the large number of terms that come directly from English into Spanish.

At the same time there is the belief that the medical terminology is precise, concise, objective and even neutral, as recommended by Terminology ISO standards and many manuals and studies on medical terminology (Bello, 2016; Navarro, 2016; Delàs, 2005). However, from different perspectives it has been found that such a belief cannot be true, as language is significantly complex and communicative situations in medicine are very diverse. It must be remembered that medical terminology is not only used by medical professionals, but also by the entire population —primarily patients and their families— in order to express opinions, fears, concerns and doubts related to their health and illness.

---

[1] The complete analysis can be found in R. Estopà (Coord.) (2020), *Los informes médicos: estrategias lingüísticas para favorecer su comprensión*

[2] In this paper we will focus only in the lexical analysis since we are interested in showing the results regarding the terminology used in medical reports.

In linguistics, terminological units are lexical units which belong to the lexicon of a language. And the lexicon of any language is exponentially complex and almost never complies with the attributes that are presupposed for the scientific lexicon: neutrality, objectivity, monosemy (Navarro, 2016). It is true, however, that there are some terms that we could label as univocal, descriptive and neutral, such as *poliomyelitis*, which has a "unique" meaning, since it represents a concept in its totality and corresponds to an object "constructed" from reality in a specific conceptual structure (that of medicine). But it is evident that on many occasions medical terms are polysemous (for example, the acronym *AA* is used to refer to *acute abdomen*, but also to *amino acid*, *abdominal appendicitis*, *ascending aorta* and *abdominal aorta*); and they also might variate, in other words, have synonyms (for example, a *stroke* is also known as a *brain attack*, a *cerebrovascular accident*, a *cerebrovascular insult*, a *cerebral vascular accident*, a *haemorrhagic stroke*, an *ischemic stroke*, etc.; and it is also referred to with acronyms such as: *CVA* or *CVI*).

This diversity of designations and diversity of senses, in the case of polysemy, results in confusion amongst specialists and in uncertainty amongst patients. For which uncertainty intermingles with the emotional burden that comes with dealing with a disease (García Palacios, 2004). Ultimately, as Wermuth and Verplaetse (2018, pp. 87) summarize: "Although classical terms still represent the foundation of medical terminology, also words from general language, abbreviations and acronyms, eponyms, slang and jargon words, synonyms, metaphors and metonyms, and made-up words are substantial parts of today's medical language". And, as part of medical language, medical reports also include all these types of units.

3. Use of Terms in Medical Reports

Medical reports record the diagnosis, or the therapeutic procedures carried out during any healthcare visit. This type of text has very particular linguistic characteristics which, taken as a whole, make it difficult to be fully understood. Currently, medical reports are mainly expository documents (Estopà and Domènech-Bagaria, 2018). This means that nominalisation in them is very high and, therefore, there are not so many verbs; consequently, the presence of terminology[3] is very high.

Some surveys conducted on patients (Estopà and Domènech-Bagaria, 2018) and on doctors (Navarro, 2016) show that terminology is one of the main obstacles to fully understand a medical report. Moreover, according to the results of the analysis carried out by Estopà and Montané (2020), terminology comprehension obstacles of a medical report can be summarised in the next four parameters:

1. **Specialised knowledge accumulation**: the number of terms contained in medical reports is very high in relation to the average number of words the text has.
2. **Semantic opacity**: terms are often not known by patients, so they are not semantically transparent.
3. **Semantic confusion**: medical terms can lead to misunderstandings as regards their meaning, especially if they correspond to terms of general use that have acquired a specific, specialised sense in medicine and which is, perhaps, different to their general sense.
4. **Semantic ambiguity**: terms variate and are subject to polysemy, which may cause them to be interpreted in different ways, which increase doubt and uncertainty.

According to these authors, these four parameters can be correlated with nine indicators that allow to determine the comprehension difficulty for a patient of a medical report:

A. Total number of terms in a medical report.
B. The percentage of terms relative to all the words in the text.
C. The percentage of abbreviations.
D. The percentage of terms formed by Greek or Latin lexical bases.
E. The percentage of terms of more general use (terms that were included in the general Spanish and Catalan language dictionaries).
F. The percentage of eponyms (terms derived from proper names, usually from scientists' last names, e.g. *Alzheimer's disease*).
G. The percentage of loanwords.
H. The percentage of defined or paraphrased terms (terms where a paraphrase is used in order to explain them).
I. Number of cases of formal terminological variation.

4. Do Patients Understand Terminology in Medical Reports?

In order to demonstrate that terminology detected and analysed in medical reports lead to comprehension problems for the patients, we implemented two different strategies that complemented each other: a general automatic readability test and a comprehension survey.

4.1 Automatic readability tests

Automatic readability tests or readability formulas are tools that indicate if a text is easily readable or not according to quantitative data (e.g. number and length of words, number and length of sentences). There exist different formulas of this nature developed mainly for English texts, formulas such as the *Reading Ease Score* (Flesch, 1948), the *SMOG test* (McLaughlin, 1969), the *Flesch-Kincaid test* (Smith and Kinkaid, 1970) or the *Gunning FOG test* (Gunning, 1952); but some have also been developed for Spanish: the *Fernández-Huerta index* (Fernández Huerta, 1959), the *Szgriszt index* (Szigriszt-Pazos, 1993) or the *INFLESZ tool* (Barrio Cantalejo et al., 2008). Most of these tests or formulas are open access and available online, so we could easily apply them to the medical reports we analysed.

INFLESZ	very difficult	quite difficult	normal	easy
	14.9%	40.4%	36.2%	8.5%

Table 1. INFLESZ test results for the CORPUS-ER

For example, with one of the most recent test developed for Spanish (Table 1), as well as with the remaining tests[4], results showed that medical reports are in general difficult

---

[3] Terms are prototypically nouns (e.g., *dermatographia, dermatitis, dermatology, dermatologist, dermatomycosis, dermatome*), since *noun* is the category that, by definition, binds knowledge together in a referential manner.

[4] For all the details and results of these tests you can check the works of Porras-Garzón and Estopà (2019 and 2020).

to read, hence the need to go further and check qualitatively some of the texts was evident in order to know if they were as difficult to read as the automatic tests reported.

Further qualitative comparison showed that preliminary results of the automatic tests were neither reliable nor discriminating, because these tools are not designed to deal with highly specialised texts (high number of medical terms) such as medical reports. Therefore, it was likely that the actual readability level was even more difficult than what the automatic analysis showed.

4.2 Comprehension survey

The second strategy implemented to confirm the results of the tests and to demonstrate there is a real comprehension problem for the users of medical reports, consisted in a survey which was conducted to a set of people (all of them have been patients and some of them currently are or will in the future be patients).

4.2.1 How was the survey done?

The next steps were followed to carry out the comprehension survey:

1. Selection of one of the medical reports from the CORPUS-ER after the qualitative analysis considering the mean of terminological density and extension.
2. Drafting of a linguistically and cognitively enriched version of said report.
3. Preparation of two comprehension surveys, one for each version of the report (original and enriched), with identical structure and similar questions.
4. An in-person implementation of both surveys was carried out with a group of 100 people. The group was divided into two subgroups: in the first stage, survey A was conducted to group 1 and survey B to group 2; and in the second stage, A to 2 and B to 1 (in this way we avoided the problem of participants learning or getting used to the content of the report from one survey to the other).
5. Statistical treatment of the results (paired-sample t-test in the case of lexical-related numerical variables).
6. Analysis of the results.

So, once the linguistic and terminological parameters that cause comprehension problems had been detected and analysed, we selected a real medical report from our corpus and then produced a new version of it in which said problems were addressed, in order to ensure the maximum understanding by the patient. Although some of the changes made during the enrichment process are in line with the recommendations of the so-called *plain language*, or *simplified language* (NARA guide, 2012), we chose to call the new version of the report a *linguistically and cognitively enriched version*, since no information was removed from it and no terms were discarded nor information paragraphs were altered. The steps taken to enrich the report were the following:

1. correction of grammatical errors (e.g., punctuation marks, missing verbs, order of the elements of a sentence) and typographical inadequacies (e.g., font);
2. **including descriptions and paraphrases of ambiguous or highly specialised lexical elements (terms, phraseology)**;
3. construction of simple phrases that match with Catalan and Spanish prototypical sentence structure of SVO (subject, verb, object);
4. **controlling and expanding abbreviations (abbreviations, acronyms, symbols)**; and
5. personalising the text to bring it closer to the patient (explicit subject, personal verbal form).

In this way, we avoided lowering the cognitive load of these texts, while writing specialised information (term related) in a more explicit way, enriching the report, since the main premise was that patients are not usually able to infer from the text the information naturally inferred by health professionals (e.g. not knowing unexpanded abbreviations or semantically opaque terms). Therefore, a medical report enriched from different perspectives (expanding abbreviations, paraphrasing terms, formulating sentences with conjugated verbs and explicit subjects...) allows the healthcare provider to ensure that the text is explicit, prevents the patient from making erroneous inferences, favours an adequate interpretation of the information and a correct understanding of the full text.

Based on these considerations, from both versions of the medical report (the original and the enriched one), two comprehension surveys with an identical structure were prepared which included the following sections:

- General data for control (sex, age, level of education, mother tongue and profession).
- Answering questions related to previous general perceptions about the comprehension of medical reports.
- Reading the corresponding medical report for the survey (original or enriched version).
- Answering different questions intended to measure the perception about the understanding of the read medical report (original and enriched version). Questions such as *If you didn't understand one section of the text, what do you think is the cause? a) Unknown words, b) Known words that I don't fully understand, c) Unknown acronyms and symbols, d) Unfamiliar expressions, e) Other causes, if so, which?*
- Answering questions intended to measure the actual understanding of the read medical report (term related questions included).
- Comparing fragments of the two versions of the report to know explicitly which of the two was better understood and which of the two was preferred by the patient considering that the information was the same.

Once the general survey parameters were applied, it was essential to carry out a pilot measurement survey (Scheaffer et al., 1987; Sampieri et al., 2000) on a small sample of 25 participants to test its functionality. Testing the survey allowed us to verify the parameters and modify them when needed. After the pilot, the survey was conducted to a total of 100 participants of different ages and level of studies. Participants were divided into two groups of 50 and all of them responded both surveys. On a first stage, the original report survey was conducted on one group and the enriched report survey on the other group; on a final stage the opposite was done: each group took the corresponding remaining survey. This allowed us to ensure there was no learning between one survey and the other.

4.2.2 Discussion of the results

The results obtained after both surveys were highly significant and discriminating. For example, in the case of the lexical-related numerical variables a paired-sample t-test was performed in order to establish the significance value for the difference between means (the mean of comprehension results of the first survey and the mean of the second one), and the p-value was $p < 0.0001$. So, this allowed us to conclude that most of the participants: a) had difficulties in understanding the original version of the medical report —even participants with a higher educational degree—; b) did not have as many difficulties in understanding the enriched version of the medical report— even the participants with a lower educational degree—; and c) understood the enriched version of the report better than the original version.

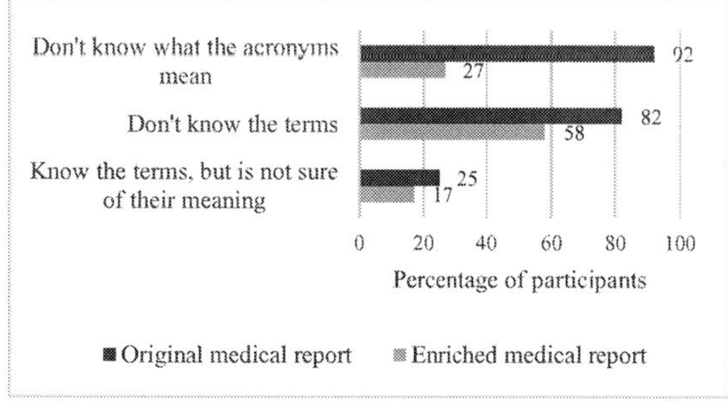

Chart 1: Perception of comprehension of the term related information in the medical reports

The results shown in Chart 1 correspond to the questions intended to measure the patient's perception of comprehension of terms and acronyms within the text. Here participants had to choose what they believed made more difficult to understand the report they just read. We can observe that in general patients perceived the original medical report as more semantically opaque. For example, regarding the unexpanded acronyms, for the original report almost all the participants (92%) selected as a comprehension obstacle the fact that acronyms were not easy to understand, while in the adapted text only 27% of participants felt the same way. Almost the same happens with the perception of unknown terms and, in a lower degree, the perception of barely known terms.

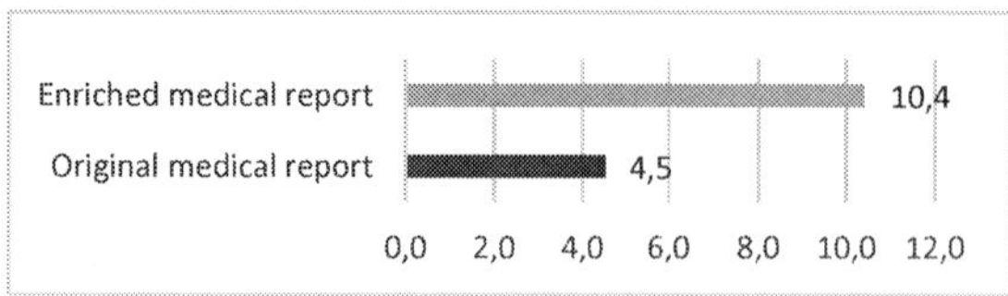

Chart 2: Actual comprehension of the term related questions

In Chart 2 the results regarding the actual comprehension of the term/acronym-related questions (e.g. *what does CBZ refer to?* or *What is nefrocalcinosis?*[5]) are displayed. In order to test/evaluate the participant's comprehension, we scored each answer from 0 to 3 (3 = answers correctly; 2 = answers imprecisely; 1 = doesn't answer or doesn't know; 0 = answers incorrectly [because it is more dangerous for a patient's health to act incorrectly than not to act at all due to not knowing something]). Since there were 4 questions measured, the highest possible result for any participant was 12, and the lowest, 0. So, results in Chart 2 are

evidence of the difference of means (which we already said they were highly significant $[p < 0.0001]$) in text comprehension between the original and the enriched version. While after reading the original texts, patients failed the test (4.5 out of 12), after reading the enriched version of the same text, they successfully approved the test (10.4 out of 12).

5. Can we Automatically Enrich Medical Reports?

So far, we have seen that the lack of understanding in medical reports is largely —although not entirely— due to the high concentration of opaque terms and acronyms. Section 4.2.2 demonstrates that actions, like including descriptions or paraphrases of highly specialised lexical elements and expanding abbreviations, can substantially improve the text understanding. However, manually carrying out this lexical enrichment is a time-consuming and labour-intensive task, hence, there is a need to automate linguistic tasks.

In computer science, the process of modifying natural language to reduce its complexity towards improving readability and comprehension is called text simplification (TS) (Shardlow, 2014), and it may involve modifications to the syntax, the lexicon or both.

Starting in the nineties with the first TS application: a grammar checker for Boeing's commercial aircraft manuals (Hoard et al., 1992) there has been much work in TS mainly for the English language. However, since the early 2000s TS started to emerge across different languages and various categories of readers. For example, tools in Japanese (Inui et al., 2003) and Bulgarian (Lozanova et al., 2013) for hearing-impaired people, in French (Max, 2006) and Spanish (Bott and Saggion, 2011) for people with aphasia, in Brazilian Portuguese (Aluísio et al. 2008) for low literacy people, and finally in Italian (Barlacchi and Tonelli, 2013) and French (Brouwers et al., 2014) for schoolchildren or second language learners. Regardless of the language and purpose of simplification tools, there are different methods within the TS field. Systems can use them individually or in combination since they are not mutually exclusive. The most common approaches are lexical, syntactic and explanation generation.

- Lexical approach. Lexical simplification is the task of identifying and replacing complex words with simpler substitutes (Shardlow, 2014). This approach does not attend grammar issues, it only focuses on vocabulary aspects. It also comprises the expanding of abbreviations.
- Syntactic approach. Syntactic simplification is the process of reducing the grammatical complexity of a text, while retaining its information content and meaning (Siddharthan, 2006).
- Explanation generation. Often called semantic simplification, is the process of taking difficult concepts in a text and augment them with extra information. It usually consists of generating an automatic explanation by hierarchically and/or semantically related terms.

Within the medical domain automatic text simplification tools have been developed for different type of texts such

---

[5] These are real examples of terms used in the analysed medical reports.

as journals articles (Abrahamsson et al., 2014), medical records (Kandula et al., 2010; Zeng-Treitler et al., 2007), information pamphlets (Leroy et al., 2012) and patient information leaflets (Delaere et al., 2009; Segura-Bedmar and Martínez, 2017).

5.1 A prototype for automatic text enrichment

As part of an ongoing doctoral project, we are building an online software so that it will be available from anywhere using a web browser and it will allow to deal with medical reports written in Spanish about rare diseases. It focuses on the sections with the highest concentration of terms: diagnosis and treatment. The strategies to deal with the terminological issues are a) synonym enrichment and b) explanation insertion. To the best of our knowledge, there is no similar tool in Spanish devoted to improving the comprehension of medical reports. Although there are systems for simplifying drug package leaflets (Segura-Bedmar and Martínez, 2017) and to help hearing-impaired people (Bott and Saggion, 2011).

5.1.1 Synonym enrichment

This first task is meant to enrich highly specialised lexical elements by selecting their less specialised versions and **adding them** within the text. It also includes the identification of abbreviations and their expansion into their full form.

For most abbreviations (e.g. *AVC*) their full form will be added (e.g. *AVC - accidente vascular cerebral*), but the patient-friendly abbreviations such as *ADN* will not have their full form (*ácido desoxirribonucleico*) displayed. Patient-friendly abbreviations are manually annotated as *preferred term* within our database.

Our main datasource for abbreviations and their corresponding full forms is the *Diccionario de siglas médicas* (Dictionary of medical abbreviations) from the *Sociedad Española de Documentación Médica* (SEDOM [Spanish Society of Medical Documentation]). Disambiguation of polysemous abbreviations is not yet solved in this first version of the prototype thus, all the associated full forms will be shown.

Regarding the highly specialised lexical elements, we chose the Spanish version of SNOMED CT to map them with a less specialised term.

SNOMED CT is a multilingual structured clinical vocabulary collection of medical terms providing codes, synonyms and definitions (SNOMED, 2017). Our tool searches within SNOMED for synonyms of a highly specialised lexical element and retrieve the patient-friendly term. For example, if the term *hepatomegalia* is found in a medical report, then the tool searches for it in the database and grabs its SNOMED identifier (*80515008* in this case). This identifier serves as a link to other synonyms and therefore, allows to select the best candidate, based on predefined parameters. In the example, *hígado grande* would be the associated element to pick and would be displayed as *hepatomegalia (hígado grande)*.

5.1.2 Explanation insertion

There are cases where no suitable terms to display are found, then it is necessary to include a short explanation for such terms. For example, the SNOMED identifier 48638002 has associated only one term, *nefrocalcinosis*. The added explanation to the medical report would be *nefrocalcinosis (trastorno en el cual hay demasiado calcio depositado en los riñones)*.

We are currently gathering, analysing and processing explanations for this kind of terms. Since a good comprehension is directly related to the quality of the information provided, we have chosen not to perform automatic explanation generation but to manually review trusted sites (e.g. Spanish version of MedlinePlus website) and adapt the information found. The main parameters we have defined to consider an explanation as valid are the following: information should always come from trusted sources, must be short, dictionary-like, homogenous and with an appropriate level of specialisation.

6. Conclusion

Dealing with any disease represents an emotional burden to patients and this burden increases significantly when they do not understand the medical reports they receive after a healthcare visit. These medical reports have a specific linguistic structure which, from the lexicon point of view, is characterised by an excessive use of medical terms and acronyms which mean for the patient: additional cognitive load, semantic opacity, semantic confusion and semantic ambiguity.

Said comprehension barriers can be breached by cognitively and linguistically enriching the medical report, as has been seen in the results of the surveys. Hence, the ICT and computational techniques to automate text enrichment can be beneficial to doctor-patient communication. Our prototype aims to be used, on one hand, as a support for the healthcare professionals to generate a more patient-friendly document and, on the other, as a query tool for the patients to have a better understanding of what they are reading.

Nevertheless, it is important to note that language is complex, and software may lead to mistakes so computational tools should be used only as an aid. Further work on our proposal might explore different branches like working with syntactic issues, including abbreviation disambiguation to enhance lexical enrichment, or widening the scope of application to other medical reports besides rare diseases.

7. Acknowledgements

This research paper has been written as part of the research project *TOGETHER: overcoming socio-educational barriers and promoting literacy on the interferences and difficulties in understanding information and documentation aimed at families of children affected by rare diseases.* RecerCaixa 2015. Avancem amb la ciència. ACUP I Obra Social "La Caixa".

The proposal of a prototype for automatic text enrichment is developed within the doctoral thesis of Alejandra López-Fuentes: *Automatic adaptation of biomedical terms for non-experts: the case of medical reports* supervised by Rosa Estopà and Julio Collado-Vides.

This work was also supported by the project *TERMMED: Analysis of lexical change and terminological variation for the creation of linguistic resources in the medical field.* Research group IULATERM (Lexicon and Technology, ref. 2017SGR1530). (FFI2017-88100-P, Ministry of Economy and Competitiveness [MINECO]).

8. Bibliographical References

Abrahamsson, E., Forni, T., Skeppstedt, M., and Kvist, M. (2014). Medical text simplification using synonym replacement: Adapting assessment of word difficulty to a compounding language. In Proceedings of the 3rd Workshop on Predicting and Improving Text Readability for Target Reader Populations. Association for Computational Linguistics, pp. 57–65.

Aluísio, S. M., Specia, L., Pardo, T. A. S., Maziero, E. G., and Fortes, R. P. M. (2008). Towards Brazilian Portuguese automatic text simplification systems. In Proceedings of the 8th ACM Symposium on Document Engineering. New York: ACM Digital Library, pp. 240–248.

Anderson, D. (2016). Medical Terminology: The Best and Most Effective Way to Memorize, Pronounce and Understand Medical Terms. D. A. Medical Handbooks.

Barlacchi, G., and Tonelli, S. (2013). ERNESTA: A sentence simplification tool for children's stories in Italian. In A. Gelbukh (Ed.), Proceedings of the 14th international conference on Computational Linguistics and Intelligent Text Processing. Vol. 2, pp. 476–487.

Barrio Cantalejo, I. M., Simón Lorda, P., Melguizo, M., Escalona, I., Marijuán, M. I., y Hernando, P. (2008). Validación de la Escala INFLESZ para evaluar la legibilidad de los textos dirigidos a pacientes. *Anales del Sistema Sanitario de Navarra*, 31(2):135–152.

Bello, P. (2016). Aprendiendo a redactar mejor tus informes. In AEPap (Ed.), *Curso de Actualización de Pediatría*. Madrid: Lúa Ediciones 3.0, pp. 391–400.

Bernabeu-Mestre, J., Perujo Melgar, J. M., Forcadell Saport, J. V., Alberola, P., Borja i Sanz, J., Cortés Orts, C., and Martínez, C. (1995). El llenguatge de les ciències de la salut. Generalitat de València, Conselleria de Sanitat i Consum, Valencia.

Bonavalot, M. (Dir.). (1978). Le vocabulaire médical de base. Étude par l'étymologie. Sociétés d'Études Techniques et Fiduciaires, Paris.

Bott, S., and Saggion, H. (2011). Spanish text simplification: An exploratory study. *Procesamiento de Lenguaje Natural*, 47:87–95.

Brouwers, L., Bernhard, D., Ligozat, A.-L., and François, T. (2014). Syntactic Sentence Simplification for French. In Proceedings of the 3rd Workshop on Predicting and Improving Text Readability for Target Reader Populations. Association for Computational Linguistics, pp. 47–56.

Cabré, M. T. (1999). La terminología. Representación y comunicación. Una teoría de base comunicativa y otros artículos. Institut Universitari de Lingüística Aplicada, Barcelona.

Delaere, I., Hoste, V., Peersman, C., Van Vaerenbergh, L., & Velaerts, P. (2009). ABOP, automatic optimization of patient information leaflets. In International symposium on Data and Sense Mining, Machine Translation and Controlled Languages (ISMTCL). Université de Franche-Comté, pp. 74-81.

Delàs, J. (Coord.). (2005). Quaderns de la bona praxis. Informes clínics, eines de comunicació. Col·legi Oficial de Metges de Barcelona, Barcelona.

Estopà, R. (Coord.) (2020). Los informes médicos: estrategias lingüísticas para favorecer su comprensión. Delhospital Ediciones, Buenos Aires, Argentina.

Estopà, R., and Domènech-Bagaria, O. (2018). Diagnóstico del nivel de comprensión de informes médicos dirigidos a pacientes y familias afectados por una enfermedad rara. Communication presented in the *36º Congreso Internacional de AESLA: «Lingüística aplicada y transferencia del conocimiento: empleabilidad, internacionalización y retos sociales»*. April 2018, Cádiz.

Estopà, R. and Montané, A. (2020). La terminología: principal obstáculo para la comprensión de los informes médicos. In R. Estopà (Coord.), *Los informes médicos: estrategias lingüísticas para favorecer su comprensión*. Buenos Aires: Delhospital Ediciones, pp. 59–78.

Falcón, M., and Basagoiti, I. (2012). El paciente y la Alfabetización en Salud. In I. Basagoiti (Coord.), *Alfabetización en salud: de la información a la acción* Valencia: Itaca/TBS, pp. 65–96.

Fernández Huerta, J. (1959). Medidas sencillas de lecturabilidad. *Consigna*, 214:29–32.

Flesch, R. (1948). A new readability yardstick. *Journal of Applied Psychology*, 32(3):221–233.

García Palacios, J. (2004). El lenguaje médico, algo más que información. *Panace@*, 5(16):135–140.

Gunning, R. (1952). The Technique of Clear Writing. McGraw-Hill Book Co., New York.

Gutiérrez Rodilla, B. (1998). La ciencia empieza en la palabra. Análisis e historia del lenguaje científico. Península, Barcelona.

Hoard, J. E., Wojcik, R., and Holzhauser, K. (1992). An Automated Grammar and Style Checker for Writers of Simplified English. In *Computers and Writing*. Springer Netherlands, pp. 278–296.

Inui, K., Fujita, A., Takahashi, T., Iida, R., and Iwakura, T. (2003). Text simplification for reading assistance. In Proceedings of the second international workshop on Paraphrasing. Morristown, NJ, USA: Association for Computational Linguistics, pp. 9–16.

Kandula, S., Curtis, D., and Zeng-Treitler, Q. (2010). A semantic and syntactic text simplification tool for health content. In Proceedings of the AMIA Annual Symposium. American Medical Informatics Association, pp. 366–370.

Leroy, G., Endicott, J. E., Mouradi, O., Kauchak, D., and Just, M. L. (2012). Improving perceived and actual text difficulty for health information consumers using semi-automated methods. In Proceedings of the AMIA Annual Symposium. American Medical Informatics Association, pp. 522–531.

López Piñero, J. M., and Terrada Ferrandis, M. L. (1990). Introducción a la terminología médica. Manuales Salvat, Barcelona.

Lozanova, S., Stoyanova, I., and Leseva, S., and Koeva, S., and Savtchev, B. (2013). Text Modification for Bulgarian Sign Language Users. In Proceedings of the Second Workshop on Predicting and Improving Text Readability for Target Reader Populations. pp. 39–48.

Max, A. (2006). Writing for language-impaired readers. In A. Gelbukh (Ed.), *CICLing '06:* Proceedings of the 7th international conference on Computational Linguistics and Intelligent Text Processing (Vol. 3878 LNCS). Springer-Verlag, pp. 567–570.

McLaughlin, G. H. (1969). SMOG Grading-a New Readability Formula. *Journal of Reading*, 12(8):639–646.

NARA Style Guide. (2012). National Archives and Records Administration. Retrieved from https://www.archives.gov/files/open/plain-writing/style-guide.pdf

Navarro, F. (2001). El inglés, idioma internacional de la medicina. Causas y consecuencias de un fenómeno actual. *Panace@*, 2(3):35–51.

Navarro, F. (2016). La precisión del lenguaje en la redacción médica. *Cuadernos de la Fundación del Dr. Antonio Esteve.* 17:89–104.

Porras-Garzón, J. M. and Estopà, R. (2019). Recursos para hacer análisis de comprensión a textos médicos escritos: análisis cuantitativo de tres casos médicos. In TERMCAT (Ed.), Proceedings of the XIII Jornada Realiter. Terminología per a la normalització i terminología per a la internacionalització. Barcelona: Realiter and Universitat Politècnica de Catalunya, pp. 107–114.

Porras-Garzón, J. M. and Estopà, R. (2020). Metodología para el análisis lingüístico de informes médicos. In R. Estopà (Coord.), *Los informes médicos: estrategias lingüísticas para favorecer su comprensión.* Buenos Aires: Delhospital Ediciones, pp. 59–78.

Sampieri R. H., Collado F. C. and Lucio P. B. (2000) Metodología de la Investigación. Second Edition. Mc. Graw Hill, Buenos Aires.

Scheaffer, R. L., W. Mendenhall and Ott, R. L. (1987). Elementos de Muestreo. Grupo Editorial Iberoamérica, México.

Segura-Bedmar, I., and Martínez, P. (2017). Simplifying drug package leaflets written in Spanish by using word embedding. *Journal of biomedical semantics*, 8(1), 45.

Shardlow, M. (2014). A Survey of Automated Text Simplification. *International Journal of Advanced Computer Science and Applications*, 4(1):58–70.

Siddharthan, A. (2006). Syntactic simplification and text cohesion. *Research on Language and Computation*, 4(1):77–109.

Smith, E. A., and Kinkaid, J. P. (1970). Derivation and Validation of the Automated Readability Index for Use with Technical Materials. *The Journal of the Human Factors and Ergonomics Society*, 12(5):457–464.

Szigriszt-Pazos, F. (1993). Sistemas predictivos de legibilidad del mensaje escrito: fórmula de perspicuidad (PhD dissertation). Universidad Complutense de Madrid, Madrid.

SNOMED CT Starter Guide. (2017). International Health Terminology Standards Development Organisation.

Wermuth, C., and Verplaetse, H. (2018). Medical terminology in the Western world. In A. Alsulaiman and A. Allaithy (Eds.), *Handbook of Terminology: Terminology in the Arab World.* Amsterdam: John Benjamin Publishing Company, pp. 84–108.

Wulff, H. R. (2004). The Language of Medicine. *Journal of the Royal Society of Medicine*, 97: 187–188.

Zeng-Treitler, Q., Goryachev, S., Kim, H., Keselman, A., and Rosendale, D. (2007). Making texts in electronic health records comprehensible to consumers: a prototype translator. In Proceedings of the AMIA Annual Symposium. American Medical Informatics Association, pp. 846–850.

Proceedings of the 6th International Workshop on Computational Terminology (COMPUTERM 2020), pages 50–54
Language Resources and Evaluation Conference (LREC 2020), Marseille, 11–16 May 2020
© European Language Resources Association (ELRA), licensed under CC-BY-NC

A study of semantic projection from single word terms to multi-word terms in the environment domain

Yizhe Wang[1], Béatrice Daille[2], Nabil Hathout[1]
CLLE, CNRS & University of Toulouse[1], LN2S, CNRS & University of Nantes [2]
yizhe.wang@univ-tlse2.fr, nabil.hathout@univ-tlse2.fr, Beatrice.Daille@univ-nantes.fr

Abstract

The semantic projection method is often used in terminology structuring to infer semantic relations between terms. Semantic projection relies upon the assumption of semantic compositionality: the relation that links simple term pairs remains valid in pairs of complex terms built from these simple terms. This paper proposes to investigate whether this assumption commonly adopted in natural language processing is actually valid. First, we describe the process of constructing a list of semantically linked multi-word terms (MWTs) related to the environmental field through the extraction of semantic variants. Second, we present our analysis of the results from the semantic projection. We find that contexts play an essential role in defining the relations between MWTs.

Keywords: semantic projection, multiwords terms, terminological relations

1. Introduction

Terminology is structured by semantic relations between terms. The relations may be identified by experts, obtained from existing resources or extracted from corpora. They include synonymy, quasi-synonymy, hypernymy, hyponymy, etc. In this study, we focus on the identification of terminological relations between multi-word terms (MWTs) using the semantic projection method. We built a set of French MWT candidates related to the environment domain and containing two lexical words such as *réchauffement climatique* 'global warming'. Three relation categories (antonymy, quasi-synonym, and hypernymy) between single word terms (SWTs) are extended to these candidates. A subset of these MWT pairs has been validated by three judges to assess the preservation and the validity of the inferred relations between MWTs. The main finding of the evaluation is that the context is crucial for the assessment because they determine the actual meaning of the MWTs.

The remaining of the paper is organized as follows. Section 2. presents the related work. Section 3. outlines the projection of the semantic relations on the MWT pairs. Section 4. describes the data and resources used for the generation of semantically linked MWTs (Section 5.). The manual evaluation and an analysis of the projection results are presented in Section 6.. A short conclusion is then given in Section 7..

2. Related work

Several approaches to semantic relation recognition have been proposed in the literature. They may be classified into three types: lexicon-based approaches (Senellart and Blondel, 2008); pattern-based approaches (Wang et al., 2010; Ravichandran and Hovy, 2002); distributional approaches (Rajana et al., 2017; Shwartz and Dagan, 2019). Since MWTs are compositional or at least weakly compositional (L'homme, 2004), the semantic projection method, also known as semantic variation and often referred to as a compositional method, is widely used to generate MWTs and predict relations between them from semantically related SWTs.

Synonymy is an important relation in terminology and is addressed in several studies, like Hamon et al. (1998) who identify synonymous term candidates through inference rules. The authors extract MWT candidates from a corpus on electric power plants and analyze the candidate terms (*ligne d'alimentation* 'supply line') as being made up of a head (*ligne* 'line') and an expansion (*alimentation* 'supply'). They then replace the head or the expansion (or both) by their synonyms obtained from a general dictionary. They assume that the substitution preserves the synonymy relation. In their study, 396 MWT pairs have been validated by an expert; 37% are real synonyms. The same method is used by Hamon and Nazarenko (2001) in order to detect synonymous MWTs in specialized corpora on nuclear power plants and coronary diseases. Their results show that general language dictionaries complement specialized hand-built lexical resources for the detection of semantic variants.

In a similar study, Morin (1999) uses inference rules to identify hierarchical relations (hypernymy) between MWTs. Instead of using relations from the general dictionary, they take as reference semantically linked SWTs extracted from the AGROVOC terminology. They not only add syntactic and semantic constraints on the reference rules but also use the semantic relations with morphological relations to detect the semantic variants. They then compare the relations generated from AGROVOC with relations generated from a general language dictionary and show that the latter has a significantly lower precision. More recently, Daille and Hazem (2014) have generalized the projection method to all types of lexical relations while Hazem and Daille (2018) use it to extract synonymous MWTs with variable lengths.

The main difference between our study and the ones presented above is that we use the context to validate the inferred relations. In our experiment, we have extracted from the corpus 5 contexts for each candidate in the validation dataset. We consider that the projection is valid if the meaning of two MTWs in at least two of their contexts is in the relation stated between the two SWTs that yielded them. The above studies do not use the context except (Hamon and Nazarenko, 2001) who checks whether the two MWT candidates can be substituted one for the other in one context. In other words, one contribution of our study is to take into account the possible ambiguity of the MWTs, and the way contexts determine their meanings.

3. Composition method

Our method is based on the assumption that MWT meaning is compositional. One consequence of this hypothesis is that when two MWTs t_1 and t_2 only differ by one of their components c_1 and c_2, the semantic relation between c_1 and c_2 is identical to the one between t_1 and t_2 because c_1 and c_2 contribute in the same way to the meanings of t_1 and t_2. For instance, the relation between the MWTs *croissance de la population* 'population growth' and *diminution de la population* 'population decline' is the same as the one between the SWTs *croissance* 'growth' and *diminution* 'decline', that is antonymy. Our hypothesis is actually a bit stronger because we consider that the equivalence holds even when t_1 and t_2 do not have the same (syntactic) structure. More formally, let t_1 and t_2 be two MWTs such as $\mathbf{voc}(t_1) = \{u_1, v_1\}$ and $\mathbf{voc}(t_2) = \{u_2, v_2\}$ where $\mathbf{voc}(x)$ is the set of the content words of x. If u_1 and u_2 are SWTs, if $v_1 = v_2$ and if there is a semantic relation R between u_1 and u_2, then R also holds between t_1 and t_2. In other words, if $\mathcal{M}$ is a set of MWTs of a domain and $\mathcal{S}$ is a set of SWTs, the hypothesis can be stated as follows:

$$\forall t_1 \in \mathcal{M}, \forall t_2 \in \mathcal{M} \text{ such as } \exists u_1, v_1, u_2, v_2/$$
$$\mathbf{voc}(t_1) = \{u_1, v_1\} \wedge \mathbf{voc}(t_2) = \{u_2, v_2\}$$
$$\wedge u_1 \in \mathcal{S} \wedge u_2 \in \mathcal{S},$$
$$[v_1 = v2 \wedge \exists R, R(u_1, u_2) \Rightarrow R(t_1, t_2)]$$

4. Data and resources

4.1. Corpus

The corpus used for extracting MWT candidates is a specialized monolingual French corpus in the environment domain (ELRA-W0065) created in the framework of the PANACEA project[1]. The corpus contains 35453 documents (about 50 million words) with different levels of specialization. The corpus has been preprocessed: extraction of the text, normalization of the characters, lemmatization with TreeTagger (Schmid, 1994).

4.2. TermSuite

The MWT candidates were extracted from the PANACEA corpus through TermSuit, a terminology extraction tool developed at LS2N[2] (Cram and Daille, 2016). TermSuit only extracts noun phrases; the candidates are provided with their part of speech, specificity, and frequency. Table 1 illustrates the extracted candidates. For this study, we only consider the candidates composed of two lexical words (e.g. *milieu naturel* 'natural environment').

---

[1]http://www.panacea-lr.eu/en/info-for-researchers/data-sets/monolingual-corpora
[2]https://www.ls2n.fr

#	type	pattern	pilot	freq	spec
3	T	N A	parc national	10198	4.17
3	V[s]	N A A	parc naturel national	59	1.94
4	T	A	communautaire	8864	4.11
13	T	T	biomasse	6239	3.96
17	T	N A	diversité biologique	5412	3.90
21	T	N A	milieu naturel	4328	3.80
21	V[s]	N A A	milieu naturel aquatique	23	1.54

Table 1: Excerpt of the TermSuite output

4.3. Reference list of linked terms

The semantic relations between MWT candidates are predicted from relations between SWTs. These semantically linked SWTs are taken from a dataset made available by Bernier-Colborne and Drouin (2016). This reference list (RefCD) is extracted from DiCoEnviro (L'Homme and Lanneville, 2014), a specialized dictionary of the environment field which describes the meaning of 1382 entry terms of various sub-fields: energy, climate change, transportation, etc. RefCD is composed of 1314 term pairs, mainly SWTs, connected by four relation categories:

1. **Quasi-synonyms (QSYN):** synonyms (*diesel* 'diesel' ↔ *gazole* 'diesel'); quasi-synonyms (*conserver* 'preserve' ↔ *protéger* 'protect'); close meanings (*électricité* 'electricity' ↔ *énergie* 'energy'); variants (*autopartage* 'car sharing' ↔ *auto-partage* 'car sharing').

2. **Hierarchical relations (HYP):** hyponyms (*autoroute* 'highway' → *route* 'road'); hypernyms (*combustible* 'fuel' → *pétrole* 'oil'). Because HYP mixes hyponyms and hypernyms, the pairs it connects are not in order.

3. **Opposites (ANTI):** antonyms (*accélérer* 'accelerate' ↔ *ralentir* 'slow down'); contrastives (*flore* 'flora' ↔ *faune* 'fona').

4. **Derivatives (DRV):** terms with the same meaning but different parts of speech (*sensibilité* 'sensitivity' ↔ *sensible* 'sensible').

Because we are focusing on the projection of lexical-semantic relations, we did not use the 259 DRV pairs and excluded them from RefCD. We also excluded the 225 pairs of verbs because TermSuite only extracts noun phrases. Since RefCD does not contain information between simple terms describing other relations, like co-hyponyms, our study on semantic relations between MWTs concentrates on QSYN, HYP, and ANTI. The distribution of the three relation categories is imbalanced, as shown in table 2.

	ANTI	HYP	QSYN	total
Pairs	116	191	523	830
Terms	107	122	415	429

Table 2: Number of terms and semantic relations in RefCD

5. Generation of semantically-linked MWTs

5.1. Raw projection

We extracted all the MWT candidates which contain two content words and formed all the MWTs pairs that share a common word and where the two other words are a pair of SWTs connected in RefCD. We did not impose any other restriction on PoS, the order of the constituents, nor the patterns of the MWT candidates. 18,382 pairs of MWT candidates have been created. Table 3 presents their distribution over the three relation categories.

ANTI	HYP	QSYN	total
3414	3696	11,272	18,382

Table 3: MWTs yielded by the semantic projection

5.2. Data filtering

The raw projection yields symmetrical pairs of MWT candidates because some of the SWT pairs in RefCD are in random order. For instance, the projection produced the couple *climat régional : climat local* 'regional climate : local climate' and the couple *climat local : climat régional*. Therefore, we deleted the symmetries of hierarchical relationships. Table 4 shows the number of pairs that remained after the data filtering.

ANTI	HYP	QSYN	total
2065	2403	6777	11,245

Table 4: Number of unordered pairs of MWT candidates

5.3. Selection of a validation subset

In order to assess the hypothesis that MWT meaning is compositional and that semantic relations between SWTs are preserved when they are projected on MWTs, we performed a manual validation on a subset of the MWT candidate pairs we have extracted. Since our study focuses on the preservation and the validity of the semantic relations, we do not want to include the quality of candidates in the validation (are they terms of the environmental field?). For instance, a candidate like *lutte contre le changement* 'fight against the change' is not a term because it is syntactically incomplete, and the actual term is *lutte contre le changement climatique* 'fight against climate change'. Additionally, a candidate like *cadre régional* 'regional framework' does not belong to the environment domain.

Therefore, we choose to check the term status of the MWT candidates through three online terminological dictionaries, namely TERMIUM Plus[3], Le Grand Dictionnaire[4] and IATE[5] (Interactive Terminology for Europe). We consider any candidate present in any of these resources is a term of the environmental field since it was extracted from a specialized corpus of this domain. Since many of the extracted terms are specific, such as *conservation du papillon* 'butterfly conservation', only a fraction of the pairs have both of their MWT candidates present in one of the resources. As shown in Table 5, the validation subset is rather small.

In general, all selected candidates are noun phrases because all MWT candidates extracted by TermSuite are noun

[3]https://www.btb.termiumplus.gc.ca/tpv2alpha/alpha-fra.html?lang=fra
[4]http://www.granddictionnaire.com/
[5]https://iate.europa.eu/

ANTI	HYP	QSYN	total
80	51	100	231

Table 5: Validation subset

phrases. In addition, most of the valid pairs are composed of two candidates having the same patterns, NA or NPN.

NA-NA	NA-NPN	NN-NN	NN-NPN	NPN-NPN
123	1	1	2	104

Table 6: Distribution of pattern pairs of the validation subset

6. Evaluation of semantic projection

6.1. Contexts

The meaning of a word strongly depends on the contexts where it is used. In this study, we show that the context also determines the meaning of MWTS and the relations that connect them. The annotation of the MWT pairs is based on the relation between the two SWTs they contain and five contexts (i.e., sentences) extracted from the corpus for each MWT. The validity of the projected relation is decided based on the meanings of the MWT occurrences in the extracted contexts. The relation is valid if it holds between the meanings of at least one occurrence of each of the MWTs.

The context may help the judges understand the meaning of a MWT like *zone de recharge* 'recharge zone' which refers to a free aquifer where water collects. It can be used to disambiguate a term like *air frais* 'fresh air' which does not mean cool air but air from the outside (1). Contexts may also highlight the polysemy of MWTs like *changement du climat* 'climate change' which has two meanings: 'global warming' in (2a) and 'climate variability' in (2b).

(1) *la ventilation est à double flux (l'air vicié intérieur réchauffe l'**air frais** entrant)*

  'the ventilation is double flow (the inside stale air heats the incoming **fresh air**)'

(2) a. *il a établi que le **changement du climat** était « sans équivoque » et que les émissions de gaz à effet de serre provenant des activités humaines étaient responsables (avec 90% de certitude) de l'augmentation des températures depuis cent ans*

  'it established that the **climate change** was "unequivocal" and that greenhouse gas emissions from human activities were responsible (with 90% certainty) for the increase in temperatures over the past hundred years'

  b. *à quelle vitesse la réduction des concentrations atmosphériques de GES de courte durée entraînerait un **changement du climat***

  'how quickly reducing short-lived atmospheric GHG concentrations would cause **climate change**'

6.2. Criteria

The selected pairs have been annotated according to two criteria: the preservation of semantic relations and their validity in the environment domain. Both criteria are based on the expert knowledge of judges on semantic relations and the contexts in which the MWT candidates appear.

1. We consider that a relation is preserved when the relation that holds between two SWTs also holds between two MWT candidates generated from these two SWTs, regardless of its validity as an instance of its category. In other words, the relation is preserved when $SWT_1:SWT_2::MWT_1:MWT_2$ form an analogy.

2. We consider that a relation between two MWT candidates is valid in the domain when it actually belongs to the category to which it is assigned.

We assessed the preservation of the relation and its validity separately because we have slightly changed the scope of the relation categories. We consider that co-hyponyms are not quasi-synonyms and cannot belong to QSYN. Furthermore, we consider the relationship between a pair of contrastive co-hyponym terms as an instance of ANTI.

6.3. Preservation

The preservation of the relation only depends on the relations between the two SWTs and the two MWTs. If the relations are identical, the relation is considered as being preserved as in the case of *temps froid : temps chaud* 'cold weather : warm weather' (3) with respect to *froid : chaud* 'cold' : 'warm'.

(3) a. *par **temps froid**, cette technique consiste à ne pas laisser tourner son moteur au ralenti plus de 30 secondes*

   'by **cold weather**, this technique consists in not leaving the engine idling for more than 30 seconds'

   b. *par **temps chaud**, le compromis entre confort et pratique est difficile à trouver*

   'by **warm weather**, the compromise between comfort and practicality is difficult to find'

On the other hand, *diversité* is a hypernym *biodiversité* in RefCD, but the contexts in (4) show that the relation between the MWTs *gestion de la diversité* 'management of diversity' and *gestion de la biodiversité*
'management of biodiversity' is different since they are used with the same meaning.

(4) a. *les variétés paysannes, issues de millénaires de **gestion de la diversité** par les agriculteurs sont trop vivantes pour se plier aux critères d'inscription*

   'peasant varieties, coming from millennia of **diversity management** by farmers are too alive to comply with the criteria for registration'

b. *elle même distincte de l'utilisation (par les agriculteurs) des semences, la **gestion de la biodiversité** cultivée réunit dans un processus continu*

   'itself distinct from the use (by farmers) of seeds, the cultivated **management of biodiversity** unites in a continuous process'

6.4. Domain validity

Relations that are not preserved are considered as invalid. However, not all preserved relations are valid in the domain. For instance, *agriculture* 'agriculture' is a hypernym of *élevage* 'lifestock farming' in RefCD, and the relation holding between these SWTs is preserved in the MWTs *agriculture biologique* 'organic agriculture' and *élevage biologique* 'organic lifestock farming'. However, a context like (5) shows that these MWTs are actually co-hyponyms because hypernyms cannot be coordinated in this way. The reason is that agriculture is polysemous and may also mean cultivation. In this context, *agriculture* and *élevage* are co-hyponyms, and the inferred relation is not valid because it is not a relation of hypernymy.

(5) ... *expérience avec une matrice agricole "sans pesticides ni intrants chimiques" (agriculture ou élevage biologique ou de prairies ...*

   '... experience with an agricultural matrix "without pesticides or chemical inputs" (agriculture or organic farming or meadows ...'

6.5. Analysis of the inferred relations

Three judges have annotated the pairs of the validation subset. Table 7 shows that the inter-annotator agreement measured by Fleiss' kappa is substantial. The cases where the judges disagreed were then resolved.

ANTI	HYP	QSYN
0.77	0.68	0.61

Table 7. Fleiss' kappa

The results (Table 8) show that most of MWTs have compositional meaning, which confirms the claim of (L'homme, 2004). They also show that the preservation and the validity of the projected relations vary with their category.

	Preservation			Validity		
	ANTI	HYP	QSYN	ANTI	HYP	QSYN
Yes	68	27	85	68	27	74
No	12	24	15	12	24	26

Table 8: Results of the validation

Even if no restriction on the patterns was used for the generation of the MWT pairs, we observed that in all of the valid pairs, the MWTs have the same patterns and the SWTs that they contain appear in the same positions.

51 out of 231 pairs of MWTs are not preserved. They fall into three groups. (*i*) The MWTs do not have the same structure like *eau de surface* 'surface water' and *surface de la terre* 'Earth's surface'. *eau* 'water' and *terre* 'land' are linked by ANTI relation but the MWTs are not because

eau and *terre* do not appear in the same position. (*ii*) The meaning of the SWTs is not preserved in the MWTs as in *route maritime : autoroute maritime* 'shipping route : marine highway'. *route* 'road' is a hypernym of *autoroute* 'highway', but *route maritime* and *autoroute maritime* are synonyms in the contexts extracted for these two MWTs. (*iii*) The change in meaning may also come from the content word shared by two MWTs as in *air libre : eau libre* 'outdoor : open water'. The 62 pairs where the relation has been considered invalid are mainly co-hyponyms formed by SWTs linked by a QSYN relation like *trafic ferroviaire : trafic routier* 'rail traffic : road traffic'.

7. Conclusion and Future Works

In this study, we have created a dataset of MWT pairs linked by semantic relations. These relations are projected from a reference list of SWTs connected by the same relations. The annotation of a subset of the data highlighted the importance of the contexts because they determine the real meaning of MWTs and subsequently, the semantic relation that holds between them. The following step in this research is to design a method to automate the annotation on the basis of the semantic relations between SWTs and contextual semantic model like BERT (Devlin et al., 2019).

8. References

Bernier-Colborne, G. and Drouin, P. (2016). Evaluation des modeles sémantiques distributionnels: le cas de la dérivation syntaxique. In *Proceedings the 23rd French Conference on Natural Language Processing (TALN)*, pages 125–138.

Cram, D. and Daille, B. (2016). Terminology extraction with term variant detection. In *Proceedings of ACL-2016 System Demonstrations*, pages 13–18.

Daille, B. and Hazem, A. (2014). Semi-compositional method for synonym extraction of multi-word terms. In *Proceedings of the Ninth International Conference on Language Resources and Evaluation (LREC'14)*, pages 1202–1207, Reykjavik, Iceland, May. European Language Resources Association (ELRA).

Devlin, J., Chang, M.-W., Lee, K., and Toutanova, K. (2019). BERT: Pre-training of deep bidirectional transformers for language understanding. In *Proceedings of the 2019 Conference of the North American Chapter of the Association for Computational Linguistics*, pages 4171–4186, Minneapolis, Minnesota.

Hamon, T. and Nazarenko, A. (2001). Detection of synonymy links between terms: experiment and results. *Recent advances in computational terminology*, 2:185–208.

Hamon, T., Nazarenko, A., and Gros, C. (1998). A step towards the detection of semantic variants of terms in technical documents. In *Proceedings of the 17th international conference on Computational linguistics-Volume 1*, pages 498–504. Association for Computational Linguistics.

Hazem, A. and Daille, B. (2018). Word embedding approach for synonym extraction of multi-word terms. In *Proceedings of the Eleventh International Conference on Language Resources and Evaluation (LREC 2018)*.

L'homme, M.-C. (2004). *La terminologie: principes et techniques*. Pum.

L'Homme, M.-C. and Lanneville, M. (2014). Dicoenviro. dictionnaire fondamental de l'environnement. *Consulté à l'adresse http://olst. ling. umontreal. ca/cgibin/dicoenviro/search. cgi*.

Morin, E. (1999). Projecting corpus-based semantic links on a thesaurus. In *Proceedings of the 37th Annual Meeting of the Association for Computational Linguistics*, pages 389–396.

Rajana, S., Callison-Burch, C., Apidianaki, M., and Shwartz, V. (2017). Learning antonyms with paraphrases and a morphology-aware neural network. In *Proceedings of the 6th Joint Conference on Lexical and Computational Semantics (* SEM 2017)*, pages 12–21.

Ravichandran, D. and Hovy, E. (2002). Learning surface text patterns for a question answering system. In *Proceedings of the 40th annual meeting on association for computational linguistics*, pages 41–47. Association for Computational Linguistics.

Schmid, H. (1994). Probabilistic part-of-speech tagging using decision trees. In *Proceedings of the International Conference on New Methods in Language Processing*, pages 44–49.

Senellart, P. and Blondel, V. D. (2008). Automatic discovery of similarwords. In *Survey of Text Mining II*, pages 25–44. Springer.

Shwartz, V. and Dagan, I. (2019). Still a pain in the neck: Evaluating text representations on lexical composition. *arXiv preprint arXiv:1902.10618*.

Wang, W., Thomas, C., Sheth, A., and Chan, V. (2010). Pattern-based synonym and antonym extraction. In *Proceedings of the 48th annual southeast regional conference*, page 64. ACM.

Proceedings of the 6th International Workshop on Computational Terminology (COMPUTERM 2020), pages 55–61
Language Resources and Evaluation Conference (LREC 2020), Marseille, 11–16 May 2020
© European Language Resources Association (ELRA), licensed under CC-BY-NC

The NetViz terminology visualization tool and the use cases in karstology domain modeling

Senja Pollak[1], Vid Podpečan[1], Dragana Miljkovic[1], Uroš Stepišnik[2] and Špela Vintar[2]
[1]Jožef Stefan Institute, Ljubljana, Slovenia
{senja.pollak,vid.podpecan,dragana.miljkovic}@ijs.si
[2]Faculty of Arts, University of Ljubljana, Slovenia
{uros.stepisnik,spela.vintar}@ff.uni-lj.si

Abstract

We present the NetViz terminology visualization tool and apply it to the domain modeling of karstology, a subfield of geography studying karst phenomena. The developed tool allows for high-performance online network visualization where the user can upload the terminological data in a simple CSV format, define the nodes (terms, categories), edges (relations) and their properties (by assigning different node colors), and then edit and interactively explore domain knowledge in the form of a network. We showcase the usefulness of the tool on examples from the karstology domain, where in the first use case we visualize the domain knowledge as represented in a manually annotated corpus of domain definitions, while in the second use case we show the power of visualization for domain understanding by visualizing automatically extracted knowledge in the form of triplets extracted from the karstology domain corpus. The application is entirely web-based without any need for downloading or special configuration. The source code of the web application is also available under the permissive MIT licence, allowing future extensions for developing new terminological applications.

Keywords: Terminology visualization, Karstology, Domain modeling, Networks

1. Introduction

Visual representations of specialized domains are becoming mainstream for several reasons, but firstly as a natural response to the fact that "concepts do not exist as isolated units of knowledge but always in relation to each other" (ISO 704, 2009). In recent terminological projects, visualization has been considered an important asset (Faber et al., 2016; Carvalho et al., 2017; Roche et al., 2019). We believe that the visualization of terminological knowledge is especially well-suited to the needs of frame-based terminology, aiming at facilitating user knowledge acquisition through different types of multimodal and contextualized information, in order to respond to cognitive, communicative, and linguistic needs (Gil-Berrozpe et al., 2017). Moreover, it has been shown that domain experts are often able to interpret information faster when viewing graphs as opposed to tables (Brewer et al., 2012). More generally, as has become evident in the rising field of digital humanities, digital content, tools, and methods are transforming the entire field of humanities, changing the paradigms of understanding, asking new research questions and creating new knowledge (Hughes et al., 2015; Hughes, 2012).

As this workshop demonstrates, terminological work has undergone a significant change with the emergence of computational approaches to extracting various types of terminological knowledge (e.g., term extraction, definition extraction, semantic relation extraction), which enhances the potential of visualization not only to represent manually annotated data, but also for automatically and semi-automatically extracted knowledge, which we also show in our use cases.

We focus on the field of karstology, the study of specific relief which develops on soluble rocks such as limestone and is characterized by caves, typical depressions, karst springs, ponors and similar. It is an interdisciplinary subdomain of geography bordering on geomorphology, geology, hydrology and chemistry. In karstology, the main objects of interest are its typical landforms usually described through their form, size, location and function, and the environmental and chemical processes affecting their development such as dissolution and weathering.

The proposed semantic network visualization tool NetViz[1] used in the presented karstology domain modeling experiments, complement our previous research in the TermFrame project including work of Vintar et al. (2019) where frame-based annotation of karst definitions is presented, Pollak et al. (2019) presenting results of term and definition extraction from karst literature, Miljkovic et al. (2019) with term co-occurrence network extraction and Grčić-Simeunović and De Santiago (2016) where semantic properties of karst phraseology are explored.

2. Related Work

There are several projects which consider *terminology visualization* as an important asset of specialized knowledge representation. One such project is the EndoTerm, a knowledge-based terminological resource focusing on endometriosis (Carvalho et al. 2016, Roche et al. 2019). EndoTerm includes a visual concept representation developed via CMap Tools and organizes knowledge into semantic categories linked with different types and levels of relations, while ensuring compatibility with existing medical terminology systems such as SNOMED. The most closely related project to ours using a visual representation of specialized knowledge is the EcoLexicon (Faber et al., 2016), where terms are displayed in a semantic network linking the central query term to related terms and its translation equivalents in up to 5 other languages. The edges of the network represent three types of relations, namely the generic-

---

[1]https://biomine.ijs.si/netviz/

specific (is_a) relation, the part-whole relation and a set of non-hierachical relations (made_of, located_at, affects etc.). While the EcoLexicon remains impressive with the abundance and complexity of data it offers, our own approach differs mainly in that we use natural language processing techniques to infer data, and that we envisage different types of visual representation depending on the task or end-user.

In terms of *domain modeling of terminological knowledge*, we can first mention the field of terminology extraction. In automatic terminology first the distinction was between linguistic and statistical approaches, but most state-of-the-art systems are hybrid. Many terminology extraction algorithms are based on the concepts of termhood and unithood (Kageura and Umino, 1996), where termhood-based approaches include work by Ahmad et al. (2000) and Vintar (2010), while Daille et al. (1994) and Wermter and Hahn (2005) use unithood-based measures, such as mutual information and t-test, respectively. More recently, deep learning and word embeddings (Mikolov et al., 2013) have become very popular in natural language processing, and several attempts have already been made to utilize these techniques also for terminology extraction (Amjadian et al., 2016; Zhang et al., 2017; Wang et al., 2016) and terminology expansion (Pollak et al., 2019). Next, for defining relations between terms, there are several relation extraction methods, which can roughly be divided into categories: co-occurrence-based, pattern-based, rule-based and machine-learning approaches (Bui, 2012; Sousa et al., 2019). Co-occurrence is the simplest approach which is based on the assumption that if two entities are frequently mentioned together in the same sentence, paragraph or document, it is probable that they are related (Song et al., 2011). The pattern- and the rule-based differ in that the former use template rules, whereas the latter might additionally implement more complex constraints, such as checking negation, determining the direction of the relation or expressing rules as a set of procedures or heuristic algorithms (Kim et al., 2007; Fundel-Clemens et al., 2007). Machine-learning approaches usually set the relations extraction tasks as classification problems (Erkan et al., 2007). Recently, the proposed approaches often use the power of neural networks as in Lin et al. (2016), Sousa et al. (2019), Luo et al. (2020). The focus of this paper is the visualization tool and its use in karstology domain modeling. For data extraction, we employ several techniques mentioned above. Pattern-based methods (Pollak et al., 2012) are used for definition extraction in the first use case (Section 4.3.) providing definition candidates for further manual annotation of domain knowledge, while in the second use case (Section 4.4.) we use statistical term extraction techniques (Vintar, 2010; Pollak et al., 2012) coupled with co-occurrence analysis and relation extraction using Reverb (Fader et al., 2011).

3. NetViz

Network visualization is of key importance in domains where an optimized graphical representation of linked data is crucial in revealing and understanding the structure and interpreting the data with the aim to obtain novel insights and form hypotheses. There is a plethora of software which deals with network analysis and visualization. For example, Gephi (Bastian et al., 2009), Pajek (Batagelj and Mrvar, 2002) and Graphviz (Ellson et al., 2001) are among the most popular classic software tools for these tasks and have been used in very diverse domains. However, every domain and every task poses specific requirements and using tools which are too general is often a poor choice which has adverse effects on usability. Therefore, our aim was to provide a minimal environment which enables zero effort network visualization for specific tasks such as terminology. We developed NetViz (`https://biomine.ijs.si/netviz/`), a web application which enables interactive visualization of networks. NetViz builds upon our previous work on visualization and exploration of heterogeneous biological networks (Podpečan et al., 2019). where several large public databases are merged into a network which can then be explored, analyzed and visualized. We applied the same principles and created a domain independent network visualization tool which was then applied to karstology domain modeling and exploration.

3.1. Features

- **Open source**. Netviz is available under the liberal MIT license on the open source portal GitHub[2].

- **Single page, client-only web application**. NetViz is implemented as a client-only web application. As a result, NetViz requires no hosting and server configuration and can be also run locally simply by downloading and opening its html page in a web browser.

- **High performance network visualization**. NetViz implements a user interface around the `vis-network` module of the `vis.js` visualization library. `vis-network` is a fast, highly configurable library for network visualization in the browser and NetViz builds upon its visualization engine.

- **Visualization and editing features**. A set of fundamental network editing and visualizaton features are implemented. The network can be modified after visualization by adding or removing nodes and edges. Several settings controling the physics simulation which does the layouting can be adjusted before, during or after the visualization. Context menus which are available on all elements (node, edges and the canvas itself) provide a few basic options which can be extended according to the requirements of the specific domain.

- **CSV data format**. In order to make the use of NetViz as simple as possible its data input format is a comma separated file (CSV) with header. Two files are used: the first one which is mandatory defines edge properties while the optional second file defines node properties. The header for edge definition file supports the following columns: `node1`, `node2`, `arrow`, `label`, `text`, `color`, and `width` where `node1`, `node2`, and `arrow` are mandatory and the rest is optional. The header for node definition file supports the following columns:

---

[2]`https://github.com/vpodpecan/netviz`

`node`, `text`, `color`, and `shape`. We expect that the list of supported columns (features) will grow and adapt to specific domains where NetViz will be used. We will also add the option to export the current network so that the user modifications of the network will not be lost upon closing the application.

The intended users are domain experts in the process of construction of a domain ontology, terminologists, as well as students and teachers. It also has potential for being used by larger public with some modifications and a fixed domain knowledge base.

4. Karstology Domain Modeling

4.1. The TermFrame Project

The context for this research is the TermFrame project which employs the frame-based approach to build a visual knowledge base for karstology in three languages, English, Slovene and Croatian. The main research focus of the project is to explore new methods of knowledge extraction from specialized text and propose novel approaches to knowledge representation and visualization (see previous work in the project described in Vintar et al. (2019), Pollak et al. (2019), Miljkovic et al. (2019)).

The frame-based approach in terminology (Faber, 2012; Faber, 2015) models specialized knowledge through conceptual frames which simulate the cognitive patterns in our minds. According to this view, a frame is a mental structure consisting of concept categories and relations between them. Unlike hand-crafted ontologies, frame-based terminology uses specialized corpora to induce frames or event templates, thus consolidating the conceptual and the textual level of a specialized domain.

Such an approach to knowledge and terminology modeling has a lot to gain from graph-like representations, because its building blocks are concept categories, concepts and terms as nodes, and various types of hierarchical and non-hierarchical relations as edges. By selecting different layers of representation it is thus possible to visualize the dynamic and multidimensional nature of specialized knowledge.

In the TermFrame project we combine manual and computational methods to extract domain knowledge. However, in an ideal scenario, as many steps as possible would be automated requiring only minimal manual validation. The main steps of our proposed domain modeling workflow can be summarized as follows:

- Convert documents to plain text format.

- Identify domain terms.

- Identify domain definitions.

- Identify semantic categories.

- Identify semantic relations.

- Select information for network visualization.

- Visualize the network.

- Interactively explore and modify the terminological resource.

Details on automated knowledge extraction for several of these steps are provided in Pollak et al. (2019). In the following subsections, we present the corpus, as well as two experiments on karstology domain modeling, where a subset of steps above are performed manually or automatically, before the final steps of visualization and interactive exploration using NetViz, which is the focus of this paper and common to both experiments.

4.2. Corpus

The English part of the TermFrame corpus, which was used in these experiments, contains 56 documents of different length, all pertaining to karstology. It includes books, research articles, theses and textbooks (for more details see Vintar et al. (2019)). We used Google Documents feature for conversion of documents from pdf to text format. Frequently such conversion introduced errors into the document such as additional line breaks or orphaned figure captions in the middle of paragraphs. Such errors were corrected in the post-processing phase either manually or using simple scripts.

4.3. Visualizing Manually Annotated data

In this experiment we use manual annotations of domain definitions. Specialized definitions were first either identified in dictionaries and glossaries or using definition extractor from domain texts (Pollak et al., 2012)[3], and next annotated with a hierarchy of semantic categories and a set of relations which allow to describe karst events. For an example of annotated definition see Figure 1. The annotation process—performed by linguists and domain experts—is described in detail in Vintar et al. (2019) and briefly summarized below.

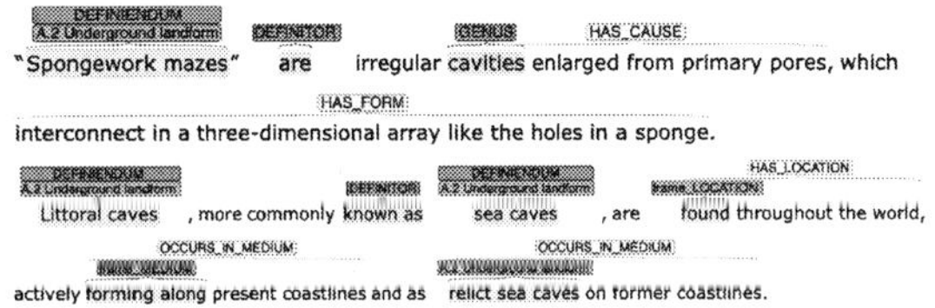

Figure 1: Manual annotation of automatically extracted definitions.

The semantic categories were inspired by the concept hierarchy in the EcoLexicon[4] and adapted to karstology by domain experts. The first three top-level categories, LANDFORMS, PROCESSES and GEOMES, are the most relevant for domain modeling as they contain terms specific to karst, while the rather broad group of ELEMENTS, ENTITIES and PROPERTIES contains broader terms from geography, chemistry, botany and similar. INSTRUMENTS and METHODS are used to categorize karstology-specific

---

[3]The evaluation of automated definition extraction is described in detail in Pollak et al. (2019). About 30% of extracted definition candidates were judged as karst or neighbouring domain definitions, while about 16% of definition candidates were evaluated as karst definitions used for the fine-grained manual annotation.

[4]https://ecolexicon.ugr.es/en/index.htm

research and/or measurement procedures, but were found to occur rarely in our set of definitions.

The second important level of annotation identifies the semantic relations which describe specific aspects of karst concepts. According to the geomorphologic analytical approach (Pavlopoulos et al., 2009), landforms are typically described through their spatial distribution (HAS_LOCATION; HAS_POSITION), morphography (HAS_FORM; CONTAINS), morphometry (HAS_SIZE), morphostructure (COMPOSITION_MEDIUM), morphogenesis (HAS_CAUSE), morphodynamics (HAS_FUNCTION), and morphochronology (OCCURS_IN_TIME). The ideal definition of a landform would include all of the above aspects, but in reality most definitions extracted from the corpus or domain-specific glossaries specify only two or three. In total, 725 definitions were annotated, 3149 terms were assigned categories.

In this experiment we focus on the visualization of the taxonomy built from manually annotated categories of DEFINIENDUM and their hypernyms, connected by IS_A relation to their subcategories and categories (LANDFORM, PROCESS, GEOME, ELEMENT/ENTITY/PROPERTY, and INSTRUMENTS/METHODS). The top level—taxonomy of categories—can be observed in Figure 2. In Figure 3, we can see lower levels, which correspond to terms from definitions, more specifically terms (definiendums) assigned to specific subcategories of Hydrological forms and Underground landforms. It allows the user to quickly grasp the main conceptual properties of hydrological forms, namely that water in karst continuously submerges underground (*sinking creek, losing streamflow, swallow hole etc.*) and reemerges to the surface (*karst spring, resurgence, vauclusian spring etc.*), depending on the porosity of the underlying bedrock. Amongst underground landforms we can quickly discern various types of caves (*crystal cave, lava cave, active cave, bedding-plane cave, roofless cave*) and typical underground formations found in them (*straw stalactites, flute, capillary stalagmite, column, cave pearl*). The network also shows that certain terms belong to both categories (*blue hole, inflow cave*) as certain forms are both underground and submerged in water or have a hydrological function in karst. In addition, we have noticed that graph-based visualization facilitates the identification and correction of inconsistencies in the manual expert annotation. The final goal is to integrate the visual, graph-based representation into a multimodal knowledge base where frames (Cause, Size, Location, Function etc.) as defined in Vintar et al. (2019) will be presented to the user together with corpus examples, images and geolocations.

4.4. Visualizing Automatically Extracted Knowledge

In this experiment we used sentences where automatically extracted terms co-occurred, and then identified relations between them. The resulting knowledge is shown in Figure 4. The relation extraction was done using Re-Verb (Fader et al., 2011), which is a program that au-

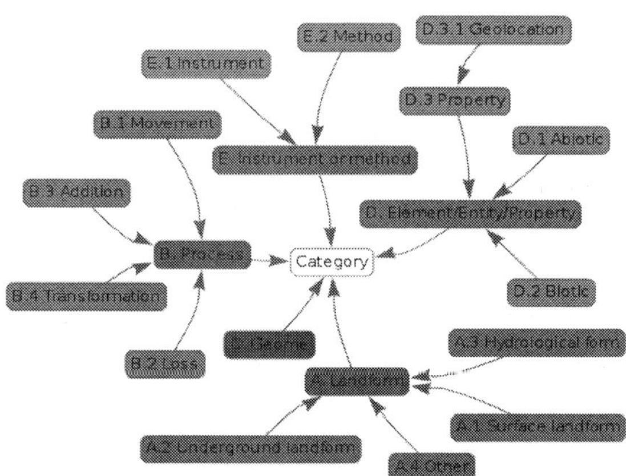

Figure 2: The taxonomy of categories visualized in NetViz.

tomatically identifies and extracts relationships from English sentences, output the triplets in form <argument1, relation phrase, argument2>, usually corresponding to subject-verb-object. It is designed for cases where the target relations cannot be specified in advance, which corresponds to the requirements of this experiment with knowledge discovery in mind. The preprocessing includes tokenization, lemmatization and POS tagging. We used the lemmatized forms. We are interested in triplets that include as arguments only terms from the karst domain. The terms were extracted using (Pollak et al., 2012) and were further validated by domain experts.[5] We also used terms in karstology term list QUIKK [6]. The validated list of domain-specific terms contained 3,149 terms, and triplet arguments extracted with ReVerb were matched against this list. In this way, a huge general triplet network containing less relevant information for domain exploration is reduced and thus made easier for manual inspection. After filtering we retained 302 triplets where arguments exactly match the terms from the list. The most frequent relations include: *be, fill_with, exceed, form_in, associate_with, be_source_of,....*

5. Conclusion and future work

We presented the NetViz terminology visualization tool and two examples of its use for knowledge modeling in the domain of karstology. First, we have demonstrated the visual representation of domain knowledge as extracted from manually annotated definitions. The multi-layer annotations include conceptual categories (Landform, Process, Geome, Element/Entity/Property, Instrument/Method) and their subcategories with which the terms are labelled, and the resulting network can be used by experts, teachers, students or terminologists to explore related groups of concepts, identify knowledge patterns or spot annotation mistakes. Next, we visualized the relations as proposed by the automated term and triplet extraction. This approach is complementary to the manual annotation and may point to previously unknown connections or knowledge structures.

---

[5]A detailed evaluation of term extraction process is presented in Pollak et al. (2019), ranging from 19.2% for strictly karst terms and 51.6% including broader domain terms and names entities.

[6]http://islovar.ff.uni-lj.si/karst

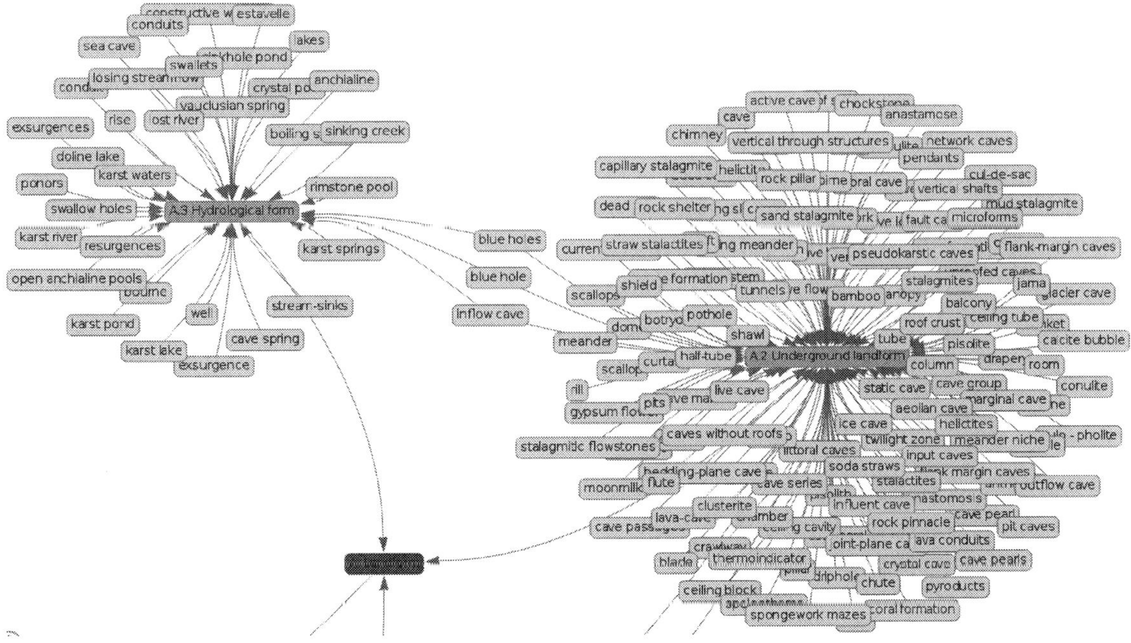

Figure 3: A visualization of a part of categories network which includes hydrological and underground landforms.

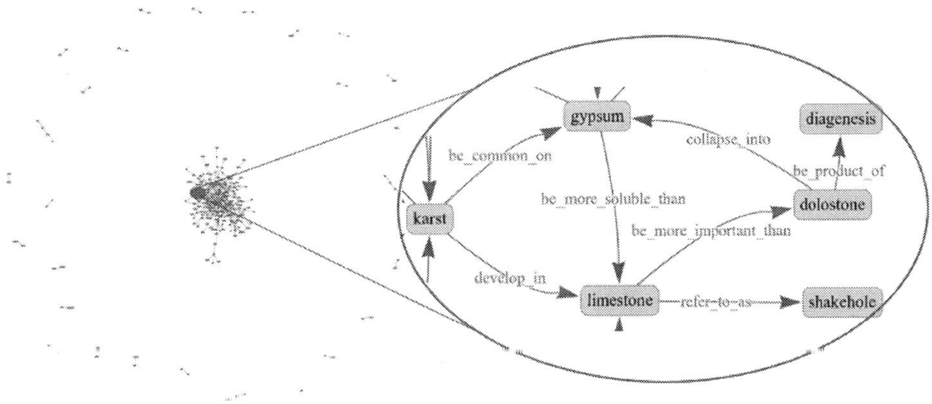

Figure 4: Graph with triplet relations extracted with ReVerb where subject and object match the manually validated list of karst terms.

The simplicity of NetViz allows users to prepare their own input data in the CSV format and create customized visualizations to support their research. For example, in the TermFrame project NetViz is currently used to explore cases where identical or similar concepts have been defined through different hypernyms (e.g. *karst* is a kind of *landscape / terrain / topography / product of processes / phenomenon / area*).

As future work and the end-result, of the TermFrame project we plan to develop an integrated web-based environment for karst exploration which will combine graphs with textual information, images and geolocations. Since a large number of natural monuments worldwide are in fact karst phenomena, we see the potential of such knowledge representations not just for science but also for education, environment and tourism.

6. Acknowledgements

The authors acknowledge the financial support from the Slovenian Research Agency for research core funding for the programme Knowledge Technologies (No. P2-0103) and the project TermFrame - Terminology and Knowledge Frames across Languages (No. J6-9372). This paper is also supported by European Union's Horizon 2020 research and innovation programme under grant agreement No. 825153, project EMBEDDIA (Cross-Lingual Embeddings for Less-Represented Languages in European News Media).

7. Bibliographical References

Ahmad, K., Gillam, L., Tostevin, L., and Group, A. (2000). University of surrey participation in trec 8: Weirdness indexing for logical document extrapolation and retrieval (wilder). 03.

Amjadian, E., Inkpen, D., Paribakht, T., and Faez, F. (2016). Local-global vectors to improve unigram terminology extraction. In *Proceedings of the 5th International Workshop on Computational Terminology (Computerm2016)*, pages 2–11.

Bastian, M., Heymann, S., and Jacomy, M. (2009). Gephi: An open source software for exploring and manipulating networks. In *Proceedings of the International AAAI Conference on Weblogs and Social Media*.

Batagelj, V. and Mrvar, A. (2002). Pajek— analysis and visualization of large networks. In Petra Mutzel, et al., editors, *Graph Drawing*, pages 477–478, Berlin, Heidelberg. Springer Berlin Heidelberg.

Brewer, N., Gilkey, M., Lillie, S., Hesse, B., and Sheridan, S. (2012). Tables or bar graphs? presenting test results in electronic medical records. *Medical decision making : an international journal of the Society for Medical Decision Making*, 32(4):545–553.

Bui, Q.-C. (2012). Relation extraction methods for biomedical literature. *Structure*, 01.

Carvalho, S., Costa, R., and Roche, C. (2017). Ontoterminology meets lexicography: the multimodal online dictionary of endometriosis (mode). In *GLOBALEX 2016: Lexicographic Resources for Human Language Technology Workshop at the 10th International Conference on Language Resources and Evaluation (LREC'16)*, pages 8–15, Portorož, Slovenia.

Daille, B., Gaussier, E., and Langé, J.-M. (1994). Towards automatic extraction of monolingual and bilingual terminology. In *Proceedings of the 15th Conference on Computational Linguistics - Volume 1*, COLING '94, page 515–521, USA. Association for Computational Linguistics.

Ellson, J., Gansner, E., Koutsofios, L., North, S., Woodhull, G., Description, S., and Technologies, L. (2001). Graphviz — open source graph drawing tools. In *Lecture Notes in Computer Science*, pages 483–484. Springer-Verlag.

Erkan, G., Ozgur, A., and Radev, D. (2007). Semi-supervised classification for extracting protein interaction sentences using dependency parsing. In *In Proceedings of the Conference of Empirical Methods in Natural Language Processing (EMNLP '07)*, pages 228–237, 01.

Faber, P., León-Araúz, P., and Reimerink, A. (2016). EcoLexicon: new features and challenges. In *Proceedings of GLOBALEX 2016: Lexicographic Resources for Human Language Technology in conjunction with the 10th edition of the Language Resources and Evaluation Conference*, pages 73–80.

Faber, P. (2012). *A Cognitive Linguistics View of Terminology and Specialized Language*. Berlin, Boston: De Gruyter Mouton.

Faber, P. (2015). Frames as a framework for terminology.

In Hendrik Kockaert et al., editors, *Handbook of Terminology*, page 14–33. John Benjamins.

Fader, A., Soderland, S., and Etzioni, O. (2011). Identifying relations for open information extraction. In *Proceedings of the Conference of Empirical Methods in Natural Language Processing (EMNLP '11)*, Edinburgh, Scotland, UK, July 27-31.

Fundel-Clemens, K., Küffner, R., and Zimmer, R. (2007). Relex - relation extraction using dependency parse trees. *Bioinformatics (Oxford, England)*, 23:365–71, 03.

Gil-Berrozpe, J., León-Araúz, P., and Faber, P. (2017) Specifying hyponymy subtypes and knowledge patterns: A corpus-based study. In *Electronic lexicography in the 21st century. Proceedings of eLex 2017 conference*, pages 63–92.

Grčić-Simeunović, L. and De Santiago, P. (2016). Semantic approach to phraseological patterns in karstology. In T. Margalitadze et al., editors, *Proceedings of the XVII Euralex International Congress*, pages 685–693. Ivane Javakhishvili Tbilisi State University.

Hughes, L. M., Constantopoulos, P., and Dallas, C. (2015). Digital methods in the humanities: Understanding and describing their use across the disciplines. In J. Unsworth S. Schreibman, R. Siemens, editor, *A New Companion to Digital Humanities*, pages 150–170). John Wiley & Sons.

Hughes, L. M. (2012). ICT methods and tools in arts and humanities research. In Lorna M. Hughes, editor, *Digital Collections: Use, Value and Impact*, pages 123–134. London, UK: Facet Publishing.

ISO 704. (2009). ISO 704:2009: Terminology work-principles and methods. Standard, ISO, Switzerland.

Kageura, K. and Umino, B. (1996). Methods of automatic term recognition: A review. *Terminology International Journal of Theoretical and Applied Issues in Specialized Communication*, 3(2):259–289.

Kim, J.-H., Mitchell, A., Attwood, T. K., and Hilario, M. (2007). Learning to extract relations for protein annotation. *Bioinformatics*, 23(13):i256–i263, 07.

Lin, Y., Shen, S., Liu, Z., Luan, H., and Sun, M. (2016). Neural relation extraction with selective attention over instances. In *Proceedings of the 54th Annual Meeting of the Association for Computational Linguistics (Volume 1: Long Papers)*, pages 2124–2133, Berlin, Germany, August. Association for Computational Linguistics.

Luo, L., Yang, Z., Cao, M., Wang, L., Zhang, Y., and Lin, H. (2020). A neural network-based joint learning approach for biomedical entity and relation extraction from biomedical literature. *Journal of Biomedical Informatics*, 103:103384, 02.

Mikolov, T., Chen, K., Corrado, G., and Dean, J. (2013). Efficient estimation of word representations in vector space. In *Proceedings to The International Conference on Learning Representations 2013*.

Miljkovic, D., Kralj, J., Stepišnik, U., and Pollak, S. (2019). Communities of related terms in Karst terminology co-occurrence network. In *Proceedings of eLex 2019*.

Pavlopoulos, K., Evelpidou, N., and Vassilopoulos, A.

(2009). *Mapping Geomorphological Environments.* Berlin Heidelberg:Springer.

Podpečan, V., Ramšak, v., Gruden, K., Toivonen, H., and Lavrač, N. (2019). Interactive exploration of heterogeneous biological networks with biomine explorer. *Bioinformatics*, 06.

Pollak, S., Vavpetič, A., Kranjc, J., Lavrač, N., and Špela Vintar. (2012). Nlp workflow for on-line definition extraction from English and Slovene text corpora. In Jeremy Jancsary, editor, *Proceedings of KONVENS 2012*, pages 53–60. ÖGAI, September. Main track: oral presentations.

Pollak, S., Repar, A., Martinc, M., and Podpečan, V. (2019). Karst exploration : extracting terms and definitions from Karst domain corpus. In *Proceedings of eLex 2019*.

Roche, C., Costa, R., Carvalho, S., and Almeida, B. (2019). Knowledge-based terminological e-dictionaries The EndoTerm and al-Andalus Pottery projects. *Terminology. International Journal of Theoretical and Applied Issues in Specialized Communication*, 25(2):259–290.

Song, Q., Watanabe, Y., and Yokota, H. (2011). Relationship extraction methods based on co-occurrence in web pages and files. In *Proceedings of the 13th International Conference on Information Integration and Web-Based Applications and Services*, iiWAS '11, page 82–89, New York, NY, USA. Association for Computing Machinery.

Sousa, D., Lamurias, A., and Couto, F. M. (2019). Using neural networks for relation extraction from biomedical literature.

Vintar, Š., Saksida, A., Stepišnik, U., and Vrtovec, K. (2019). Modelling specialized knowledge with conceptual frames: The TermFrame approach to a structured visual domain representation. In *Proceedings of eLex 2019*, pages 305–318.

Vintar, Š. (2010). Bilingual term recognition revisited: The bag-of-equivalents term alignment approach and its evaluation. *Terminology*, 16(2):141–158, 12.

Wang, R., Liu, W., and McDonald, C. (2016). Featureless domain specific term extraction with minimal labelled data. In *Proceedings of the Australasian Language Technology Association Workshop 2016*, pages 103–112.

Wermter, J. and Hahn, U. (2005). Paradigmatic modifiability statistics for the extraction of complex multi-word terms. In *Proceedings of Human Language Technology Conference and Conference on Empirical Methods in Natural Language Processing*, pages 843–850, Vancouver, British Columbia, Canada, October. Association for Computational Linguistics.

Zhang, Z., Gao, J., and Ciravegna, F. (2017). Semrerank: Incorporating semantic relatedness to improve automatic term extraction using personalized pagerank. *arXiv preprint arXiv:1711.03373*.

Proceedings of the 6th International Workshop on Computational Terminology (COMPUTERM 2020), pages 62–71
Language Resources and Evaluation Conference (LREC 2020), Marseille, 11–16 May 2020
© European Language Resources Association (ELRA), licensed under CC-BY-NC

Towards Automatic Thesaurus Construction and Enrichment

Claudia Lanza†, Amir Hazem§, and Béatrice Daille§
†University of Calabria, Italy
§ LS2N - UMR CNRS 6004, Université de Nantes, France
c.lanza@dimes.unical.it, amir.hazem@ls2n.fr, beatrice.daille@ls2n.fr

Abstract

Thesaurus construction with minimum human efforts often relies on automatic methods to discover terms and their relations. Hence, the quality of a thesaurus heavily depends on the chosen methodologies for: (i) building its content (terminology extraction task) and (ii) designing its structure (semantic similarity task). The performance of the existing methods on automatic thesaurus construction is still less accurate than the handcrafted ones of which is important to highlight the drawbacks to let new strategies build more accurate thesauri models. In this paper, we will provide a systematic analysis of existing methods for both tasks and discuss their feasibility based on an Italian Cybersecurity corpus. In particular, we will provide a detailed analysis on how the semantic relationships network of a thesaurus can be automatically built, and investigate the ways to enrich the terminological scope of a thesaurus by taking into account the information contained in external domain-oriented semantic sets.

Keywords: Automatic thesaurus construction, Terminology extraction, Semantic similarity.

1. Introduction

In computational linguistics and terminology, a thesaurus is often used to represent the knowledge of a specific domain of study as a controlled vocabulary. This paper aims at presenting an analysis of the best performing NLP approaches, i.e., patterns configuration, semantic similarity, morpho-syntactic variation given by term extractors, in enhancing a semantic structure of an existing Italian thesaurus about the technical domain of Cybersecurity. Constructing thesauri by carrying out minimum handcrafted activities is currently highly demanded (Azevedo et al., 2015). Hence, several methods to automatically build and maintain a thesaurus have been proposed so far (Güntzer et al., 1989; Morin and Jacquemin, 1999; Yang and Powers, 2008a; Schandl and Blumauer, 2010). However, the quality of automatically generated thesauri tends to be rather weaker in their content and structure with respect to the conventional handcrafted ones (Ryan, 2014). To guarantee the currency of a thesaurus (Batini et al., 2009) it is crucial to whether improve existing methods or to develop new efficient techniques for discovering terms and their relations. On the perspective of using existing NLP tools for constructing a thesaurus, choosing the most appropriate ones is not an easy task since the performance varies depending on the domain (Nielsen, 2001), the supported languages, the applied strategies, etc. Selecting a highly performing NLP procedure to build on a knowledge representation resource does also contemplate maintenance and enrichment phases aimed at empowering the application usages of these semantic sources.
This work aims at presenting an analysis of which of the NLP approaches, i.e., patterns configuration, semantic similarity, morpho-syntactic variation given by term extractors, could be considered the best performing in enhancing a semantic structure of an existing Italian thesaurus about the technical domain of Cybersecurity. The paper starts firstly from a description of how the current thesaurus has been constructed (Broughton, 2008), following the rules included in the main reference standards for building thesauri (ISO/TC 46/SC 9 2011 and 2013), and of the source corpora composition from which the thesaurus construction has taken its basis. In detail, the paper is organized as follows: Section 2 presents a state-of-the-art on the main works about the construction of terminological knowledge bases, as well as on those that dealt with the semantic relations discovering approaches, such as, the distributional similarity ones. Section 3 describes the former configuration of the handcrafted thesaurus for Cybersecurity and of the source corpus used to build the controlled vocabulary on the Cybersecurity domain, i.e., the Italian corpus made up of legislation and domain-oriented magazines. Section 4 provides an outline of the data sets, i.e., a ranked summary of the terminological lists, including the ones considered as the main gold standards to which rely on; in this part a set of representative examples for each existing relation, which has been extracted from the draft thesaurus to use as data meant to be ameliorated, is given. Section 5 to 7 describe the methods used to automatize the hierarchical, associative and synonymous configuration of the Italian Cybersecurity thesaurus along with their experiments and results. Section 8 combines the results to determine which approach is the best performing with respect to the desired thesaurus output to achieve. Finally, Section 8 presents the conclusion.

2. Objectives

The main purpose presented in this paper is to guarantee a higher-quality management of the Italian Cybersecurity thesaurus' domain-oriented terminology. In particular, this paper explores which could be considered the best performing NLP tool among a plethora of selected ones to be used in order to empower an existing thesaurus of a highly technical domain, the Cybersecurity one. The source language of this semantic resource is the Italian, and the methods pursued to provide reliable candidate terms structures, meant to be included in the thesaurus, are based on sophisticated terminological extractor tools. With the objective of carrying out a study on how to automatically generate the semantic networking systems proper to theauri, these terms extraction software represent the basis from which to begin the non-manually construction of a thesaurus outline. Specifically, the approaches undertaken are the following:

1. Pattern based system: the causative patterns aim at enhancing the associative relationship proper to thesauri configuration;

2. Variants recognition: semantic variation is useful to detect hierarchical and associative sets;

3. Distributional analysis: this procedural methodology helps in identifying the synonymy connection.

Automatically constructing a thesaurus aims at obtaining, as output, an improved knowledge organization system on the Cybersecurity area of study from a semantic correlation construction point of view. This system should provide an advanced hierarchical structuring that is meant to overcome a current thesaurus outline, as well as the associative and equivalence terms organization. Indeed, as described in the following sections, the handcrafted thesaurus categorization sometimes proves to be either subjective and not completely explicit in representing associations among domain-specific terms.

3. Related Works

3.1. Terms Extraction

A thesaurus can be considered as a controlled system that organizes the knowledge of a specific domain of study through a network of semantic relations linked to the hierarchy, synonymy and association structures (Broughton, 2008). Terms included in the thesauri have to keep a unambiguous value, as affirmed in the standard NISO TR-06-2017, Issues in Vocabulary Management: "Controlled vocabulary: A list of terms that have been enumerated explicitly. This list is controlled by and is available from a controlled vocabulary registration authority. All terms in a controlled vocabulary must have an unambiguous, non-redundant definition". Constructing an efficient terminological system usually implies the acquisition of domain-oriented information from texts, specifically those that can provide semantic knowledge density and granularity about the lexicon that is meant to be represented (Barrière, 2006). These structures are in literature known as TKBs (Terminological Knowledge Bases) (Condamines, 2018), and, indeed, they support the modalities of systematizing the specialized knowledge by merging the skills proper to linguistics and knowledge engineering. The ways in which the candidate terms are extracted from a specific domain-oriented corpus (Loginova Clouet et al., 2012) usually follow text pre-processing procedures and extraction of single and multi-word units (Daille and Hazem, 2014) from texts filtered out by frequency measures, then they can undergo a phase of variation recognition (Weller et al., 2011) and other statistical calculations to determine the specificity, accuracy, similarity in the texts from which they come from (Cabré et al., 2001). The reason why the domain-oriented terms are called 'candidates' (Condamines, 2018) is linked to the fact that in the terminologists' activity the need of experts' validation is frequently required, this because just the subjective selection by terminologists might not be exhaustive and fully consistent with the domain expertise (ISO/TC

46/SC 9 2013).

Thesauri's realization is commonly connoted by a manual semantic work that assumes a terminologists' activity in selecting terms from a list of candidate ones, extracted, in turn, from a reference corpus (Condamines, 2007) and, consequently, arranging them in a structure that follows the guidelines given by ISO standards for constructing thesauri (ISO/TC 46/SC 9 2011 and 2013) which aim at normalizing the information meant to be shared by a community of users. For the seek of gaining time to terminologists in defining thesauri's structure (Rennesson et al., 2020), their construction phases are supported by using computer engineering techniques and followed by an evaluation phase that sees experts of the domain involved in the decision-making process about the insertion of the terms in the semantic resource. Even though, a process of appropriateness' check by experts isn't entirely suitable to demonstrate that the TKBs comply with the specialized corpus knowledge flow. Hence, together with certain groups of experts' supervision, other tools support the accuracy validation, i.e., the gold standards (Barrière, 2006). This task is meant to give results on the way terms that have been selected to be part of a semantic resource – designed to represent a specialized language – can be aligned with others included in reference texts. These target texts can be in the same language as the one of the source corpus, and could present less difficulties in the matching system, or multilingual (Terryn et al., 2018), in these cases using translations from existing semantic resources could represent a solution. In this paper, the gold standards taken into account are in Italian language or have been translated in Italian – Nist and Iso – this reflects the native purpose of the project that was intended to provide a guidance for the understanding of the Cybersecurity domain in Italian language.

3.2. Semantic Relations

This paper is going to give a description of the exploited methodologies in automatizing the way thesauri, specifically for the case of study, i.e., Cybersecurity, can be constructed by means of semantic similarity procedures and patterns configuration related to the causative connections. The automatized methodologies used for the configuration of thesauri's structure (Yang and Powers, 2008b; Morin and Jacquemin, 1999), can quicken the process related to the arrangement of textual relations network to shape the informative tissue of a domain. To achieve this framework system different approaches can be pursued, starting from lexico-syntactic patterns conformation (Condamines, 2007), and experimenting other solutions such as the ones proposed by (Grefenstette, 1994) with "Sextant", or (Kageura et al., 2000) with their methodology in considering the common entries in two different thesauri and constructing pairs of codes. As linguistic structures that are very frequent within a corpus of documents (Lefeuvre, 2017), patterns allow to discover among terms which are the conceptual relations (Bernier-Colborne and Barrière, 2018). The study of patterns dates way back, at the end of 90' the works of Hearst (1992) were, for instance, firstly focused on the configuration of Noun Phrases followed by other morpho-syntactic structures to be found in texts. Many authors in the literature studied the ways nominal and verbal phrases allow to identify semantic relations between terms through syntagmatic or phrasal structures (Girju et al., 2006). The typologies of lexico-syntactic markers help in retrieving the desired semantic information about the terminology proper to a specialized domain (Nguyen et al., 2017), that's the case of the casual relationships between terms. This particular kind of connection is notably described in the works of Barrière (2002) in which the author gives a wide-ranging perspective for investigating the causal relationships in informative texts. As the author underlines, it is not an easy task to group the causative verbs that should isolate the representative terms of a domain to be linked through a cause-effect relation. Nevertheless, grouping some of them can help in identifying the semantic associations to be reflected in a controlled vocabulary given the domain-oriented nature of the casual connections. Indeed, retrieving this type of patterns is a context-dependent procedure: in considering the source area of study and having some technical knowledge about it, terminologists can much easily analyse in an autonomous and accurate way a combination of semantic relationships (Condamines, 2008).

For what concerns semantic similarity methods in the literature, they have firstly been applied to single word terms (SWTs) using a variety of approaches such as: lexicon-based approaches (Blondel and Senellart, 2002), multilingual approaches (Wu and Zhou, 2003; van der Plas and Tiedemann, 2006; Andrade et al., 2013), distributional approaches (Hagiwara, 2008; Hazem and Daille, 2014) and distributed approaches such in (Mikolov et al., 2013; Bojanowski et al., 2016). This procedure helps in configuring the associations between terms with respect to synonyms connections retrieved from corpora. On this point, it is important to highlight the relevance of extracting reliable lists of candidate terms that could represent the starting point from which to set up a conceptual modeling of a thesaurus as well as a basis to analyse and define the internal domain-specific synonyms and hyperonyms (Meyer and Mackintosh, 1996).

4. Thesaurus Structure on Cybersecurity

At this stage, the Italian Cybersecurity thesaurus, on which our paper focuses to describe automatic thesauri construction methodologies, contains 246 terms in the source language (it) and most of them have their definition, or Scope Notes (SN) according to standardized tags (ISO/TC 46/SC 9 2011), taken from the texts from which they derive inside the corpus or the translated gold standards definitions, i.e. Nist and Iso. The thesaurus has been built on the basis of the thesauri construction guidelines from ISO/TC 46/SC 9 2011 and 2013: terms have been formalized in order to guarantee the sharing of information in a standardized way, the concepts of the source corpus have been represented by preferred terms organized according to a network of hierarchical, synonymous and associative semantic relationships. This system allows to set up a knowledge organization oriented towards a creation of semantic connections that, in turn, can create a reflection of the informative scope inside the corpus texts.

The structure phase of the thesaurus for Cybersecurity has started by evaluating the list of terms extracted by using a semi-automatic semantic tool, TextToKnowledge (T2K) (Dell'Orletta et al., 2014), specifically taking into account the frequency scores of the most representative terms and isolating them as being the main candidate terms to be sent to experts' validation process. It was thanks to the co-working process with domain experts that the first list of candidate terms has been filtered out and the first categories, from which the thesaurus structure was developed, provided. This phases resulted after having taken into account several terminological passages:

- the matching process between the output lists derived from the semantic extraction and the taxonomies contained in the gold standards of Nist and Iso; these lists of terms have been translated into Italian language by using an automatic translation software, TRADOS, and a multi/crosslingual terminological platform, IATE;

- the inverse frequency ranks in the term lists;

- the head-term grouping system T2K processed.

In this way, merging the output of a semantic extractor tool, the terminology competencies and the group of experts' validation and supervision, the four main top entry categories have been selected: **Cybersecurity, Cyberbullism, Cyber defence, Cybercriminality**. The goal of the research activity presented in this paper is to improve the decision-making process towards the thesaurus construction by means of approaches that rely on patterns configuration and semantic similarity measures in order to enrich the informative tissue inside the controlled vocabulary.

5. Data Sets

5.1. Corpora

In this section the sets of documents from which the candidate terms have been extracted by using several approaches are presented. The first one refers to the Italian gold standard corpus, i.e., Clusit, and the other, i.e., Cybersecurity corpus, is the one used to build on the source corpus. Taking in consideration a highly specialized field of knowledge with plenty of words in English meant to create a shared base of information among users, the terms extrated resulted to be a hybrid syllabus of English and Italian terms. This because the domain of Cybersecurity owns several technical terms that can be maintained in their English version even providing variants, e.g., *hackers* or *exploit*.

5.1.1. Clusit Corpus

Clusit corpus indicates the reports that have been published by an Italian Cybersecurity organization which shares some of the main cyber threats and attacks together with descriptions, reviews, and a final glossary.

5.1.2. Cybersecurity Corpus

Designing a corpus (Leech, 1991), from which to develop a strong terminological knowledge base that guarantees a rich-context dependency to transmit a reliable representation of a domain, leads to generate a semantic fundamental dataframe that can be representative of the area of study to be analysed (Condamines, 2018). The Cybersecurity corpus is composed of 220 laws documents and 342 5-sector-oriented magazines. The collection of the texts that compose the source corpus is heterogeneous, this means that the information included takes its ground from legislative documents, regulations, norms, directives, guidelines as well as domain-oriented magazines in order to provide an exhaustive resource to assemble the information representation about the field of knowledge. The information included within the divulgative corpus, with respect to the law data set, provided higher accurate terminology, more targeted kind of concepts to be represented with terms. Table 1 summerizes the number of words (#Words) and the number of documents (#Documents) of the used corpora (Clusit and Cybersecurity).

Corpus	#Words	#Documents
Clusit	385,544	6
Cyber	7,179,829	562

Table 1: Number of words and documents of the Italian corpora: Clusit and Cybersecurity.

5.2. Terminology Lists

For evaluation, we used five terminological lists:

Clusit The Clusit term list contains the main domain specific terms of the reports gathered in a glossary which is composed by a syllabous of these latter followed by their definitions;

Glossary The Glossary term list contains terms with their definitions published by a political intelligence organism, this characteristic has to be taken into account in considering the accuracy and appropriateness of its derived terminology that seems to be weaker than the other more technical domain-oriented resources;

Nist The Nist 7298 - Glossary of Key Information Security Terms (Kisserl, 2013) term list is a complex of terms alphabetically ordered and accompanied by their definitions, also derived from other reference standards. It's considered as a main authoritative data set for Cybersecurity experts on the same level as the Iso list;

Iso The Iso term list refers to the International Standard (ISO/IEC 27000, 2016) for Security and Technology, and it contains, as the Nist, the terms alphabetically ordered with their definitions;

Cyber The Cybersecurity term list contains candidate terms taken from the post-processed texts connected together through the main semantic relationships proper to thesauri (Broughton, 2008), i.e., hierarchical, synonymy, association. These relations are respectively formalized by standard tags (ISO/TC 46/SC 9 2011 and 2013):

> **broader term** broader term (BT) that stands for hyperonyms;

> **narrower term** narrower term (NT) that stands for hyponyms;

> **used for** used for (UF) and **use** (USE) that represent the synonymy relation;

> **related term** related term (RT).

Hereafter some examples of the four addressed relations: hyperonymy (Hyp), synonymy (Syn), related terms (Rel) and cause (Cause).

Hypernym Spam/Phishing, Spam/Smishing, Crypto miner malware/Bitcoin Virus, DoS/DDoS;

Synonym Crackers/Black hat, Sotware malevoli (*malicious software*)/Malware, Cyber minacce (*cyber threats*)/Cyber Threat Actors;

Related Blockchain/Proprietà di sicurezza (*security properties*), Crackers/Hacking, Cyber defence/Cybersecurity;

Causative verb Spoofing/Attacchi informatici (*cyber attacks*) (*to alterate*), Integrità (*integrity*)/Cyber minacce (*cyber threats*) (*to damage*), Attacco (*attack*)/Malware (*implicate*).

Tables 2 and 3 respectively illustrate the size of the term evaluation lists and the distributions of each semantic relation.

	Clusit	Glossary	Nist	Iso	Cyber
#terms	202	284	1282	89	247

Table 2: Size of the 5 term lists.

	Hyp	Syn	Rel	Cause
#terms	172	63	110	68
#pairs	169	35	260	54

Table 3: Semantic similarity evaluation list size. #terms indicates the total number of terms per semantic relation type, and #pairs indicates the number of pairs for each semantic relation.

6. Term Extraction Approaches

6.1. Term Extraction Tools

In this section we provide a description of the chosen tools to execute the terminology extraction.

6.1.1. TermSuite - Variants Detection Tool

TermSuite (Cram and Daille, 2016) is a toolkit for terminology extraction and multilingual term alignment. Its performance is quite immediate when it runs over big data sets. The term extraction provided by TermSuite is a list of representative terms that are presented together with different properties, e.g., their frequency, accuracy, specificity. Terms are therefore ordered according to their unithood and application to the domain. One of the main feature that shapes the quality of this software is its syntactic and morphological variants detection among terms, e.g, lexical reduction, composition, coordination, derivation (Lanza and Daille, 2019). Variants identification given by the output list in TermSuite represents one of the methods selected to retrieve hyperonyms as well as synonyms in the source corpus. In fact, through the denominative, conceptual and linguistic variants included in the terminological output it is possible to detect in which ways terms are expanded by other semantic elements, reduced, related to an opposite one, or appearing in several linguistic conformations, e.g., *cyber security* or *cybersecurity*. Below a list of few examples to show the variations given by the outputs in TermSuite terminological extraction for Cybersecurity domain in Italian language that can help in detecting semantic associations to be included in the thesaurus:

- **denominative variants:**
  NPN: **hacker (21 matches)** del telefono (*mobile hacker*)→ NA: hacker telefonico

- **conceptual variants:**
  NPN: **worm (8 matches)** → NPNPNA: worm del genere del famigerato nimda (*worm, the infamous nimda kind one*)

- **linguistic variants**:
  N: **antivirus (6 matches)** → A: anti-virus

In the next paragraphs we show how these terms included in the examples above are returned in different ways by the other systems, T2K and PKE.

6.1.2. T2K - Language Design Tool

T2K is an Italian software to automatically extract linguistic information from domain-oriented data sets (Dell'Orletta et al., 2014). The software takes a corpus and processes it according to a default or customized configuration given in input. The list of terms is sorted by the inverse frequency measure or indexed by grouping them according to head-terms ordering. One of the advantages of this semantic extractor is the possibility to personalize the patterns meant to be exploited to execute the extraction of domain-oriented terminology; in this way a more precise semantic chains output can be achieved. On the other hand, though this software shows many benefits related to its flexibility in adapting the configuration to the terminology needs, it performs very slowly when it comes to analyse big corpora. Also for T2K we provide a small set of terms that appear differently from TermSuite's output, or are given with a larger number of results (this is because in T2K the terminological extraction is numerically higher than TermSuite) referred to the aforementioned examples. They provide as well some extra information that can help in orientating the structure outline of the thesaurus blocks:

- **hacker (519 matches)** → hackeraggio (*hacking*)

- **worm (102 matches)** → worm via posta elettronico (*worm via e-mail*)

- **antivirus (127 matches)** → antivirus affetto da trojan (*antivirus affected by trojan*)

6.1.3. Pke - Keyphrases Identification Tool

PKE (Boudin, 2016) is an open-source python keyphrase extraction toolkit that implements several keyphrase extraction approaches. From a linguistic point of view, PKE resulted to be very efficient in terms of providing a semi-automatic structuring of information since many candidate terms, which have been selected as being part of the Cybersecurity thesaurus, are grouped alongside with other ones that, in turn, could represent their associative semantic chains. For this section we provide as well related examples for the terms outputs precision:

- **hacker** and **worm** are found in a same keyphrase cluster → sistemi (*systems*), rete (*network*), worm analisi (*worm analysis*), password, hacker

- **antivirus/anti-virus** not present

New information is on the other hand given by terms that are not appearing in the previous two extractors and that are grouped in a way that can help in structuring their relations inside the thesaurus' outline. In the following cluster it can be observed how the candidate complex term *cyber counterintelligence* could be organized according to the surrounding terms that help in conceiving it as a *technique* or a *procedure* in the cyber intelligence and cyber defence tasks.

attività (*activities*) intelligence, controspionaggio (*counter espionage*), tecniche (*techniques*), **cyber counterintelligence**, cyber actions, difesa (*defence*)

#cand	T2K	TermSuite	PKE	BERT
Clusit	33,833	15,028	16,664	5,433
CyberSec	593,887	16,541	218,569	6,200

Table 4: Terminology extraction: number of candidate terms extracted by each tool for the Clusit and CyberSec corpora.

6.1.4. BERT

Feature-based approaches are often used for automatic term extraction (Terryn et al., 2018). However, it is often time consuming and not always straightforward to design the most appropriate features to efficiently train a classifier. In order to get rid of the handcrafted features, we chose to apply, as an alternative, a very recent deep neural network approach: Bidirectional Encoder Representations from Transformers (BERT). BERT has proven to be efficient in many downstream NLP tasks (Devlin et al., 2018) including next sentence prediction, question answering, name entity recognition (NER), etc. BERT can be used for feature extraction or for classification. In automatic term extraction (ATE) task, we use BERT as a binary classifier for term prediction. The main idea is to associate each term with its context. Hence, by analogy to next sentence prediction, the first sentence given to BERT is the one which contains the term, and the sentence to predict is the term itself. For training, we feed the model with all the context/term pairs that appear in the corpus as positive examples. The negative examples are generated randomly. Therefore, we hypothesize

		Evaluation lists														
		Clusit			Glossary			Nist			Iso			Cyber		
Corpus	coverage (%)	100			36.2			22.3			55.6			49.3		
	Tools	P	R	F1	P	R	F1	P	R	F1	P	R	F1	P	R	F1
	T2K	0.19	33.1	0.38	0.18	**21.4**	0.36	0.48	**13.1**	0.93	0.09	**37.5**	0.18	0.15	21.4	0.32
Clusit	TermSuite	0.37	27.7	0.73	0.30	15.8	0.58	0.82	9.59	1.51	0.14	23.8	0.27	0.39	23.8	0.77
	PKE	0.85	**69.8**	1.68	0.35	20.4	0.69	0.95	12.4	1.76	0.17	32.9	0.34	0.46	30.7	0.91
	BERT	**2.03**	30.6	**3.81**	**1.03**	16.5	**1.94**	**2.34**	9.59	**3.76**	**0.30**	20.4	**0.59**	**1.07**	**32.7**	**2.07**
	coverage (%)	61.3			72.5			35.3			67.0			100		
	Tools	P	R	F1	P	R	F1	P	R	F1	P	R	F1	P	R	F1
	T2K	0.01	23.7	0.02	0.02	42.2	0.04	0.05	**21.2**	0.10	0.01	**47.7**	0.02	0.01	30.7	0.02
CyberSec	TermSuite	0.10	7.92	0.19	0.37	21.8	0.73	0.77	9.98	1.41	0.12	23.8	0.25	0.20	13.7	0.40
	PKE	0.05	**49.0**	0.10	0.06	**44.0**	0.12	0.12	**21.2**	0.24	0.02	44.3	0.04	0.05	**46.5**	0.10
	BERT	**0.48**	14.3	**0.93**	**1.04**	15.1	**1.95**	**2.30**	7.10	**3.47**	**0.43**	20.4	**0.84**	**1.11**	25.9	**2.13**

Table 5: Terminology extraction results of T2K, TermSuite, PKE and BERT on the Clusit and Cybersecurity corpora. The evaluation is conducted on five lists (Clusit, Glossary, Nist, Iso and Cyber) and the results (%) are given in terms of Precision (P), Recall (R) and F-measure (F1).

that BERT can learn associations between terms and their contexts.

Term extraction systems, with the exception of BERT, include filtering methods that allow the user to set thresholds on various statistical measures above which the ranked candidate terms are kept. In order to favour recall, we decided not to apply any further filtering except for those included as default parameters. Table 4 shows the number of extracted candidates for each used tool/method. T2K software outputs come out with the largest terminological range sets and BERT with the smallest.

6.2. Term Extraction Experiments

We conduct an evaluation on five terminological lists: *Clusit, Glossary, Nist, Iso* and *Cyber* and on two corpora: Clusit (*Clusit*) and Cybersecurity (*Cyber*). The results are given in terms of Precision (P), Recall (R) and F-measure (F1). We also give the coverage of each list on each corpus.

Table 5 illustrates the obtained results on the terminology extraction task. Overall, we observe weak results for all the methods. Nonetheless, the recall is much higher especially for PKE and T2K which correlates with the number of their output candidates (see Table 4). The evaluation's list size is very small (around 200) and systems output is often around thousands of terms, which explains the very low precision. Moreover, the evaluation lists are not exhaustive and, by consequence, do not allow a fair evaluation on precision. Indeed, several correct terms which are not present in the evaluation lists have been observed. Finally, based on the F1 score, BERT obtained the best results in all the cases.

7. Semantic Relations Automatization

To address the semantic similarity task, we introduce in the following sections pattern-based and word embedding-based approaches.

7.1. Patterns-based

Among the approaches which have been used for the development of this strategy that could retrieve the semantic connections starting from a domain-oriented data set, the patterns recognition has been one of them (Rösiger et al., 2016). For the purposes of this research activity, some key verbs have been taken into account to represent the causative relationships among the terms included in all the documents of the Italian Cybersecurity source corpus. Almost all of these first verbs imply a relation of agent - cause that provokes some circumstances. The objective of this path-based configuration is to improve the accuracy of the associative relationships included in thesauri and labelled as RT, which stands for *Related Terms* (ISO/TC 46/SC 9, 2011). Indeed, as stated in (Rösiger et al., 2016) work on the achievement of good sets of semantic relationships by employing NLP techniques, the decision of certain verb object pairs relies on the domain pertinence and relevance, and also on the assumption that these pairs can be syntactically correct. In this step, the verbs considered to launch the queries meant to group the causative relationships among the candidate terms has not followed frequency drills. Almost thirty of the most common casual verbs in Italian have been exploited to retrieve the co-occurrences in the source corpus. The aim about using patterns configuration related to the causative relations (Lefeuvre and Condamines, 2015) is that of providing an improvement in the structure of the related terms in the thesaurus. In ISO Standard 25964 of 2013, when it comes to discuss about the interoperability of the systems, the associative mapping is described as a connection that "[...] may be established between concepts when they do not qualify for equivalence or hierarchical mappings, but are semantically associated to such an extent that documents indexed with the one are likely to be relevant in a search for the other." As can be further observed, the associative relationship in thesauri systematization is among the others, hierarchical and equivalence, the one that presents more ambiguity in the way it connects the domain-oriented terms. By using causative-based patterns the references from one specific term to another seem more precise and reliable.

The following list presents some examples for the selected causative verbs, some of these relations added new information about the connections among the Cybersecurity specicialized terms, i.e., the relation that occurs between *camouflage* and *password*, or *cyber threats* and the *security properties*; sometimes they confirmed the already configured outline of the thesaurus, as *cyber attacks* and *DDoS* or *spoofing*.

- **provocare** (*to provoke*):
  virus - worm
  cyber attacks - DDoS
  risks - cyber threats

- **danneggiare** (*to damage*):
  crackers - data
  cyber threats - integrity, privacy, availability

- **comportare** (*to imply*):
  cyber attacks - malware
  cyber harrassment - cyber bullism

- **alterare** (*to alter*):
  camouflage - password
  spoofing - cyber attacks

- **manomesso da** (*sabotaged by*):
  monitoring - cyber attacks
  monitoring - DoS

- **impattare** (*to impact*):
  DDoS - cyber attacks
  monitoring - cybersecurity

In summary, causative connections retrieved from source corpus provided added information to the existing ones contained in the Italian Cybersecurity thesaurus, which have already gone through an evaluation phase by a group of experts of the domain.

7.2. Word Embedding-based

Word embedding models have been showing to be very effective in word representation. They have been applied in several NLP tasks including word disambiguation, semantic similarity, bilingual lexicon induction (Mikolov et al., 2013; Arora et al., 2017; Bojanowski et al., 2016), etc. For semantic similarity, and more precisely synonym extraction of multi-word terms, two compositionality-based techniques have been proposed (Hazem and Daille, 2018). The first technique called *Semi-compositional word embeddings* is based on distributional analysis (Hazem and Daille, 2014) and assumes that the head or a tail is shared by two semantically related terms. The second technique called *Full-compositional word embeddings* is inspired by the idea that phrases can be represented by an element-wise sum of the word embeddings of semantically related words of its parts (Arora et al., 2017). In our experiments we follow the principle of the second technique and apply it to the automatic extraction of hyperonyms, synonyms, related and causative terms. The idea is to answer the question: are word embedding models able to extract semantic relations using full-compositionality? All the multi-word

terms (MWTs) are represented by a single embedding vector. Each MWT is first characterized by an element-wise sum of its word embedding elements. Then, the cosine similarity measure is applied to extract MWTs synonyms, hypernyms, causative and related terms.

7.3. Semantic Similarity Experiments

We evaluate two word embedding models: word2vec (W2V) (Mikolov et al., 2013) and fastText (Bojanowski et al., 2016). For both models we experiment the Skipgram (Sg) and the Continuous Bag of Words (CBOW) models. The results are shown in terms of precision at 100 (P@100).

	Hyp	Syn	Rel	Cause
W2V (Sg)	**5.91**	**45.7**	5.38	**13.2**
W2V (CBOW)	2.95	34.2	6.15	0.00
fastText (Sg)	4.73	34.2	**10.3**	3.77
fastText (CBOW)	3.55	22.8	**10.3**	1.88

Table 6: Results of semantic relation extraction of word2vec (W2V) and fastText using the Precision at 100 (P@100%) score.

As illustrated in Table 6, all the models fail to extract hypernyms, related, and causative relations. Only synonym extraction exibits acceptable results with Sg (45.7%). Nonetheless, the weak results, even for synonyms can be explained by the mixed nature of language in the Cybersecurity corpus terminology. Indeed, several terms are in English and their related terms in Italian or conversely. This circumstance might weaken the embedding models for low frequency terms.

8. Discussion

To draw guidelines for automatic thesaurus construction, we discuss the following questions: (i) which term extraction system to use; (ii) which system output is the most convenient to enrich an existing term list; (iii) which word embedding model is the most suitable for semantic relation extraction; and, finally, (iv) what kind of relations are extracted by word embedding models. As stated in previous work (Terryn et al., 2018), the evaluation of automatic term extraction is not an easy task. This observation is confirmed in this paper with regards to the obtained results on different evaluation lists (Clusit, Cyber, Iso, etc.). This is particularly true because our evaluation lists are not exhaustive and, for this reason, they don't reflect a real term extraction evaluation scenario. However, they do reflect the situation of thesaurus enrichment, which we stress in this work. If we cannot draw final conclusions on the term extraction performance of the evaluated systems, we can still observe their weak performance on the addressed small subset of terms on Cybersecurity. Nonetheless, this result is to be counterbalanced by encouraging new terms extracted by these systems. Indeed, a manual evaluation of BERT system output, for instance, has shown many new accurate extracted terms. This work represents the first attempt to use BERT model for terminology extraction. Overall, BERT obtained the best results with minimum supervision and no pattern analysis. This is encouraging since no careful filtering process has been applied, and opens the path for new strategies to pursue for term extraction using deep neural approaches.

For what concerns the types of relations extracted by word embedding models, for the most part the terms in the lists referred to the three semantic relations categories, i.e., hierarchy, association and causative links, prove to be quite similar in the occurrences they provided and, at times, not very faithful, e.g., *cyber gang* is connected in an hierarchical way with *criptography*. On the other hand, the synonyms detection showed better results and the findings are very exhaustive both for what concerns the retrieval of the synonyms themselves, and for the recognition, among the outputs given by the models, of other candidate related terms to add in the thesaurus.

The connections given by these models were performed using the existing thesaurus relations, which have been created following the ISO 25964:2011 rules, as source correspondences to be enhanced with sophisticated grouping procedures. Though the manual evaluation of these series of interrelations has inferred quite similar proximity among the terms extracted in all the four classes of relations, at least on a quantitative level, e.g. *rischi cyber (cyber risks)*, *anti spam*, *hackeraggio (hacking)* appear for almost all the cases, many associated terms helped in improving the thesaural systematization. It should be underlined that when evaluating these kind of lists, a minimum level of knowledge expertise about the technical domain to be studied is required since many terms connected with the head ones sometimes appear related in a very implied way, at least for the domain experts, e.g., *cavalli di troia (trojan horse)* or *zero-day*.

We provide few examples of the additional inputs provided by word embedding techniques on the Italian source corpus about Cybersecurity. It is implied that a new evaluation from the experts of the domain is necessary for the seek of reaching out high pertinence and accuracy levels in the terminological enhanced network meant to transposed in the semantic tool, which is supposed to be shared.

Hyperonyms detection

1. **gestione del rischio cyber (*risk management*)** which has as hyponym *piano di risposta al rischio cyber (risk response measures)*, has been connected with: *attacchi cibernetici (cyber attacks), cavalli di troia (trojan horse), cyber intelligence, difesa informatica (cyber security)*; this confirms the thesaurus outline regarding the top term category of *cybersecurity* and adds another one to be considered, i.e., *cyber intelligence*.

2. **intrusion detection system** - host-based, in the thesaurus is the hyponym of *network security systems*. Among the terms related in a hierarchical way, *network security systems* has been confirmed, and, in turn, other related terms have been included in the semantic structure, e.g., *hacker, mid hacking, sniffing* and *malware*.

Synonymys detection

1. **cybersecurity** has been related to the following synonyms that can be considered as positive candidates for the thesaurus: *difesa informatica (informative defence), deep security, sicurezza cibernetica (cibernetic security), protezione cibernetica (cibernetic protection), sicurezza dei sistemi informativi (informative systems security), sicurezza ict (ict security)*.

2. **malware** has been found related with these synonyms: *software malevolo (malicious software), programmi malevoli (malicious programs)*, confirming the existing synonymous structure in the thesaurus; the interesting result is that *malware* is associated in the same list with several representative terms that will be, in a future perspective, conceived as candidates to improve its semantic connections: *spyware, keylogger, firewall, exploit*.

Related terms detection

1. **zero-day** that in the thesaurus is connected on an associative level with *software vulnerabilities*, is grouped together with *trojan horse, anti spam, hacking, privacy, risk management*.

2. **cyber molestie (*cyber harassment*)**, related in the thesaurus, among others, with *cyber stalking*, has an improved structuring matches since it is found associated also with *cyber theft, hacking, threats, cyber insurance*.

Causative relations detection

1. **cyber minacce (*cyber threats*)** was connected through the causative verb *to damage* to the *security properties of data*, in these models it is linked to *cyber intelligence, difesa informatica (cyber security), hackeraggio (hacking)* and *cavalli di troia (trojan horse)*.

2. **bitcoin** was associated with *data loss* through the causative pattern verb *to prevent*, with the application of these embedding techniques it seems also related with *risk management, cyber risk, spam, hacking*.

9. Conclusion

Automatic thesaurus construction requires efficient methods to collect terminologies and to structure them in a representative way. We discussed in the present paper different approaches for the two building blocks of thesaurus construction: (i) term extraction and (ii) similarity linking. We conducted experiments on an Italian Cybersecurity corpus and reported the performance of existing methods with regards to several evaluation lists. We also proposed a new BERT-based approach that outperformed existing methods on the task of term extraction. If on a general perspective the obtained results provided not so high scores, we observed that system outputs contain accurate candidates that can be used to enrich the existing thesaurus. This is noticeable for the proposed BERT model. Also, regarding semantic similarity, word embedding models showed interesting outputs especially for synonyms and causative relations.

10. References

Andrade, D., Tsuchida, M., Onishi, T., and Ishikawa, K. (2013). Synonym acquisition using bilingual comparable corpora. In *International Joint Conference on Natural Language Processing (IJCNLP'13)*, Nagoya, Japan.

Arora, S., Yingyu, L., and Tengyu, M. (2017). A simple but tough to beat baseline for sentence embeddings. In *Proceedings of the 17th International Conference on Learning Representations (ICLR'17)*, pages 1–11.

Azevedo, C., Iacob, M., Almeida, J., van Sinderen, M., Ferreira Pires, L., and Guizzardi, G. (2015). Modeling resources and capabilities in enterprise architecture: A well-founded ontology-based proposal for archimate. *Information systems*, 54:235–262, 12.

Barrière, C. (2002a). Hierarchical refinement and representation of the causal relation. *Terminology*, 8(1):91–111.

Barrière, C. (2002b). Investigating the causal relation in informative texts. *Terminology*, 7(4):135–154.

Barrière, C. (2006). Semi-automatic corpus construction from informative texts. In Lynne Bowkes, editor, *Text-Based Studies in honour of Ingrid Meyer*, Lexicography, Terminology and Translation, chapter 5. University of Ottawa Press, January.

Batini, C., Cappiello, C., Francalanci, C., and Maurino, A. (2009). Methodologies for data quality assessment and improvement. *ACM Comput. Surv.*, 41(3), July.

Bernier-Colborne, G. and Barrière, C. (2018). CRIM at semeval-2018 task 9: A hybrid approach to hypernym discovery. In *Proceedings of The 12th International Workshop on Semantic Evaluation, SemEval@NAACL-HLT, New Orleans, Louisiana, June 5-6, 2018*, pages 725–731.

Blondel, V. D. and Senellart, P. (2002). Automatic extraction of synonyms in a dictionary. In *SIAM Workshop on Text Mining*.

Bojanowski, P., Grave, E., Joulin, A., and Mikolov, T. (2016). Enriching word vectors with subword information. *CoRR*, abs/1607.04606.

Boudin, F. (2016). pke: an open source python-based keyphrase extraction toolkit. In *Proceedings of COLING 2016, the 26th International Conference on Computational Linguistics: System Demonstrations*, pages 69–73, Osaka, Japan, December. The COLING 2016 Organizing Committee.

Broughton, W. (2008). *Costruire Thesauri: strumenti per indicizzazione e metadati semantici"*. EditriceBibliografica, 2008, Milano, Italia Cliffs, NJ.

Cabré, M. T., Bagot, R. E., and Platresi, J. V. (2001). Automatic term detection: A review of current systems. In *Recent Advances in Computational Terminology*, volume 2 of *Natural Language Processing*, pages 53–88. John Benjamins.

Condamines, A. (2007). L'interprétation en sémantique de corpus : le cas de la construction de terminologies. *Revue française de linguistique appliquée*, Vol. XII(2007/1):39–52.

Condamines, A. (2008). Taking Genre into account when Analyzing Conceptual Relation Patterns. *Corpora*, 8:115–140.

Condamines, A. (2018). Terminological knowledge bases from texts to terms, from terms to texts. In *The Routledge Handbook of Lexicography*. Routledge.

Cram, D. and Daille, B. (2016). Terminology extraction with term variant detection. In *Proceedings of ACL-2016 System Demonstrations*, pages 13–18, Berlin, Germany, August. Association for Computational Linguistics.

Daille, B. and Hazem, A. (2014). Semi-compositional method for synonym extraction of multi-word terms. In *Proceedings of the Ninth International Conference on Language Resources and Evaluation (LREC'14)*, pages 1202–1207, Reykjavik, Iceland, May. European Language Resources Association (ELRA).

Dell'Orletta, F., Venturi, G., Cimino, A., and Montemagni, S. (2014). T2K: a system for automatically extracting and organizing knowledge from texts. In *Proceedings of the Ninth International Conference on Language Resources and Evaluation (LREC'14)*, Reykjavik, Iceland, may. European Language Resources Association (ELRA).

Devlin, J., Chang, M., Lee, K., and Toutanova, K. (2018). BERT: pre-training of deep bidirectional transformers for language understanding. *CoRR*, abs/1810.04805.

Girju, R., Badulescu, A., and Moldovan, D. (2006). Automatic discovery of part-whole relations. *Computational Linguistics*, 32(1):83–135.

Grefenstette, G. (1994). *Explorations in Automatic Thesaurus Discovery*. Kluwer Academic Publisher, Boston, MA.

Güntzer, U., Jüttner, G., Seegmüller, G., and Sarre, F. (1989). Automatic thesaurus construction by machine learning from retrieval sessions. *Inf. Process. Manage.*, 25(3):265–273, May.

Hagiwara, M. (2008). A supervised learning approach to automatic synonym identification based on distributional features. In *Proceedings of the ACL-08: HLT Student Research Workshop*, pages 1–6, Columbus, Ohio, June. Association for Computational Linguistics.

Hazem, A. and Daille, B. (2014). Semi-compositional method for synonym extraction of multi-word terms. In *Proceedings of the Ninth International Conference on Language Resources and Evaluation (LREC'14)*, Reykjavik, Iceland, may. European Language Resources Association (ELRA).

Hazem, A. and Daille, B. (2018). Word Embedding Approach for Synonym Extraction of Multi-Word Terms. In *Proceedings of the Eleventh International Conference on Language Resources and Evaluation (LREC 2018)*, Miyazaki, Japan, May 7-12, 2018. European Language Resources Association (ELRA).

Hearst, M. A. (1992). Automatic acquisition of hyponyms from large text corpora. In *COLING 1992 Volume 2: The 15th International Conference on Computational Linguistics*.

ISO/IEC 27000, (2016). *Information technology – Security techniques – Information security management sys-*

tems – Overview and vocabulary. International Standard, February.

ISO/TC 46/SC 9, (2011). *ISO 25964-1:2011 Information and documentation — Thesauri and interoperability with other vocabularies — Part 1: Thesauri for information retrieval*. International Standard, August.

ISO/TC 46/SC 9, (2013). *ISO 25964-2:2013 Information and documentation — Thesauri and interoperability with other vocabularies — Part 2: Interoperability with other vocabularies*. International Standard, March.

Kageura, K., Tsuji, K., and Aizawa, A. N. (2000). Automatic thesaurus generation through multiple filtering. In *Proceedings of the 18th Conference on Computational Linguistics - Volume 1*, COLING '00, page 397–403, USA. Association for Computational Linguistics.

Kisserl, R., (2013). *Glossary of Key Information Security Terms*. National Institute of Standards and Technology, May. NISTIR 7298 Revision 2.

Lanza, C. and Daille, B. (2019). Terminology systematization for Cybersecurity domain in Italian language. In *TIA 2019 Terminologie et Intelligence Artificielle - Atelier TALN-RECITAL et IC (PFIA 2019)*, Toulouse, France, July.

Leech, G. (1991). *The state of the art in corpus linguistics*. Longman, London.

Lefeuvre, L. and Condamines, A. (2015). Constitution d'une base bilingue de marqueurs de relations conceptuelles pour l'élaboration de ressources termino-ontologiques. In *Terminology and Artificial Intelligence (TIA'2015)*, pages 183–190, Granada, Spain.

Lefeuvre, L. (2017). *Analyse des marqueurs de relations conceptuelles en corpus spécialisé : recensement, évaluation et caractérisation en fonction du domaine et du genre textuel*. Ph.D. thesis. Thèse de doctorat Sciences du langage - U. Toulouse 2.

Loginova Clouet, E., Gojun, A., Blancafort, H., Guegan, M., Gornostay, T., and Heid, U. (2012). Reference Lists for the Evaluation of Term Extraction Tools. In *Terminology and Knowledge Engineering Conference (TKE)*, Madrid, Spain.

Meyer, I. and Mackintosh, K. (1996). The Corpus from a Terminographer's Viewpoint. *International Journal of Corpus Linguistics*, 1(2):257–285.

Mikolov, T., Yih, S. W.-t., and Zweig, G. (2013). Linguistic regularities in continuous space word representations. In *Proceedings of the 2013 Conference of the North American Chapter of the Association for Computational Linguistics: Human Language Technologies (NAACL-HLT-2013)*. Association for Computational Linguistics, May.

Morin, E. and Jacquemin, C. (1999). Projecting corpus-based semantic links on a thesaurus. In *Proceedings of the 37th Annual Meeting of the Association for Computational Linguistics*, page 389–396. Association for Computational Linguistics.

Nguyen, K. A., Köper, M., Schulte im Walde, S., and Vu, N. T. (2017). Hierarchical embeddings for hypernymy detection and directionality. In *Proceedings of the 2017 Conference on Empirical Methods in Natural Language Processing*, pages 233–243. Association for Computational Linguistics.

Nielsen, M. L. (2001). A framework for work task based thesaurus design. *Journal of Documentation*, 57(6):774–797.

Rennesson, M., Georget, M., Paillard, C., Perrin, O., Pigeotte, H., and Tête, C. (2020). Le thésaurus, un vocabulaire contrôlé pour parler le même langage. *Médecine Palliative*, 19(1):15 – 23. Documentation et pratiques documentaires en soins palliatifsCoordonné par Caroline Tête.

Ryan, C. (2014). Thesaurus construction guidelines: An introduction to thesauri and guidelines on their construction. *Dublin: Royal Irish Academy and National Library of Ireland*.

Rösiger, I., Bettinger, J., Schäfer, J., Dorna, M., and Heid, U. (2016). Acquisition of semantic relations between terms: how far can we get with standard nlp tools? In *Proceedings of COLING 2016: 5th International Workshop on Computational Terminology (CompuTerm)*, Osaka, Japan.

Schandl, T. and Blumauer, A. (2010). Poolparty: Skos thesaurus management utilizing linked data. In *The Semantic Web: Research and Applications*, pages 421–425, Berlin, Heidelberg. Springer Berlin Heidelberg.

Terryn, A. R., Hoste, V., and Lefever, E. (2018). A Gold Standard for Multilingual Automatic Term Extraction from Comparable Corpora: Term Structure and Translation Equivalents. In *Proceedings of the Eleventh International Conference on Language Resources and Evaluation (LREC 2018)*, Miyazaki, Japan, May 7-12, 2018. European Language Resources Association (ELRA).

van der Plas, L. and Tiedemann, J. (2006). Finding synonyms using automatic word alignment and measures of distributional similarity. In *21st International Conference on Computational Linguistics and 44th Annual Meeting of the Association for Computational Linguistics ACL'06*, Sydney, Australia.

Weller, M., Gojun, A., Heid, U., Daille, B., and Harastani, R. (2011). Simple methods for dealing with term variation and term alignment. In *Proceedings of the 9th International Conference on Terminology and Artificial Intelligence (TIA 2011)*, pages 87–93, Paris, France, November. INALCO.

Wu, H. and Zhou, M. (2003). Optimizing synonym extraction using monolingual and bilingual resources. In *Proceedings of the second international workshop on Paraphrasing-Volume 16*, pages 72–79. Association for Computational Linguistics.

Yang, D. and Powers, D. M. (2008a). Automatic thesaurus construction. In *Proceedings of the Thirty-First Australasian Conference on Computer Science - Volume 74*, ACSC '08, page 147–156, AUS. Australian Computer Society, Inc.

Yang, D. and Powers, D. M. (2008b). Automatic thesaurus construction. In *Proceedings of the Thirty-first Australasian Conference on Computer Science - Volume 74*, ACSC '08, pages 147–156, Darlinghurst, Australia, Australia. Australian Computer Society, Inc.

Proceedings of the 6th International Workshop on Computational Terminology (COMPUTERM 2020), pages 72–79
Language Resources and Evaluation Conference (LREC 2020), Marseille, 11–16 May 2020
© European Language Resources Association (ELRA), licensed under CC-BY-NC

Supporting terminology extraction with dependency parses

Małgorzata Marciniak, Piotr Rychlik, Agnieszka Mykowiecka
Institute of Computer Science, Polish Academy of Sciences
Jana Kazimierza 5, 01-248 Warsaw, Poland
{mm, rychlik, agn}@ipipan.waw.pl

Abstract

Terminology extraction procedure usually consists of selecting candidates for terms and ordering them according to their importance for the given text or set of texts. Depending on the method used, a list of candidates contains different fractions of grammatically incorrect, semantically odd and irrelevant sequences. The aim of this work was to improve term candidate selection by reducing the number of incorrect sequences using a dependency parser for Polish.

Keywords: terminology extraction, candidates filtering, dependency parsing, prepositional phrases

1. Introduction

Extracting important domain related phrases is a part of very many NLP tasks such as information extraction, indexing or text classification. Depending on a particular scenario either more precise or more robust solutions are preferable. In our terminology extraction work, the aim is to prepare preliminary lists for building terminology resources or text indexing. As manual checking of the prepared list is expensive, we are interested in a solution in which the top of the ordered candidates list is of the highest quality. One of the problems of all term extraction methods is the fact that some extracted sequences are incorrect. The sequences recognized using statistical methods or shallow grammars can sometimes be semantically odd or even incorrect at the syntactic level. We identify two types of errors. In the first, the shallow patterns cover only part of the phrase, e.g., *resolution microscopy*. In the second, parts of two independent phrases are merged into a sequence which does not form a coherent phrase, e.g., *high resolution microscopy designed*. The aim of this work was to improve term candidate selection by reducing the number of incorrect sequences using a dependency parser for Polish. The answer to the question whether using a deep parser improves term identification would have been evident if the parsing were perfect. In such a case, at least all syntactically incorrect phrases (the errors of the second type mentioned above) would have been eliminated. However, errors of the first type are rather hard to identify on syntactic grounds.

Dependency analysis classifies all modifiers as adjuncts, some of them are necessary term parts and indicate a particular subtype, e.g., *basic income*, while others are just modifications which specify frequency, intensity or quality features and do not constitute a part of a term, e.g., *bigger income*. That is why we propose a hybrid approach, not just dependency parsing.

In this paper, we will not discuss the computational aspects of dependency parsing. Although it can significantly slow down the extraction process, it might still be useful in cases where the potential user wants to improve the quality of the output. Besides, not all sentences of the processed text need to be analyzed by a dependency parser, but only those containing examined terms.

2. Related Work

Terminology extraction (sometimes under the name of keyword/keyphrase extraction) is quite a popular NLP task which is tackled by several tools available both as open access and commercial systems. An overview of biomedical terminology extraction is presented in (Lossio-Ventura et al., 2016), several keyphrase extraction systems described in the scientific literature were later presented in (Merrouni et al., 2019). The latter paper mainly describes solutions which were proposed within the area of text mining or artificial intelligence, while quite a lot of other approaches were proposed at more natural language processing and terminology extraction oriented venues, e.g., TermSuite (Cram and Daille, 2016) and Sketch Engine (Kilgarriff et al., 2014). Competitions in automatic term extractions have been also organised, e.g., at SemEval workshop (Kim et al., 2010) or (Augenstein et al., 2017).

Terminology extraction systems can be divided into two groups. In one group, term extraction is treated as any other extraction task and is usually solved as a classification task using statistical, e.g., CRF, (Zhang, 2008), (Yu et al., 2012), or deep learning methods, e.g., (Zhang et al., 2016), (Meng et al., 2017). The other approach, also accepted by the extraction tool we use (TermoPL), comes from collocation/phrase recognition work. Most of the term extraction systems which were developed along these lines follow the standard three phase procedure consisting of text preprocessing, potential term selection and term scoring. Text preprocessing depends on the source of texts and the language in which they are written and usually consists of filtering out unnecessary information, tokenization and sometimes POS tagging. As a lot of work was done for English, most approaches for candidate selections are based on selecting just word n-grams on the basis of the simple frequency based statistics, e.g., (Rose et al., 2010) or on the shallow grammars usually written as a set of regular expressions over POS tags, e.g., (Cram and Daille, 2016). Deep syntactic grammars are hardly used at all. One solution in which dependency grammar is used to extract term candidates is described in Gamallo (2017). Dependency parses were also analyzed in Liu et al. (2018). All the above approaches to candidate selection are approximate (for different reasons), i.e. some term candidates are improper while others are omitted. In our work, we used shallow grammars with additional specification of morphological values dependencies. As Polish is an inflectional language, this approach allows a lot of grammatically incorrect phrases to be filtered out while, at the same time, it is not limited to the sequences recognized properly by a deep parser for Polish, which for a specific domain might not have enough coverage.

The second step of the process – candidate ranking – is also carried out in very different ways. The frequency of a term or frequency based coefficients play the most prominent role. The most popular is tf-idf, but the C-value (Frantzi et al., 2000), used in this paper, also became widely used. Unlike many other coefficients, the C-value takes into account not only the longest phrases or sequences of a given length, but also sequences included in other, longer, sequences.

Although in some approaches the ranking procedure may be very complex, the idea of an additional phase of filtering improperly built pre-selected phrases, as suggested in our paper, is not very popular. There are, however, some solutions with a post filtering phrase, e.g. (Liu et al., 2015), in which the candidates are compared to different external terminology resources. This approach was not adopted in our work, as it cannot be used to identify new terms and it requires resources adequate for a specific domain. Another postulated modification of the overall processing schema is the final re-ranking procedure adopted in (Gamallo, 2017).

As in many other NLP tasks, evaluation of the terminology extraction results is both crucial and hard to perform. Evaluation can either be performed manually or automatically. In the first case, apart from the cost of the evaluation, the main problem is that sometimes it is hard to judge whether a particular term is domain related or comes from general language. Automatic evaluation requires terminological resources (which, even if they exist, are usually not complete), or preparing the gold standard labelled text (which has similar problems to direct manual evaluation). In statistical methods, the automatic evaluation procedure is usually used. In (Merrouni et al., 2019), the results of several systems show the overall very poor recall (0.12-0.5) and a little higher precision (0.25-0.7) with the F1 measure usually below 0.3. Manual verification usually covers the top few hundred terms which are judged by a domain expert to be domain related terms or not. In this approach, only the precision of the results can be evaluated at reasonable cost. Gamallo (2017) reports precision of 0.93 for the first 800 terms extracted from English biomedical texts using an approach similar to that adopted by us. In (Marciniak and Mykowiecka, 2014), the then existing version of the TermoPL gave precision of 0.85 for 800 top positions of the terms list obtained from medical clinical reports. The recall counted on four reports (a very small dataset) was 0.8. The poorer results obtained for Polish data are mainly caused by the poor quality of text with many errors and missing punctuation marks (both commas and dots).

The results of the two groups of methods described above cannot be directly compared, but the good quality of the linguistically based methods is the reason why we want to develop this approach to terminology extraction.

3. Tools Description

3.1. TermoPL

As the baseline method of term selection for our experiments we chose one implemented in the publicly available tool – TermoPL (Marciniak et al., 2016). The tool operates on the text tagged with POS and morphological features values and uses shallow grammar to select the term candidates. Grammar rules operate on forms, lemmas and morphological tags of the tokens. They thus allow for imposing agreement requirements important for recognizing phrase borders in inflectional languages, such as Polish. TermoPL has a built-in grammar describing basic Polish noun phrases and also allows for defining custom grammars for other types of phrases. The program was originally developed for the Polish language so it is capable of handling the relatively complex structural tagset of Polish (Przepiórkowski et al., 2012). It is also possible to redefine this tagset and process texts in other languages. To eliminate sub-sequences with borders crossing strong collocations, the NPMI (Bouma, 2009) based method of identifying the proper sub-sequences was proposed (Marciniak and Mykowiecka, 2015). According to this method, subphrase borders are subsequently identified between the tokens with the smallest NPMI coefficient (counted for bigrams on the basis of the whole corpus). So, if a bigram constitutes a strong collocation, the phrase is not being divided in this place, and this usually blocks creation of semantically odd nested phrases.

The final list of terms is ordered according to the C-value adapted for taking one word terms into account. The C-value is a frequency dependent coefficient but takes into account not only the occurrences of the longest phrase, but also counts occurrences of its sub-sequences.

3.2. COMBO

In our experiments we use a publicly available Polish dependency parser – COMBO (Rybak and Wróblewska, 2018). COMBO is a neural net based jointly trained tagger, lemmatizer and dependency parser. It assigns labels based on features extracted by a biLSTM network. The system uses both fully connected and dilated convolutional neural architectures. The parser is trained on the Polish Dependency Bank (http://zil.ipipan.waw.pl/PDB). In our work we used the version trained on PDB annotated with a set of relations extended specifically for Polish (http://zil.ipipan.waw.pl/PDB/DepRelTypes).

4. Data Description

The experiment was conducted on the textual part of an economics articles taken from Polish Wikipedia. It was collected in 2011 as part of the Polish Nekst project (POIG.01.01.02-14-013/10). The data contains 1219 articles that have economics related headings and those linked to them.

The data was processed by the Concraft tagger (Waszczuk, 2012) which uses Morfeusz morphological dictionary and a guesser module for unknown words. The processed text has about 460K tokens in around 20,000 sentences. There are about 46,600 different token types of 17,900 different lemmas or known word forms within the text.

$$NPP \quad : \quad \$NAP\ NGEN^*;$$
$$NAP[agreement] \quad : \quad AP^*\ N\ AP^*;$$
$$NGEN[case = gen] \quad : \quad NAP;$$
$$AP \quad : \quad ADJ \mid PPAS \mid$$
$$ADJA\ DASH\ ADJ;$$
$$N[pos = subst, ger];$$
$$ADJ[pos = adj];$$
$$ADJA[pos = adja];$$
$$PPAS[pos = ppas];$$
$$DASH[form = \text{"-"}];$$

Figure 1: The built-in grammar represents noun phrases comprised of nominal phrases built from nouns or gerunds optionally modified by adjectival phrases located either before or after them. Nominal phrases can be modified by any number of nominal phrases in the genitive.

$$NP \quad : \quad NPPINST \mid PPP \mid NPAPGEN;$$
$$PPP \quad : \quad NPAPGEN\ PREP\ NAP^+;$$
$$NPPINST \quad : \quad NPAPGEN\ NINST\ NGEN^*;$$
$$NPAPGEN \quad : \quad \$NAP\ NGEN^*;$$
$$NAP[agreement] \quad : \quad AP^*\ N\ AP^*;$$
$$NGEN[case = gen] \quad : \quad NAP;$$
$$NINST[case = inst] \quad : \quad NAP;$$
$$AP \quad : \quad ADJ \mid PPAS \mid$$
$$ADJA\ DASH\ ADJ;$$
$$N[pos = subst, ger];$$
$$ADJ[pos = adj];$$
$$ADJA[pos = adja];$$
$$PPAS[pos = ppas];$$
$$DASH[form = \text{"-"}];$$
$$PREP[pos = prep];$$

Figure 2: The final grammar with added modifiers being noun phrases in the instrumental case and prepositional phrases.

5. Phrase identification

A selection of candidate phrases is performed by a shallow grammar defined over lemmatized and morphologically annotated text. TermoPL recognizes the maximal sequences of tokens which meet the conditions set out in a grammar. The built-in grammar, see Fig. 1, recognizes noun phrases where the head element can by modified by adjectives appearing before or after it, such as *międzynarodowe stosunki gospodarcze* 'international economic relations'. All these elements must agree in number, case and gender, which is marked in the rules by the *agreement* parameter. The noun phrase can be modified by another noun phrase in the genitive, e.g., *ubezpieczenie [odpowiedzialności cywilnej]$_{gen}$* 'insurance of civil responsibility'. All these elements can be combined, e.g., *samodzielny publiczny zakład [opieki zdrowotnej]$_{gen}$* 'independent public health care'. The $\$$ character marks a token or a group of tokens which should be replaced by their nominal forms when base forms are generated. It does not affect the type of phrase being recognized. In the economics texts, the built-in grammar collects 61,966 phrases when the NPMI driven selection method is used (without the NPMI it collects 82,930 phrases).

The built-in grammar does not cover noun phrases modified by prepositional phrases which quite often create important terms, e.g., *spółka z ograniczoną odpowiedzialnością* 'limited liability company'. This decision was made because it was difficult to recognize the role of a prepositional phrase in a sentence. A phrase very similar to the one above, e.g., *umowa spółki z uniwersytetem* 'a company agreement with the university' (word for word translation: ('agreement' 'company' 'with' 'university') should not lead to a conclusion that *spółka z uniwersytetem* creates a term – both nouns *firma* 'company' and *uniwersytet* 'university' are complements of the noun *umowa* 'agreement'. If the only criterion is a shallow grammar, we are unable to distinguish between such uses.

When analyzing the results obtained by the grammar defined in Fig. 1, we realised that some nominal phrases can have a noun phrase complement in the instrumental case. It applies to phrases such as, e.g., *handel [ropą naftową]$_{instr}$* 'trading in petroleum', *gospodarka nieruchomościami$_{instr}$* 'management of real estate' *opodatkowanie [podatkiem dochodowym]$_{instr}$* 'taxation of income'. But a similar problem, as for prepositional phrases, occurs for noun complements in the instrumental case, as we don't know if they are complements of a preceding nominal phrase or if they refer to another element in the sentence. For example: *rząd obłożył [papierosy] [akcyzą]$_{instr}$* (word for word translation: 'government' 'charged' 'cigarettes' 'excise duty') 'the government charged cigarettes with excise duty', where *akcyzą* 'excise duty' is the complement of *obłożył* 'charged' and not *papierosy* 'cigarettes'.

Both constructions described above, i.e. prepositional modifiers and noun complements in the instrumental case, are taken into account in the grammar given in Fig. 2. It collects 72,758 phrases when the NPMI driven selection method is used, which is over 10,000 more than for the built-in grammar (without the NPMI the grammar collects 113,687 phrases). Although the number of new terms is high, there are a couple of new top candidates on our list. The top 100 terms contains three correct phrases with prepositional modifiers *spółka z ograniczoną odpowiedzialnością* 'limited liability company', *ustawa o rachunkowości* 'accounting act' and *podatek od towarów* 'tax on goods', and no term with a noun complement in the instrumental case. The first such phrase *prawo o publicznym obrocie papierami wartościowymi* 'law on public trading of securities' is in position 637.

As we wanted to know how productive the above grammatical constructions are, we have defined two grammars describing them alone. This allows us to check how many phrases might be introduced to the term candidate list by these constructions.

type	number of phrases	
	absolute	relative
correct term	452	0.66
incorrect modification	114	0.17
incorrect – other reason	120	0.17

Table 1: Manual evaluation of the top phrases with a preposition modifier

frequency	number of phrases	
	absolute	relative
30-38	5	0.01
20-29	5	0.01
10-19	29	0.04
5-9	101	0.15
3-4	244	0.35
2	302	0.44

Table 2: Number of top phrases with a preposition modifier in different frequency groups.

The first dedicated grammar (NPPP) defines nominal phrases with a prepositional modifier. It consists of all rules given in Fig. 2 except the first, third and the seventh one. When the NPMI method is used, the grammar selects 22,150 terms. We evaluate all phrases which occurred at least 2 times and have a C-value of at least 3.0, i.e. 686 phrases. The results are given in Tab 1 – 66.6% of them are correct phrases (i.e. for these phrases precision is 0.666), 16.5% are phrases where a preposition phrase does not modify the preceding noun phrase, and for 16.9% a reason for not accepting the phrase is different. Many incorrect phrases are incomplete, such as *różnica między sumą przychodów uzyskanych* 'difference between the sum of revenues obtained' which is a part of *różnica między sumą przychodów uzyskanych z tytułu ... a kosztami uzyskania przychodów* 'difference between the sum of revenues from ... and tax deductible costs'.

The second grammar (NPInst) defines nominal phrases modified by noun phrases in the instrumental case. It consists of all rules given in Fig. 2 except the first and the second one. It selects fewer phrases, namely 1390. As there was only 44 phrases with a C-value of at least 3.0, we evaluated all 110 phrases which occurred at least twice. The results are given in Tab. 3. The example of an incorrect phrase recognised by the grammar is *budownictwo kosztorysantem* ('architecture' 'estimator') which actually is built up from two phrases and occurred three times in sentences similar to the following: *w [budownictwie kosztorysantem] jest rzeczoznawca* 'in architecture, an appraiser is an estimator'. Tab. 4 gives the frequency of the evaluated phrases. The statistics show that such constructions are not common. Moreover, we observe that only a small number of nouns and gerunds (acting as nouns) were used to create valid phrases in our data. These are: *obrót* 'trading' (21), *zarządzanie* 'management' (21), *handel* 'trade' (9), *opodatkowanie* 'taxation' (5), *gospodarka/gospodarowanie* 'management' (4).

type	number of phrases	
	absolute	relative
correct term	84	0.76
incorrect modification	10	0.09
incorrect – other reason	16	0.14

Table 3: Manual evaluation of selected phrases with an instrumental modifier.

frequency	number of phrases	
	absolute	relative
10-16	4	0.04
5-9	11	0.10
3-4	20	0.18
2	75	0.68

Table 4: Number of top phrases with an instrumental modifier in different frequency groups.

6. Filtering phrases with COMBO

In the postprocessing phase, we match the phrases found by NPPP and NPInst TermoPL grammars to some fragments of the dependency trees generated by COMBO for sentences containing these phrases. We imposed a few simple constraints that must be satisfied by matched tree fragments. The first one concerns prepositional phrases. If the preposition in the phrase being examined is associated with a part of the sentence that is not included in the phrase, then this phrase is certainly not a valid term. In other words, it means that no link in the dependency tree is allowed to connect something from outside the matched fragment with the preposition that lies inside this fragment. Examples of a good and a bad prepositional phrase are shown in Fig. 3 and 4, respectively. The first of these phrases *spółka z ograniczoną odpowiedzialnością* 'limited liability company' is a good example of an economics term. The second one *przedsiębiorstwo pod własną firmą* is a nonsense phrase that has a word for word translation 'enterprise under own company', which is equally nonsensical.

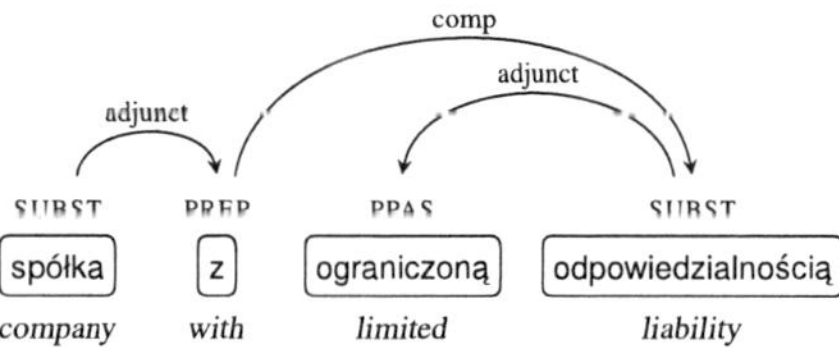

Figure 3: Dependency graph corresponding to correct prepositional phrase *spółka z ograniczoną odpowiedzialnością*.

It turns out that there are phrases that in some sentences are good candidates for terms, and in others not. A string *podatek od dochodu* which has the word for word translation 'tax from income' can be a noun modifier, e.g., *[podatek od dochodu] należy zapłacić w terminie do ...* 'income tax must be paid by ...', or it can be a valency constraint in the following sentence *Wyliczając kwotę do za-*

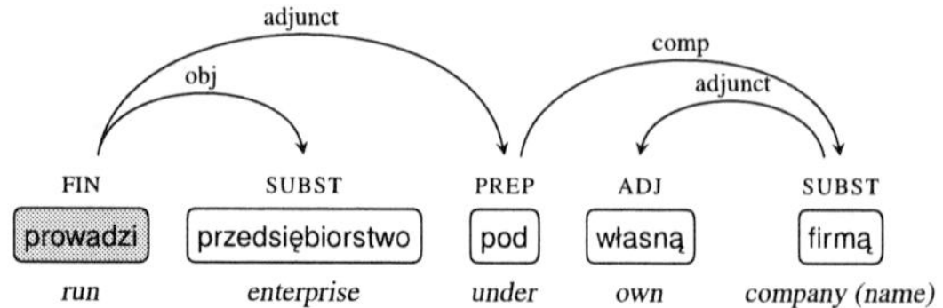

Figure 4: Dependency graph corresponding to the incorrect prepositional phrase *przedsiębiorstwo pod własną firmą*.

płaty należy odjąć [podatek] [od dochodu]. 'When calculating the amount to be paid, tax must be deducted from the income.' In the first example (see Fig. 5), the term *podatek od dochodu* is accepted by the constraint we mentioned above. In the second example, the same constraint rejects this phrase as a term (see Fig. 6).

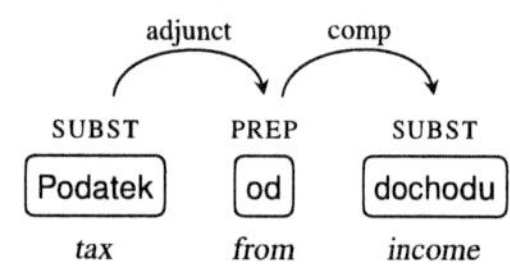

Figure 5: Accepted term *podatek od dochodu*.

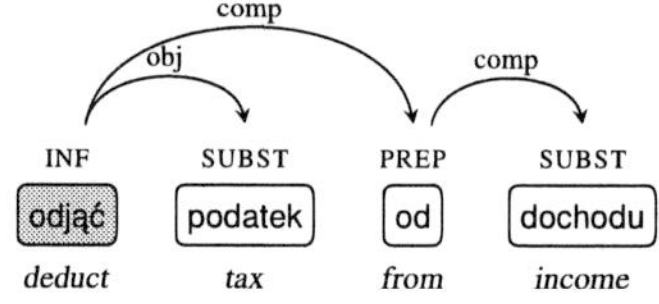

Figure 6: Rejected term *podatek od dochodu*.

The second constraint we impose on dependency graphs concerns the consistency of its matched fragment. A fragment of the graph corresponding to the examined phrase is consistent if, passing from the node considered as the head of the phrase, we pass through all its nodes. Fig. 7 presents an inconsistent graph for the phrase *koszty dojazdów środkami* (with word for word transtation 'travel costs by means'), which is syntactically correct, but without sense. However, when we consider the broader context, the phrase *pokrycie kosztów dojazdów środkami komunikacji miejscowej* 'coverage of travel costs by local transport', we obtain a phrase that makes sense and has a consistent graph. The graph for the phrase *podatek od dochodu* depicted in Fig. 6 is also inconsistent with this constraint (although it would anyway be rejected by the first rule described above). Finally, we eliminate graphs that correspond to some types of truncated phrases. They are depicted in Fig. 8-10. Fig. 8 shows an example in which a named entity phrase should not be divided. The phrase *Ustawa o Funduszu Kolejowym* 'Act on the Railway Fund' may not be shortened to the phrase *Ustawa o Funduszu* 'Act on the Fund', although it is still acceptable at the syntactic level. The other two examples show situations in which an adjective or participle, modifying an object or a complement, should not be cut

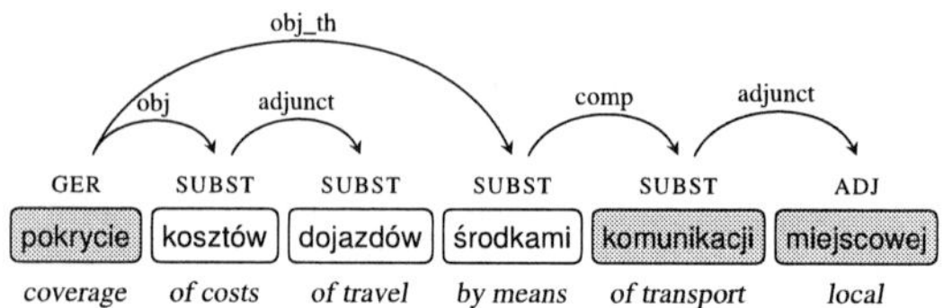

Figure 7: Graph inconsistency for the phrase *koszty dojazdów środkami*.

from the phrase on its right side, as they are usually necessary components of terms. The phrase *podatek dochodowy od osób fizycznych* 'personal income tax' (see Fig. 9) cannot be shortened to *podatek dochodowy od osób*. Similarly, the phrase *opodatkowanie podatkiem dochodowym* 'taxation on income' (see Figure 10) cannot be shortened to *opodatkowanie podatkiem*.

Sometimes, truncated phrases can be identified by their inconsistent graphs as shown in Fig. 7.

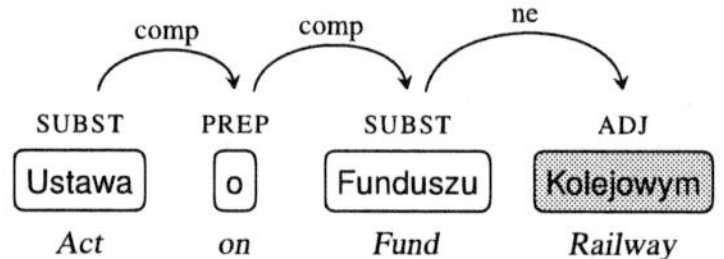

Figure 8: Truncated named entity (ne) phrase.

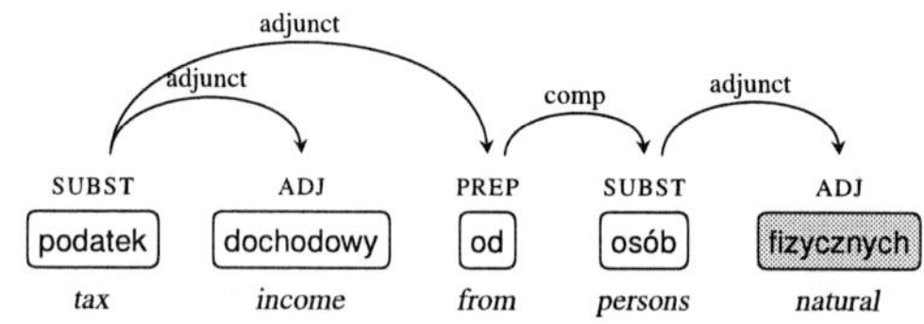

Figure 9: Truncated phrase *podatek dochodowy od osób*.

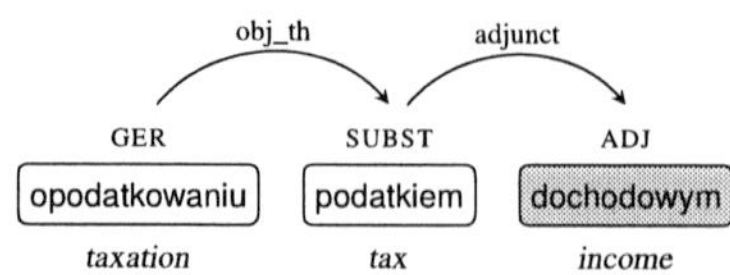

Figure 10: Rejected term *opodatkowanie podatkiem*.

We can now use all the above constraints to filter phases. If a phrase is supported by more than 50% of its dependency trees (which means that these trees satisfy all constraints), it is considered as a good term candidate. Otherwise, it is rejected.

7. Evaluation of the method

We compare the manual evaluation of all phrases obtained by two separate grammars with the results of filtering described in Sec. 6. The filtering gives the binary information: correct/incorrect phrase so we assume that the result is proper if an incorrect phrase is manually classified as incorrect modification or incorrect 'other reason'. Tables 5-6 give the evaluation of phrases with prepositional modifiers and phrases with instrumental modifiers respectively, classified by the dependency parser. The results depicted there show that the proposed approach is not precise enough. For phrases with prepositional phrases, 74% of correct phrases are correctly classified as valid terms, but there are about twenty percent of the proper terms which are discarded. There are even more incorrect sequences which are classified as correct (about quarter). For instrumental modifications, there are far fewer incorrect sequences accepted as good, while the percentage of the correct terms which are classified as bad is even higher than for prepositional modifiers. The answer to the question whether these results are due to our classification strategy not being good enough or to the insufficient quality of the parser needs further research.

Manual eval.	COMBO	correct	incorrect
correct		365	87
incorrect		131	103

Table 5: Comparison of the manual evaluation of the phrases with a preposition modifier with the dependency parser filtering. The results achieved for classification a phrase as correct by the parser: precision=0.74, recall=0.81.

Manual eval.	COMBO	correct	incorrect
correct		50	34
incorrect		4	22

Table 6: Evaluation of the phrases with an instrument modifier filtered by the dependency parser. The results achieved for classification a phrase as a correct one by the parser: precision=0.93, recall=0.60.

type	in top3.0	out top3.0	out
correct term	391	27	34
incorr modif.	67	15	32
incorr. – other	59	33	38
total	487	75	104

Table 7: Phrases with a preposition modifier – with NPMI.

8. Results

In this section, we analyze results of TermoPL using the extended grammar given in Fig. 2. A set of phrases for which the C-value is at least 3.0 are called hereinafter top3.0. For the plain method of term selection (without NPMI), the top3.0 consists of 5,935 terms. Phrases with prepositional modifiers are 11.9% of the top3.0 set. 7.6% of them are correct phrases and 4.3% are incorrect ones.

Then, we test if the NPMI method can prevent us from introducing incorrect phrases with prepositional modifiers into the top3.0 set. For some phrases, the NPMI method reduces their C-value which means they are pushed to the end of the list. Moreover, some phrases may not even appear on the term list. The top3.0 set for TermoPL with NPMI consists of 5,078 phrases. The statistics are given in Tab. 7, where the 'out top 3.0' column indicates the number of phrases whose C-value fell below the 3.0 level, and the 'out' column indicates the number of phrases which disappeared from the list. This method introduced 487 prepositional phrases into top3.0, which is 9.5%. 7.7% of them are correct phrases and 1.8% are incorrect ones. Tab. 8 gives the location of the correct 391 phrases on the top3.0 list ordered by C-value.

C-value	position	number of phrases	
		absolute	relative
<50-278)	1-78	1	0.2%
<20-50)	79-343	9	2.3%
<10-20)	344-899	31	7.9%
<5-10)	900-2129	113	28.9%
<3-5)	2130-5078	237	60.6%

Table 8: Distribution of the correct phrases with prepositional modifiers in top3.0 of TermoPL with NPMI.

type	in top3.0
correct-accepted	365
incorrect-accepted	131
correct-deleted	86
incorrect-deleted	101

Table 9: Phrases with a preposition modifier filtered by the dependency parser from the plain TermoPL results.

As we expected, application of the NPMI method in candidate phrase recognition reduces the number of incorrect phrases in the top3.0. In our experiment, they drop from 4.3% to 1.8% of all the top3.0. It slightly declines the share of phrases with prepositional modifiers on the top3.0 list from 11.9% to 9.5%. Moreover, it seems that this method works better for phrases which are incorrect because of 'other reasons' (e.g. truncated ones), as from the top3.0, it eliminates 71 of 130 such phrases (i.e. 54.6%) while for incorrect modifiers it eliminates 47 of 114 phrases which is 41.2%.

For nominal phrases with instrumental modifiers only 37 correct and 2 incorrect (because of 'other reasons') were on the top3.0 list generated without NPMI. Statistics are given in Tab. 3. It gives 0.66% of all top3.0 phrases, where 0.62% are correct new phrases. When the NPMI method is used, the top3.0 list contains 30 correct and 2 incorrect phrases with instrumental modifiers, which gives 0.63% of all top3.0 phrases including 0.59% correct new phrases.

To assess the usefulness of the dependency parsing we checked how many phrases with prepositional modifiers were accepted or deleted from the top3.0 of the TermoPL results generated without NPMI. The results for preposition modifiers are given in Tab. 9. So, filtering prepositional phrases by dependency grammar results in removing 187 phrases, where 101 of them were incorrect (i.e., their removal was justified).

9. Conclusion

The purpose of this work was to test whether dependency parsing can be useful in filtering out incorrectly constructed phrases in automatic terminology extraction. We tested this approach on phrases containing prepositional modifiers and nominal modifiers in the instrumental case.

We realised that noun phrases with prepositional modifiers are important in the terminology extraction task, as they constitute about 10% of the top term phrases. The phrases with instrumental case modifiers are much less important as they create only 0.65% of the top phrases. However, it is worth noting that there are only two incorrect such phrases among the top3.0. These constructions are much rarer and the most frequent phrases usually form correct terms.

There are about 6% of correct and 2% of incorrect preposition phrases on the top3.0 list generated without applying NPMI and filtered with the dependency parser. These results seem slightly worse than the results obtained by the NPMI method alone. It occurs that dependency parsing filters out an additional 43 incorrect phrases from the top3.0 list when the NPMI method is applied. Unfortunately, it also filters out 85 correct phrases. This observation requires further investigation.

As the quality and efficiency of the dependency parsing is constantly improving, we hope that these methods will better support the selection of term candidates. We also plan to check how the proposed filtering methods will work on terms with other syntactic structures.

Acknowledgements

Work financed as part of the investment in the CLARIN-PL research infrastructure funded by the Polish Ministry of Science and Higher Education.

Bibliographical References

Augenstein, I., Das, M., Riedel, S., Vikraman, L., and McCallum, A. (2017). SemEval 2017 task10: ScienceIE extracting keyphrases and relations from scientific publications. In *Proceedings of the 11th International Workshop on Semantic Evaluation*, pages 546–555. Association for Computational Linguistics.

Bouma, G. (2009). Normalized (pointwise) mutual information in collocation. In Christian Chiarcos, et al., editors, *From Form to Meaning: Processing Texts Automatically, Proceedings of the Biennial GSCL Conference*, pages 31–40. Tubingen: Gunter Narr Verlag.

Cram, D. and Daille, B. (2016). TermSuite: Terminology extraction with term variant detection. In *Proceedings of the 54th Annual Meeting of the Association for Computational Linguistics—System Demonstrations*, pages 13–18. Association for Computational Linguistics.

Frantzi, K., Ananiadou, S., and Mima, H. (2000). Automatic recognition of multi-word terms: the C-value/NC-value method. *Int. Journal on Digital Libraries*, 3:115–130.

Gamallo, P. (2017). Citius at SemEval-2017 task 2: Cross-lingual similarity from comparable corpora and dependency-based contexts. In *Proceedings of the 11th International Workshop on Semantic Evaluation*, pages 226–229. Association for Computational Linguistics.

Kilgarriff, A., Baisa, V., Bušta, J., Jakubíček, M., Kovář, V., Michelfeit, J., and Pavel Rychlý, V. S. (2014). The Sketch Engine: ten years on. *Lexicography*, 1:7–36.

Kim, S. N., Medelyan, O., Kan, M.-Y., and Baldwin, T. (2010). Semeval-2010 task 5: Automatic keyphrase extraction from scientific articles. In *Proceedings of the 5th International Workshop on Semantic Evaluation*, pages 21–26. Association for Computational Linguistics.

Liu, W., Chung, B. C., Wang, R., Ng, J., and Morlet, N. (2015). A genetic algorithm enabled ensemble for unsupervised medical term extraction from clinical letters. *Health Information Science and Systems*.

Liu, Y., Zhang, T., Quan, P., Wen, Y., Wu, K., and He, H. (2018). A novel parsing-based automatic domain terminology extraction method. In Shi Y. et al., editor, *Computational Science – ICCS 2018. Lecture Notes in Computer Science, vol 10862. Springer, Cham*, pages 796–802.

Lossio-Ventura, J. A., Jonquet, C., Roche, M., and Teisseire, M. (2016). Biomedical term extraction: overview and a new methodology. *Information Retrieval Journal*, pages 1573–7659.

Marciniak, M. and Mykowiecka, A. (2014). Terminology extraction from medical texts in Polish. *Journal of biomedical semantics*, 24.

Marciniak, M. and Mykowiecka, A. (2015). Nested term recognition driven by word connection strength. *Terminology*, 2:180–204.

Marciniak, M., Mykowiecka, A., and Rychlik, P. (2016). TermoPL — a flexible tool for terminology extraction. In Nicoletta Calzolari, et al., editors, *Proceedings of the Tenth International Conference on Language Resources and Evaluation, LREC 2016*, pages 2278–2284, Portorož, Slovenia. ELRA, European Language Resources Association (ELRA).

Meng, R., Zhao, S., Han, S., He, D., Brusilovsky, P., and Chi, Y. (2017). Deep keyphrase generation. In *Proceedings of the 55th Annual Meeting of the Association for Computational Linguistics (Volume 1: Long Papers)*, pages 582–592, Vancouver, Canada, July. Association for Computational Linguistics.

Merrouni, Z. A., Frikh, B., and Ouhbi, B. (2019). Automatic keyphrase extraction: a survey and trends. *Journal of Intelligent Information Systems*.

Adam Przepiórkowski, et al., editors. (2012). *Narodowy Korpus Języka Polskiego*. Wydawnictwo Naukowe PWN.

Rose, S., Engel, D., Cramer, N., and Cowley, W. (2010). Automatic keyword extraction from individual documents. *Text Mining: Applications and Theory*, pages 1 – 20, 03.

Rybak, P. and Wróblewska, A. (2018). Semi-supervised

neural system for tagging, parsing and lemmatization. In *Proceedings of the CoNLL 2018 Shared Task: Multilingual Parsing from Raw Text to Universal Dependencies*, page 45–54. Association for Computational Linguistics.

Waszczuk, J. (2012). Harnessing the CRF complexity with domain-specific constraints. The case of morphosyntactic tagging of a highly inflected language. In *Proceedings of the 24th International Conference on Computational Linguistics (COLING 2012)*, pages 2789–2804.

Yu, F., Xuan, H., and Zheng, D. (2012). Key-phrase extraction based on a combination of CRF model with document structure. In *Eighth International Conference on Computational Intelligence and Security*, pages 406–410.

Zhang, Q., Wang, Y., Gong, Y., and Huang, X. (2016). Keyphrase extraction using deep recurrent neural networks on twitter. In *Proceedings of the 2016 Conference on Empirical Methods in Natural Language Processing*, pages 836–845, Austin, Texas, November. Association for Computational Linguistics.

Zhang, C. (2008). Automatic keyword extraction from documents using conditional random fields. *Journal of Computational Information Systems*, 4(3):1169–1180.

Proceedings of the 6th International Workshop on Computational Terminology (COMPUTERM 2020), pages 80–84
Language Resources and Evaluation Conference (LREC 2020), Marseille, 11–16 May 2020

Computational Aspects of Frame-Based Meaning Representation in Terminology

Laura Giacomini, Johannes Schäfer
Institute for Information Science and Natural Language Processing, University of Hildesheim
Universitätsplatz 1, 31141 Hildesheim (Germany)
laura.giacomini@uni-hildesheim.de, johannes.schaefer@uni-hildesheim.de

Abstract

Our contribution is part of a wider research project on term variation in German and concentrates on the computational aspects of a frame-based model for term meaning representation in the technical field. We focus on the role of frames (in the sense of Frame-Based Terminology) as the semantic interface between concepts covered by a domain ontology and domain-specific terminology. In particular, we describe methods for performing frame-based corpus annotation and frame-based term extraction. The aim of the contribution is to discuss the capacity of the model to automatically acquire semantic knowledge suitable for terminographic information tools such as specialised dictionaries, and its applicability to further specialised languages.

Keywords: frame-based terminology, term extraction, technical terminology

1. Introduction

In the context of a larger study on variation in technical terminology carried out at the Institute for Information Science and Natural Language Processing of Hildesheim University, we have devised and implemented a method for ontology- and frame-based term variation modeling for texts concerning technical products. In this paper, we will concentrate both on already performed tests and on ongoing work. Our aim is to introduce our frame-based model and its advantages for representation of term meaning in lexicographic and terminographic resources, providing details on our method for frame-based corpus annotation, ranging from corpus preprocessing to semantic labeling.

Examples cited in this paper come from a 5.2-million-word corpus of specialised German texts concerning thermal insulation products and specifically built for this project.

2. Synonymous Term Variation

The relatively low degree of standardization of many technical subfields is one of the main reasons for the thriving of terminological variation in technical language. Synonymy, in particular, appears to be a pervasive phenomenon that is in strong contradiction with the traditional Wüsterian conception of terminology (Wüster, 1974). In particular, texts by the same source (or even the same text) often contain multiple (near) synonymous variants. These variants are sometimes characterized by the coexistence of morphologically divergent technical terms (e.g. *Hard Disk* vs. *Festplatte, technische Hydromechanik* vs. *Hydraulik, dämmen* vs. *isolieren*) but, more often, they consist of clusters of single word and multiword terms displaying morphological similarity (Giacomini, 2017). This is given in (1):

(1) Holzweichfaserdämmplatte,
Weichholzfaserdämmplatte,
Holzfaserdämmplatte,
Holzfaserplatte zur Dämmung von...,
Platte aus Holzfasern zur Dämmung von...

Morphological similarity is here referred to variants sharing lexical morphemes. The relationship between members of a variant cluster (such as the one in (1)) can normally be described in terms of the syntactic rules proper of a language, but their actual presence in texts may escape predictability and be motivated by contingent factors which are cognitive or discursive in nature (Freixa, 2006). We have developed a method for semi-automatically detecting variation in technical texts by relying, on the one hand, on the morphological similarity of variants and, on the other hand, on a frame-based approach to terminology (Faber, 2012/ 2015), according to which a cluster of synonymous variants takes on the same semantic role (or combination of semantic roles) within a specific conceptual scenario (frame).

3. The Frame-Based and the Ontological Description Layer

Our frame-based approach to terminology presupposes the description of the frame that is most apt to identify the topics dealt with by specialized texts contained in a corpus. It also presupposes that the technical products we aim to cover are similar in nature and function. A frame is a cognitive structure describing a situation made up of a set of specific semantic roles (frame elements, in the following named FEs) played by terms used in that situation (cf. Frame Semantics, Fillmore and Baker 2010). On the one hand, we take into account investigations showing a comparable approach (Corcoglioniti et al., 2016, Gómez-Moreno and Castro, 2017, Anić and Zuvela, 2017 among others). On the other hand, we also look at studies concerning the automation of frame-based semantic analysis for the German general language (especially Burchardt et al., 2009), as well as studies on the application of a frame-based approach to specific semantic aspects (e.g. sentiment analysis, for instance in Reforgiato Recupero, 2015).

We specify frames with reference to a previously defined domain ontology. For the field of thermal insulation products, an OWL-specified ontology has been built based on existing resources such as the upper ontologies SUMO and DOLCE, wordnets, technical dictionaries, and specialized literature. Three ontological macroclasses, MATERIAL, FORM, and FUNCTION, are first of all identified: they include several classes of ontological entities involved in the extralinguistic reality of insulation products (Giacomini, 2017/ 2019). Among suitable frames for the description of thermal insulation products (Giacomini, 2020), we concentrate on the frame FUNCTIONALITY and manually create an initial set of core frame elements, for instance the MATERIAL of which a product is made, the DELIVERY FORM in which a product is sold, the TECHNIQUE by means of which a product is applied, or the PROPERTY of a product.

We identified the following frame elements by analyzing corpus texts and automatically extracted candidates:

MATERIAL, MATERIAL CLASS, MATERIAL ORIGIN, MATERIAL PRODUCTION TECHNIQUE, PROPERTY, DELIVERY FORM, PACKAGING, MANUFACTURING FEATURE, TARGET, TARGET MATERIAL, COMPLEMENT, APPLICATION TECHNIQUE, TOOL, USER, PROJECT, SYSTEM, GOAL, RESULT, PRODUCT.

Each FE signals the semantic role played by a term (e.g. *Platte* (board) corresponds to the FE FORM) or part of a term (e.g. *Matte* (batt) in the compound *Steinwollematte* (stone wool batt) also corresponds to the FE FORM), and thus enables us to recognize this role across different terms, especially if they are morphologically similar. In the following example, an excerpt from a variant cluster of German terms for *extruded polystyrene insulation board* is manually annotated with POS and FE labels (e.g. N: FORM):

Platte aus extrudiertem Polystyrol :
N:FORM aus V:MAT_TECH N:MAT

Dämmplatte aus extrudiertem Polystyrol :
(V:GOAL N:FORM) aus V:MAT_TECH N:MAT

Polystyrol-Extruderschaum-Dämmplatte :
N:MAT - (V:MAT_TECH N:MAT_CLASS) - (V:GOAL N:FORM)

XPS-Platte :
(V:MAT_TECH N:MAT - N:MAT_CLASS)- N:FORM

Any term in the cluster includes the following, minimal FE combination:

MATERIAL (MAT), DELIVERY FORM (FORM), MATERIAL PRODUCTION TECHNIQUE (MAT_TECH),

whereas the frame element MATERIAL CLASS (MAT_CLASS) may additionally appear in some cases as a further specification of MATERIAL.

4.   Creating a String-Based Seed Lexicon

The frame-based tagset used in our study is made up of the core frame elements found for the frame FUNCTIONALITY. In order to perform initial annotation, a number of terminological strings derived from extracted terms needs to be attributed to the frame-based tags. This leads to a seed lexicon of string-tag associations. The strings can either be full words, roots or stems depending on factors such as inflectional and derivational properties of the terms to which they belong, or their occurrence within compounds (all different cases are collected and described in a guideline).

It needs to be pointed out that a preliminary experiment of compound splitting using COMPOST (Cap, 2014) had failed to return sufficiently robust results for the German language. Moreover, the choice of employing different types of strings can be generally explained with the morphological orientation of our approach. Some string examples will be now mentioned together with the corresponding FE tag:

MATERIAL: baumwoll, glas, holz, cellulose,...
MATERIAL ORIGIN: natur, pflanz, herkunft,...
MATERIAL PRODUCTION TECHNIQUE: bläh, back,...
PROPERTY: beständig, brenn, dicht, fein,...
APPLICATION TECHNIQUE: blas, klemm, verschraub,...

For the sake of avoiding multiple and, above all, incorrect annotation, we sometimes allow for overstemming and understemming (e.g. we include all these strings: *pore, porig, porös,* and *dämm, dämmung, dämmen*). Generally speaking, priority is given to the recognition of small groups of semantically homogenous words, which is particularly important in the case of the verb *dämmen* (to insulate) and its derivatives: *dämmen*, for instance, refers to the FE GOAL, the nominalization *Dämmung* (insulation) can either refer to a GOAL, a RESULT, or a PRODUCT.

5.   Semantic Annotation and Variant Extraction

The collection of technical texts is first tokenized and annotated with part-of-speech tags and lemmata using the RFTagger (Schmid and Laws, 2008). An automatic correction step is applied to make a best guess for those word forms that are unknown to the tagger lexicon. For efficient querying, the annotated corpus is then encoded for the IMS Open Corpus Workbench (CWB) (Evert and Hardie, 2011).

We then annotate these texts using the abovementioned frame elements (Section 5.1) and extract terms and variants from the encoded corpus (Section 5.2).

5.1   Semantic Annotation Employing Frame Elements

We automatically annotate tokens with the frame-based tags if they contain any of the predefined strings from the seed lexicon. Here, we exclude one frequent special case and decide not to annotate PROPERTY whenever a match of the string *offen* (open) in words containing *stoffen* (materials) is given, since this would cut the word stem. It should be noted that our string-based technique might produce other linguistically incorrect annotations, however we accept this noise for the sake of finding a higher number of potential terms in a liberal approach aiming for high recall. Tokens containing strings which are attributed to multiple frame element tags, for example the string *dämmung*, are annotated with this ambiguity, i.e. in this example GOAL/RESULT. In cases where multiple strings are matched in a single token and thus multiple frame element tags have been annotated, a special treatment to check for recursive matches is applied.

An overlapping of seed strings does not occur since they have been chosen in such a way as to exclude this. However, embedding is allowed, for example, the word *Wärmeleitfähigkeit* (thermal conductivity) contains the four PROPERTY strings *wärme, leitfähig, leit* and *fähig*. In this case, since *leit* and *fähig* are embedded in the string *leitfähig*, we only annotate *wärme* and *leitfähig* as primary annotation and *wärme*, *leit* and *fähig* as alternative (or embedded) annotation.

In the annotation of embedded FEs, we exclude morphologically incorrect cases of string matching. First, we do not consider the string *latte* as being embedded in the string *platte*. Second, we do not consider the strings *zell* or *lose* as being embedded in the string *zellulose*. In both cases the shorter, embedded string is not annotated if the longer one is also matched. In general, our string comparison is not case-sensitive, except for strings which are specifically in upper case, for example, abbreviations such as *PUR* (Polyurethane). Finally, the annotation of matched FE tags is also encoded into the CWB corpus.

5.2 Frame-Based Extraction of Terms and Variants

We first use the IMS Open Corpus Workbench and adapt the terminology extraction approach presented in Schäfer et al. (2015) to our purposes, obtaining a list of nouns and nominal multiword candidate terms ranked according to termhood measures (for details about the termhood measures, cf. Giacomini, 2020). Category metadata are included in the output, listing for each candidate term lemma the different associated word forms, its part-of-speech annotation, and example sentences from the corpus. Term candidates and concepts from the domain ontology are employed to define a relevant frame-based tagset (cf. Section 3). This tagset, in turn, is used to semantically annotate the corpus. We then extract terms and variants using our annotation of frame element tags. In a first step, we consider all tokens which are annotated with multiple frame element tags, typically compounds. We filter these compounds by only selecting tokens with a maximum of five frame element tags, since we observed that tokens with more tags are mostly unwanted, probably results of erroneous spelling or tokenization.

Word forms are then grouped according to their frame element tags. Here we consider both primary and alternative frame element tag annotations. In a second step, we extract multiword variants for each of these compounds as follows. Initially we consider the frame element tags of a compound as a set, and compute all possible variant shapes as parts of the partition (without the original set) of this set.

For example, the compound *Vakuumisolationspaneel* (vacuum insulated panel) with the three contained strings *vakuum*, *isolation* and *paneel*, in set form: s={vakuum, isolation, paneel}, has the four different variant shapes:

s_v1 = {{vakuum}, {isolation}, {paneel}},
s_v2 = {{vakuum, isolation}, {paneel}},
s_v3 = {{vakuum}, {isolation, paneel}} and
s_v4 = {{vakuum, paneel}, {isolation}}.

Here, every set in each variant shape corresponds to a separate word, e.g. for s_v3 we would search for variants of the compound 's' consisting of two words, one containing a string annotated with {vakuum} and a second one containing strings annotated with {isolation, paneel}. Furthermore, we consider every possible order of these words and consequently search for all permutations of each variant shape set. For instance, for s_v3 we take both {{vakuum}, {isolation, paneel}} and {{isolation, paneel}, {vakuum}} into consideration. However, we constrain our search to variants for which all FE-tagged words are found in a single sentence.

We group all found variants by their ordered variant shape and extract for each match the corresponding word forms and part-of-speech tags. To detect further variants when computing variant shapes, we also leave single strings associated to a certain frame element tag. For example, given the abovementioned set 's', we also search for any other word annotated as FORM together with {vakuum, isolation} in a sentence, thus looking for the more general pattern {{vakuum, isolation}, {FORM}}. This is a more liberal method which produces more errors and less relevant terms, and which has therefore been employed as a secondary option.

By automatically applying ontological restrictions to FE combinations and syntactic restrictions to multiword terms, we are also able to identify previously unknown string constellations. Also extracted variants in which a component (head or non-head) is expanded, e.g. *Dachdämmung - Steildachdämmung* (roof insulation - pitched roof insulation) are particularly interesting, since they can potentially reveal new words which might be exploited for extending the domain ontology. We plan to release the data in 2020.

6. Statistics

In this section, we provide the results of the semantic annotation and term extraction on our 5.2-million-word corpus.

6.1 Statistics on Semantic Annotation

In total, 869,158 tokens in our corpus were matched with the defined seed strings and automatically annotated with frame element tags. Out of these, 162,462 also have an alternative annotation. Table 1 shows the distribution of the different tags in the corpus by their frequencies. Here we count occurrences in the primary and alternative annotation.

Frame Element Tag	Frequency
PROPERTY	273,129
TARGET	253,891
MATERIAL	151,924
RESULT	129,165
DELIVERY FORM	88,528
GOAL	86,774
APPLICATION TECHNIQUE	61,499
PROJECT	60,456
TARGET MATERIAL	35,322
PRODUCT	33,478
SYSTEM	28,691
MATERIAL ORIGIN	27,836
MATERIAL CLASS	14,724
MATERIAL PROD. TECHNIQUE	13,144
USER	9,917
PACKAGING	9,669
MANUFACTURING FEATURE	6,579
COMPLEMENT	4,509
TOOL	3,659

Table 1: Annotated frame elements

Figures indicated in the table correspond to the expected performance of the different frame elements: PROPERTY and TARGET are, together with MATERIAL, the conceptually most important elements of the frame, and identify the largest sets of strings in the seed lexicon. PROPERTY, in particular, comprehensively refers to chemical and physical properties of insulation products and insulation materials, but also to physical quantities. Semantic content related to insulation materials, other than in the case of PROPERTY, has been distributed across several frame elements (MATERIAL, MATERIAL CLASS, MATERIAL ORIGIN, MATERIAL PRODUCTION TECHNIQUE), which explains the lower number of tags which have been attributed e.g. to MATERIAL alone.Since we focus during extraction on compounds with multiple frame element tags, we analyze the number of tags for each annotated token. Most annotated tokens only match one of our frame element tag strings, precisely 615,171 out of the 869,158, which is approximately 71%. With an increasing number of tags per token, the frequency decreases.

6.2 Statistics on Term Extraction

Our approach to term and variant extraction uses the annotation of the predefined frame element tags with strings as previously described. As a result, we extract combinations of these annotated tags in single word terms and multiword terms at sentence level. Our 5.2-million-word corpus contains 3,124 unique word-level FE combinations (with a frequency of at least 5 to avoid excessive fragmentation).

Each base term lists any of the possible variants with their corresponding word forms if they were found at least five times in the corpus. Table 2 shows the distribution in numbers of variants for the 3,124 compounds we extracted. Our domain corpus accounts for variation of most compounds, while only 461 (approximately 15%) of the compounds have no variants. We observe that the most frequent case for more than half of the compounds is that they have two variants. The average number of extracted variants per compound is approximately 1.82.

Variants per compound	Number of compounds
0	461
1	754
2	1,604
3	58
4	69
5	49
> 6	128

Table 2: Annotated variants

7. Conclusions

We have introduced a promising method for analyzing term variation in texts, which allows for the semantically grounded detection of variant shapes of a given string set, and with noise tolerated in favor of high recall.

Results have been later refined by applying both ontological restrictions to FE combinations and syntactic restrictions to multiword terms. Tests performed on other technical fields also demonstrate that the method is generalizable at least to domains that show similar conceptualization and standardization traits.

In future work, the integration of a new compound splitting approach into the current method could be tested, with the goal of restricting annotation to those strings which do not violate the splits.

Validation and evaluation steps have been performed in the context of the main study by applying the method to a new corpus and comparing our results with those obtained by other term extraction tools.

8. Bibliographical References

Anić, A. O. and S. K. Zuvela (2017). The conceptualization of music in semantic frames based on word sketches. In 9th International Corpus Linguistics Conference.

Burchardt, A., K. Erk, A. Frank, A. Kowalski, S. Padó, and M. Pinkal (2009). Using FrameNet for the semantic analysis of German: Annotation, representation, and automation. In Boas H. C. (Ed.), Multilingual FrameNets in Computational Lexicography, pp. 209-244. De Gruyter Mouton.

Cap, F. (2014). Morphological processing of compounds for statistical machine translation. Dissertation, Institute for Natural Language Processing (IMS), Universität Stuttgart.

Corcoglioniti, F., M. Rospocher, and A. P. Aprosio (2016). Frame-based ontology population with pikes. IEEE Transactions on Knowledge and Data Engineering 28(12), 3261–3275.

Evert, S. and A. Hardie (2011). Twenty-first century corpus workbench: Updating a query architecture for the new millennium. http://cwb.sourceforge.net/index.php

Faber, P. (2012). A cognitive linguistics view of terminology and specialized language, Volume 20. Walter de Gruyter.

Faber, P. (2015). Frames as a framework for terminology. Handbook of terminology 1, 14–33.

Fillmore, C. J. and C. Baker (2010). A frames approach to semantic analysis. In B. Heine and H. Narrog (Eds.), The Oxford handbook of linguistic analysis, pp. 313–339. Oxford University Press.

Freixa, J. (2006). Causes of denominative variation in terminology: A typology proposal. Terminology. International Journal of Theoretical and Applied Issues in Specialized Communication 12(1), 51–77.

Giacomini, L. (2020). Ontology – Frame – Terminology. A method for extracting and modelling variants of technical terms (Forthcoming).

Giacomini, L. (2019). Phraseology in technical texts: a frame-based approach to multiword term analysis and extraction. In Proceedings of Europhras 2019, Santiago de Compostela (ES).

Giacomini, L. (2017). An ontology-terminology model for designing technical e-dictionaries: formalisation and presentation of variational data. In Proceedings of eLex 2017, September 2017, Leiden (NL).

Gómez-Moreno, J. M. U. and M. B. Castro (2017). Semantic and conceptual aspects of volcano verb collocates within the natural disaster domain: A frame-based terminology approach. Cognitive Approaches to Specialist Languages, 330.

Reforgiato Recupero, D., V. Presutti, S. Consoli, A.

Gangemi and A. G. Nuzzolese (2015). Sentilo: Frame-Based Sentiment Analysis. Cognitive Computation 7, pp. 211–225.

Schäfer, J., I. Rösiger, U. Heid, and M. Dorna (2015). Evaluating noise reduction strategies for terminology extraction. In TIA, pp. 123–131.

Schmid, H. and F. Laws (2008). Estimation of conditional probabilities with decision trees and anapplication to fine-grained pos tagging. In Proceedings of the 22nd International Conference on Computational Linguistics-Volume 1, pp. 777–784. Association for Computational Linguistics.

Wüster, E. (1974). Die allgemeine terminologielehre–ein grenzgebiet zwischen sprachwissenschaft, logik, ontologie, informatik und den sachwissenschaften. Linguistics 12(119), 61–106.

Proceedings of the 6th International Workshop on Computational Terminology (COMPUTERM 2020), pages 85–94
Language Resources and Evaluation Conference (LREC 2020), Marseille, 11–16 May 2020
© European Language Resources Association (ELRA), licensed under CC-BY-NC

TermEval 2020: Shared Task on Automatic Term Extraction Using the Annotated Corpora for Term Extraction Research (ACTER) Dataset

Ayla Rigouts Terryn*, Veronique Hoste*, Patrick Drouin, Els Lefever***

(*) LT³ Language and Translation Technology Team, Ghent University;
(**) Observatoire de Linguistique Sens-Texte, Université de Montréal;
(*) firstname.lastname@ugent.be, (**) patrick.drouin@umontreal.ca

Abstract

The TermEval 2020 shared task provided a platform for researchers to work on automatic term extraction (ATE) with the same dataset: the Annotated Corpora for Term Extraction Research (ACTER). The dataset covers three languages (English, French, and Dutch) and four domains, of which the domain of *heart failure* was kept as a held-out test set on which final f1-scores were calculated. The aim was to provide a large, transparent, qualitatively annotated, and diverse dataset to the ATE research community, with the goal of promoting comparative research and thus identifying strengths and weaknesses of various state-of-the-art methodologies. The results show a lot of variation between different systems and illustrate how some methodologies reach higher precision or recall, how different systems extract different types of terms, how some are exceptionally good at finding rare terms, or are less impacted by term length. The current contribution offers an overview of the shared task with a comparative evaluation, which complements the individual papers by all participants.

Keywords: ATE, automatic term extraction, terminology

1. Introduction

Automatic Term Extraction (ATE) can be defined as the automated process of identifying terminology from a corpus of specialised texts. Despite receiving plenty of research attention, it remains a challenging task, not in the least because terms are so difficult to define. Terms are typically described as "lexical items that represent concepts of a domain" (Kageura and Marshman, 2019), but such definitions leave room for many questions about the fundamental nature of terms. Since ATE is supposed to automatically identify terms from specialised text, the absence of a consensus about the basic characteristics of terms is problematic. The disagreement covers both practical aspects, such as term length and part-of-speech (POS) pattern, and theoretical considerations about the difference between words (or collocations/phrases) and terms. This poses great difficulties for many aspects of ATE, from data collection, to extraction methodology, to evaluation.

Data collection, i.e. creating domain-specific corpora in which terms have been annotated, is time and effort consuming. When manual term annotation is involved, inter-annotator agreement is notoriously low and there is no consensus about an annotation protocol (Estopà, 2001). This leads to a scarcity in available resources. Moreover, it means that the few available datasets are difficult to combine and compare, and often cover only a single language and domain. While the manual annotation bottleneck has often been circumvented by starting from existing resources, such as ontologies or terminological databases, specialised dictionaries, or book indexes, such strategies do not have the same advantages as manual annotation and will rarely cover all terms in an entire corpus.

This is linked to the evaluation of ATE, for which the accepted metrics are precision (how many of the extracted terms are correct), recall (how many of the terms in the text have correctly been extracted), and f1-score (harmonic mean of the two). To calculate recall (and, therefore, also f1-score), it is necessary to know all true terms in a text. Since manual annotation is such an expensive operation, and relatively few resources are currently available, evaluation is often limited to either a single resource, or the calculation of precision.

The ATE methodology itself, most notably the types of terms a system is designed to find, is impacted as well. Some of the most fundamental differences are term length (in number of tokens), term POS-pattern (sometimes only nouns and noun phrases, sometimes adjectives, adverbs, and verbs are included), and minimum term frequency. Differences which are more difficult to quantify are, for instance, how specialised or domain-specific a lexical unit needs to be before it is considered a term. These three aspects are closely related, since different systems and evaluation methods will be suited for different datasets. This combination of difficulties creates a hurdle for clear, comparative research.

All of this can slow down the advance of ATE, especially now that (supervised) machine learning techniques are becoming more popular for the task. The TermEval shared task on ATE, using the ACTER Annotated Corpora for Term Extraction Research, was designed to lower these hurdles. The ACTER dataset contains specialised corpora in three languages (English, French, and Dutch), and four domains (corruption, dressage (equitation), heart failure, and wind energy), which have been meticulously, manually annotated according to transparent guidelines. Both the texts and the annotations have been made freely available. The current version of the dataset presents the annotations as unstructured lists of all unique annotated terms (one term and its label per line), rather than providing the span of each occurrence of annotated terms in their context (which may be provided in future releases). The shared task brought together researchers to work on ATE with the same data and evaluation setup. It allowed a detailed comparison of different methodologies. Standard evaluation methods (precision, recall, f1-score) were used for the basic evaluation and ranking; these are elaborated with more detailed evaluations as presented both in the current overview paper and in participants' contributions.

The following sections start with a brief overview of current datasets and methodologies for ATE. In section 3, the ACTER dataset is described in some detail. The fourth section contains an overview of the shared task itself and the results. The final section is dedicated to a discussion and the conclusions.

2. Related Research

2.1. Manually Annotated Gold Standards for ATE

Two of the most commonly used annotated datasets are GENIA (Kim et al., 2003), and the ACL RD-TEC 2.0 (Qasemizadeh and Schumann, 2016), both of which are in English. GENIA is a collection of 2000 abstracts from the MEDLINE database in the domain of bio-medicine, specifically "transcription factors in human blood cells". Over 400k tokens were annotated by two domain experts to obtain 93,293 term annotations. The ACL-RD-TEC 2.0 contains 300 annotated abstracts from the ACL Anthology Reference Corpus. Again, two experts performed the annotation of 33k tokens, which resulted in 6818 term annotations. They claim three main advantages over GENIA: first, the domain (computational linguistics) means that ATE researchers will have a better understanding of the material. Second, the ACL RD-TEC corpus covers three decades, which allows some research of the evolution of terms. Third and finally, the annotation is more transparent, with freely available annotation guidelines and the possibility to download the annotations of both experts separately. There are other examples as well, such as the CRAFT corpus, another English corpus in the biomedical domain (99,907 annotations over 560k tokens) (Bada et al., 2012), an English automotive corpus (28,656 annotations over 224,159 tokens) (Bernier-Colborne, 2012; Bernier-Colborne and Drouin, 2014), a diachronical English corpus on mechanical engineering (+10k annotations over 140k words) (Schumann and Fischer, 2016), the TermITH French corpus on language sciences (14,544 unique validated terms found over 397,695 words) (TermITH, 2014; Billami et al., 2014), a small German corpus on DIY, cooking, hunting and chess which focused on inter-annotator agreement between laypeople (912 annotations on which at least 5 out of 7 annotators agreed, over 3075 words) (Hätty and Schulte im Walde, 2018b) and, within the framework of the TTC project (Loginova et al., 2012), lists of 107-159 annotated terms in corpora in seven languages and two domains (wind energy and mobile technology). While this is a non-exhaustive list, it illustrates an important and logical trend: either the created gold standard is quite large, with over 10k annotations, or it covers multiple languages and/or domains.

While this is not necessarily problematic, the annotation guidelines for all of these corpora differ, and, therefore, the annotations themselves as well. That does create difficulties, since comparing ATE performance on multiple corpora will not necessarily reflect differences in performance between domains or languages, but may also show the contrast between the different annotation styles. The differences can be quite substantial, e.g. in GENIA and ACL RD-TEC, nested annotations are not allowed, in CRAFT they are only allowed under certain conditions, while in the TermITH project they are allowed in most cases. Moreover, it is important to note that the annotations of both the TermITH project and the TTC project are based on the manual annotation of ATE results, rather than manual annotations in the unprocessed text. A final remark is that some corpora have been annotated with multiple term labels or have even been annotated according to large taxonomies, while others don't make any distinctions beyond terms. As will be discussed in more detail in section 3, the ACTER dataset has been specifically designed to deal with some of the issues addressed here.

2.2. ATE

Traditionally, three types of ATE methodologies are identified: linguistic (relying on linguistic information, such as POS-patterns and chunking), statistical (using frequencies, often compared to a reference corpus, to calculate termhood and unithood (Kageura and Umino, 1996)), and hybrid methods (which combine the two). It has been established for some time that hybrid methods appear to outperform the other two (Macken et al., 2013). These methods typically select candidate terms based on their POS-pattern and rank these candidate terms using the statistical metrics, thus combining the advantages of both techniques. A particular difficulty is defining the cut-off threshold for the term candidates, which can be defined as the top-n terms, the top-n percentage of terms, or all terms above a certain threshold score. Manually predicting the ideal cut-off point is extremely difficult and can result in a skew towards either precision or recall, which can be detrimental to the final f1-score (Rigouts Terryn et al., 2019a).

While this typology of linguistic, statistical, and hybrid systems is sometimes still used today, in recent years, the advance of machine learning techniques has made such a simple classification of ATE methodologies more complicated (Gao and Yuan, 2019). Methodologies have become so diverse that they are no longer easily captured in such a limited number of clearly delineated categories. For instance, apart from the distinction between statistical and linguistic systems, one could also distinguish between rule-based methods and machine learning methods. However, rather than a simple binary distinction, there is quite a range of options: methods that rely on a single statistical score (Drouin, 2003; Kosa et al., 2020), systems that combine a limited number of features with a voting algorithm (Fedorenko et al., 2013; Vivaldi and Rodríguez, 2001), an evolutionary algorithm that optimises the ROC-curve (Azé et al., 2005), rule-induction (Foo and Merkel, 2010), support-vector models (Ramisch et al., 2010), logistic regression (Bolshakova et al., 2013; Judea et al., 2014), basic neural networks (Hätty and Schulte im Walde, 2018a), recursive neural networks (Kucza et al., 2018), siamese neural networks (Shah et al., 2019), and convolutional neural networks (Wang et al., 2016). Within the machine learning systems, there are vast differences between supervised, semi-supervised, and unsupervised systems, as well as the distinction between sequence labelling approaches and systems that start from a limited list of unique term candidates. Splitting systems by their features is perhaps even more difficult, since research has moved far beyond using simple linguistic and statistical features. Some examples include the use of topic modelling (Šajatović et al., 2019; Bolshakova et al., 2013), queries on search engines, Wikipedia, or other external resources (Kessler et al., 2019; Vivaldi and Rodríguez, 2001), and word embeddings (Amjadian et al., 2016; Kucza et al., 2018; Qasemizadeh and Handschuh, 2014; Pollak et al., 2019). Some methods are even called "featureless" (Gao and Yuan, 2019; Wang et al., 2016).

There are many more ways in which ATE systems can vary. Some can already be deduced from the ways in which the datasets are annotated, such as support for nested terms. Another very fundamental difference is the frequency cutoff: many ATE systems only extract terms which appear above a certain frequency threshold in the corpora. This threshold is extremely variable, with some systems that do not have any threshold, others that only extract candidate terms which appear 15 times or more (Pollak et al., 2019), and still others where only the top-n most frequent terms are extracted (Loukachevitch, 2012). Term length is similarly variable, with systems that don't place any restrictions, others that extract only single-word terms, only multi-word terms, or those that extract all terms between 1 and n tokens (with n ranging from 2 to 15), where n is sometimes determined by the restrictions of a system, sometimes experimentally set to an optimal value, and at other times directly determined by the maximum term length in a gold standard. There are many other possible differences, such as POS patterns, which will not be discussed in any detail here. More information regarding both datasets for ATE and different ATE methodologies can be found in Rigouts Terryn et al. (2019b).

With such a great variety of methodologies, comparative research is essential to identify the strengths and weaknesses of the respective strategies. However, as discussed, appropriate datasets are scarce and often limited. This means that ATE systems are regularly scored solely on precision (or some variation thereof), since recall and f1-score cannot be calculated without knowing all true terms in a corpus. Considering the expense of data annotation, the extra effort required is rarely feasible. The strictness of the evaluation varies as well, such as determining how specialised a term candidate needs to be for it to be considered a true term, and validating only full matches or also partial ones. Moreover, scores for sequence labelling approaches are difficult to compare to scores for approaches that provide ranked lists of unique terms. There is even disagreement on the required expertise for annotators: do they need to be domain experts or terminologists? This disparity does not only make comparisons between systems highly problematic, it also means that many systems are evaluated on only a single domain (and language).

3. ACTER Annotated Corpora for Term Extraction Research

ACTER is a collection of domain-specific corpora in which terms have been manually annotated. It covers three languages (English, French, and Dutch) and four domains (corruption, dressage (equitation), heart failure, and wind energy). It has been created in light of some of the perceived difficulties that have been mentioned. A previous version (which did not yet bear the ACTER acronym) has already been elaborately described (Rigouts Terryn et al., 2019b), so we refer the interested reader to this work for more detailed information. However, the current version of the dataset has been substantially updated since then, to be even more consistent. All previous annotations have been double-checked, inconsistent annotations were automatically found and manually edited when necessary, and, with this shared task, a first version has been made publicly available. Therefore, the remainder of this section will focus on the up-to-date statistics of version 1.2 of the ACTER dataset (version 1.0 was the first to appear online for the shared task). The annotation guidelines have been updated as well and are freely available[1]. Discontinuous terms (e.g. in ellipses) have been annotated, but are not yet included in ACTER 1.2, and neither are the cross-lingual annotations in the domain of heart failure. The changes made between ACTER versions are indicated in detail in the included README.md file and the biggest difference between version 1.0 and 1.2 (besides some 120 removed or added annotations) is the inclusion of the label of each annotation.

The dataset contains trilingual comparable corpora in all domains: the corpora in the same domain are similar in terms of subject, style, and length for each language, but they are not translations (and, therefore, cannot be aligned). Additionally, for the domain of corruption, there is a trilingual parallel corpus of aligned translations. For each language and domain, around 50k tokens have been manually annotated (in the case of corruption, the annotations have only been made in the parallel corpus, so the comparable corpus on corruption is completely unannotated). In all domains except heart failure, the complete corpora are larger than only the annotated parts, and unannotated texts are included (separately) as well. The texts are all plain text files and the sources have been included in the downloadable version. The annotations have been performed in the BRAT annotation tool (Stenetorp et al., 2011), but they are currently provided as flat lists with one term per line. The annotations have all been performed by a single annotator with experience in the field of terminology and ATE and fluent in all three languages. However, she is not a domain-expert, except in the domain of dressage. Multiple semi-automatic checks have been performed to ensure the best possible annotation quality and inter-annotator agreement studies were performed and published (Rigouts Terryn et al., 2019b) to further validate the dataset. Furthermore, the elaborate guidelines helped the annotator to make consistent decisions and make the entire process more transparent. Nevertheless, term annotation remains an ambiguous

---

[1] http://hdl.handle.net/1854/LU-8503113

bioprosthetic valve replacement	Specific_Term
biopsies	Common_Term
biopsy	Common_Term
biosynthetic enzymes	Specific_Term
bisoprolol	Specific_Term
bisphosphonates	Specific_Term

Table 1: Sample of one of the gold standard term lists in the ACTER 1.2 dataset to illustrate the format

and subjective task. We do not claim that ours is the only possible interpretation and, therefore, when using ACTER for ATE evaluation purposes, always recommend checking the output for a more nuanced evaluation (e.g. Rigouts Terryn et al. (2019a)).

While ATE for TermEval has been perceived as a binary task (term or not), the original annotations included four different labels. There are three term labels, for which terms are defined by their degree of domain-specificity (are they relevant to the domain) and lexicon-specificity (are they known only by experts, or by laypersons as well). The three term labels defined this way are: Specific Terms (which are both domain- and lexicon-specific), Common Terms (domain-specific, not lexicon-specific), and Out-of-Domain (OOD) Terms (not domain-specific, lexicon-specific). In the domain of heart failure, for instance, *ejection fraction* might be a Specific Term: laypersons generally do not know what it means, and it is strongly related to the domain of heart failure, since it is an indication of the volume of blood the heart pumps on each contraction. *Heart* is an example of a Common Term: it is clearly domain-specific to heart failure and you do not need to be an expert to have a basic idea of what a heart is. An example of an OOD term might be *p-value*, which is lexicon-specific since you need some knowledge of statistics to know the term, but it is not domain-specific to heart failure. In addition to these three term labels, Named Entities (proper names of persons, organisations, etc.) were annotated as well, as they share a few characteristics with terms: they will appear more often in texts with a relevant subject (e.g. brand names of medicine in the field of heart failure) and, like multi-word terms, have a high degree of unithood (internal cohesion). Labelling these does not mean we consider them to be terms, but it offers more options for the evaluation and training based on the dataset.

Since TermEval was set up as a binary task, all three term labels were combined and considered as true terms. There were two separate datasets regarding the Named Entities: one including both terms and Named Entities, one with only terms. All participating systems were evaluated on both datasets. Moreover, while the evaluation for the ranking of the participating systems was based only on these two binary interpretations, the four labels were made available afterwards for a more detailed evaluation of the results. The gold standard lists of terms were ordered alphabetically, so with no relation to their labels or degree of termhood. Table 1 shows a sample of such a gold standard list, with one unique term per line followed by its label.

Tables 2 and 3 provide more details on ACTER 1.2. Table 2 shows the number of documents and words per corpus, both in the entire corpus and only the annotated part of the corpus. Table 3 provides details on the number of annotations per corpus, counting either all annotations or all unique annotations. In total, 119,455 term and Named Entity annotations have been made over 596,058 words, resulting in 19,002 unique annotations. As can be seen, the number of annotations within a domain is usually somewhat similar for all languages (since the corpora are comparable), with larger differences between the domains. Version 1.2 of ACTER only provides a list of all unique lowercased terms (and Named Entities) per corpus. The aim is to release future versions with all in-text annotation spans, where every occurrence of each term is annotated, so that it can be used for sequence-labelling approaches as well. It is important to note that, since the annotation process was completely manual, each occurrence of a term was evaluated separately. When a lexical unit was only considered a term in some contexts, it was only annotated in those specific contexts. For instance, the word *sensitivity* can be used in general language, where it will not be annotated, but also as a synonym of *recall* (true positive rate), in which case it was annotated as a term.

Additional characteristics to bear in mind about these annotations are that nested annotations are allowed (as long as the nested part can be used as a term on its own), and that there were no restrictions on term length, term frequency, or term POS-pattern (apart from the condition that terms had to contain a content word). If a lexical unit was used as a term in the text, it was annotated, even if it was not the best or most frequently used term for a certain concept. The reasoning behind this strategy was that one of the most important applications of ATE is to be able to keep up with fast-evolving terminology in increasingly more specialised domains. If only well-established, frequent terms are annotated, the rare and/or new terms will be ignored, even though these could be particularly interesting for ATE. While these qualities were all chosen to best reflect the desired applications for ATE, they do result in a particularly difficult dataset for ATE, so f1-scores for ATE systems tested on ACTER are expected to be rather modest in comparison to some other datasets.

4. TermEval Shared Task on ATE

4.1. Setup

The aim of the TermEval shared task was to provide a platform for researchers to work on the same task, with the same data, so that different methodologies for ATE can easily be compared and current strengths and weaknesses of ATE can be identified. During the training phase, participants all received the ACTER dataset as described in the previous section, with all domains apart from *heart failure*. The latter is provided during the final phase as the test set on which the scores are calculated. As described in the previous section, ACTER 1.2 consists of flat lists of unique terms per corpus, with one term per line. Since this first version of the shared task aims to focus on ATE in general, rather than term variation, all terms are lowercased, and only identical lowercased terms are merged in a single entry, without lemmatisation. Even when terms acquire

Type	Domain	Language	# Texts	# Words in entire corpus	# Words in annotated part of corpus
Parallel	Corruption	en	24	176,314	45,234
		fr	24	196,327	50,429
		nl	24	184,541	47,305
Comparable	Corruption	en	44	468,711	-
		fr	31	475,244	-
		nl	49	470,242	-
	Dressage	en	89	102,654	51,470
		fr	125	109,572	53,316
		nl	125	103,851	50,882
	Heart failure	en	190	45,788	45,788
		fr	215	46,751	46,751
		nl	175	47,888	47,888
	Wind Energy	en	38	314,618	51,911
		fr	12	314,681	56,363
		nl	29	308,742	49,582
		TOTAL	3,365,924	1194	596,058

Table 2: Number of documents and words in the entire corpus vs. the annotated part of each corpus in ACTER 1.2

Domain	Language	# Annotations Terms (all)	Terms (unique)	NEs (all)	NEs (unique)
Corruption	en	6,385	927	2,373	247
	fr	5,930	982	2,186	235
	nl	5,163	1,047	2,334	248
Dressage	en	10,889	1,155	970	420
	fr	9,397	963	467	220
	nl	11,207	1,395	295	151
Heart failure	en	14,011	2,361	526	224
	fr	10,801	2,276	319	147
	nl	10,219	2,077	433	180
Wind Energy	en	9,478	1,091	1,429	443
	fr	8,524	773	439	195
	nl	5,044	940	636	305
	TOTAL	107,048	15,987	12,407	3,015

Table 3: Number of annotations (counting all annotations separately or all unique annotations) of terms and Named Entities (NEs), per corpus in ACTER 1.2

a different meaning through different capitalisation options or POS patterns, they only count as a single annotation in this version. For example, the English corpus on dressage contains the term *bent* (verb – past tense of *to bend*), but also *Bent* (proper noun – person name). While both capitalisation and POS differ, and *bent* is not the lemmatised form, there is only one entry: *bent* (lowercased) in the gold standard (other full forms of the verb *to bend* have separate entries, if they are present and annotated in the corpus). We do not discount the importance of ATE systems that handle term variation, but a choice was made to focus on the core task for the first edition of the task.

There are three different tracks (one per language) and participants could enter in one or multiple tracks. When participants submitted their final results on the test data (as a flat list of unique lowercased terms, like the training data), f1-scores were calculated twice: once compared to the gold standard with only terms, once compared to the

gold standard with both terms and Named Entities. These double scores did not influence the final ranking based on f1-scores. The dataset has been used for more detailed evaluations as well (see section 4.3) and participants were encouraged to report scores on the training domains in their own papers as well.

4.2. Participants

Five teams participated in the shared task: TALN-LS2N (Hazem et al., 2020), RACAI (Pais and Ion, 2020), e-Terminology (Oliver and Vàzquez, 2020), NLPLab_UQAM (no system description paper), and NYU (no system description paper but based on previous work in Meyers et al. (2018)). NYU and RACAI participated only in the English track, TALN-LS2N participated in both the English and French tracks, and e-Terminology and NLPLab_UQAM participated in all tracks. We refer to their own system description papers for more details, but will provide a short summary of each of their methodologies.

Team **NYU** has applied an updated version of Termolator (Meyers et al., 2018). Candidate terms are selected based on "terminological chunking and abbreviations". The terminological chunking focuses, among others, on nominalisations, out-of-vocabulary words, and technical adjectives (based on suffixes) to find terms. Constructions where full forms are followed by their abbreviations are also taken into account. Next, three distributional metrics (e.g. TFIDF) are combined with equal weights and a "well-formedness score" is calculated, using mainly linguistic and morphological information. Additionally, a relevance score is based on the results of an online search engine. The final selection of candidate terms is made based on the product of these three metrics. Due to the timing of the shared task, Termolator was not specifically tuned to the ACTER dataset.

Team **e-Terminology** uses the TSR (Token Slot Recognition) technique, implemented in TBXTools (Oliver and Vazquez, 2015; Vàzquez and Oliver, 2018). For Dutch, the statistical version of TBXTools is employed, for English and French the linguistic version is used. Stopwords are filtered out and all candidate terms that appear below a frequency threshold of two. As a terminological reference for each language (required for the TSR technique), the IATE database for 12-Law was chosen.

Team **RACAI** uses a combination of statistical approaches, such as an improved TextRank (Zhang et al., 2018), TFIDF, clustering, and termhood features. Algorithms were adapted where possible to make use of pre-trained word embeddings and the result was generated using several voting and combinatorial approaches. Special attention is also paid to the detection of nested terms.

Team **TALN-LS2N** uses BERT as a binary classification model for ATE. The model's input is represented as the concatenation of a sentence and a selected n-gram within the sentence. If the n-gram is a term, the input is labelled as positive training example. If not, a corresponding negative example is generated.

Team **NLPLab_UQAM** applied a bidirectional LSTM. Pre-trained GloVe word embedding were used to train a neural network-based model on the training corpora.

4.3. Results

Precision, recall, and f1-scores were calculated both including and excluding Named Entities, for each team in all tracks. The scores and resulting ranking are presented in Table 3. As can be seen, TALN-LS2N's system outperforms all others in the English and French tracks. NLPLab_UQAM's system outperforms e-Terminology for the Dutch track (though their respective rankings for English and Dutch are reversed). Scores with and without Named Entities are usually very similar (average difference of one percentage point), with e-Terminology and NYU scoring slightly better when Named Entities are excluded, and the others scoring better when they are included. On average, precision is higher than recall, especially when Named Entities are included. However, there is much variation. For instance, TALN-LS2N's English system obtains 36-40% more recall than precision (the difference is

only 6-9% for their French system). Comparatively, e-Terminology obtains 20% higher precision than recall on average and NLPLab_UQAM obtains more balanced precision and recall scores. The number of extracted term candidates varies greatly as well, from 744 (e-Terminology in Dutch), to 5267 (TALN-LS2N in English). Therefore, even though TALN-LS2N achieves the highest f1-scores thanks to great recall in English, their system also produces most noise, with 3435 false positives (including Named Entities). The average number of extracted candidate terms (2038) is not too different from the average number of terms in the gold standard (2422 incl. Named Entities, 1720 without). Looking at performance of systems in multiple tracks, there does not appear to be one language that is inherently easier or more difficult. TALN-LS2N's best performance is reached for French, e-Terminology's for English, and NLPLab_UQAM's for Dutch.

As with many other task within natural language processing, the methodology based on the BERT transformer model appears to outperform other approaches. However, the large gap between precision and recall for the English model, which is much smaller for the French model, may be an indication of an often-cited downside of deep learning models: their unpredictability. For ATE, predictability is cited as at least as important as f1-scores: "for ATE to be usable, its results should be consistent, predictable and transparent" (Kageura and Marshman, 2019). Additionally, it appears that neural networks and word embeddings do not always work for this task, as demonstrated by the fact that, for English and French, NLPLab_UQAM's bidirectional LSTM approach with GLOVE embeddings is ranked last, below non-neural approaches such as NYU's.

Apart from the ranking based on f1-scores, three different aspects of the results are analysed in more detail: composition of the output, recall of terms with different frequencies, and recall of terms with different lengths. Figure 1 shows the first of these, illustrating the composition of the gold standard regarding the four annotation labels, versus the true positives from each team. The results are averaged over all languages, as the differences between the languages were small. False positives were not included, since these can be deduced from the precision scores. The graphs are relative, so they do not represent the absolute number of annotations per type, only the proportions. The order of the teams is the order of their ranks for the English track. A first observation is that all teams seem to extract at least some Named Entities, except for e-Terminology. This may be partly due to their low recall, but since they did not extract a single Named Entity in any of the languages, it does appear that their system is most focused on terms. While the differences are never extreme, the various systems do show some variation in this respect. For instance, the two lowest ranked systems can be seen to extract relatively more Common Terms. This may be an indication that they are sensitive to frequency, as many of the Specific Terms are rarer (e.g., e-Terminology employs a frequency threshold of two). Conversely, NYU's system appears to excel at extracting these Specific Terms and also extracts relatively few Named Entities. The output of two top-scoring teams has a very similar composition to the gold standard, which

Track	Rank	Team	Scores incl. NEs			Scores excl. NEs		
			precision	recall	f1-score	precision	recall	f1-score
English	1	TALN-LS2N	34.8	70.9	46.7	32.6	72.7	45.0
	2	RACAI	42.4	40.3	41.3	38.6	40.1	39.3
	3	NYU	43.5	23.6	30.6	42.2	25.1	31.5
	4	e-Terminology	34.4	14.2	20.1	34.4	15.5	21.4
	5	NLPLab_UQAM	21.4	15.6	18.1	20.1	16.0	17.8
French	1	TALN-LS2N	45.2	51.5	48.1	41.9	50.9	45.9
	2	e-Terminology	36.3	13.5	19.7	36.3	14.4	20.6
	3	NLPLab_UQAM	16.1	11.2	13.2	15.1	11.2	12.9
Dutch	1	NLPLab_UQAM	18.9	18.6	18.7	18.1	19.3	18.6
	2	e-Terminology	29.0	9.6	14.4	29.0	10.4	15.3

Table 4: Scores (as percentages) and rank for all teams per track

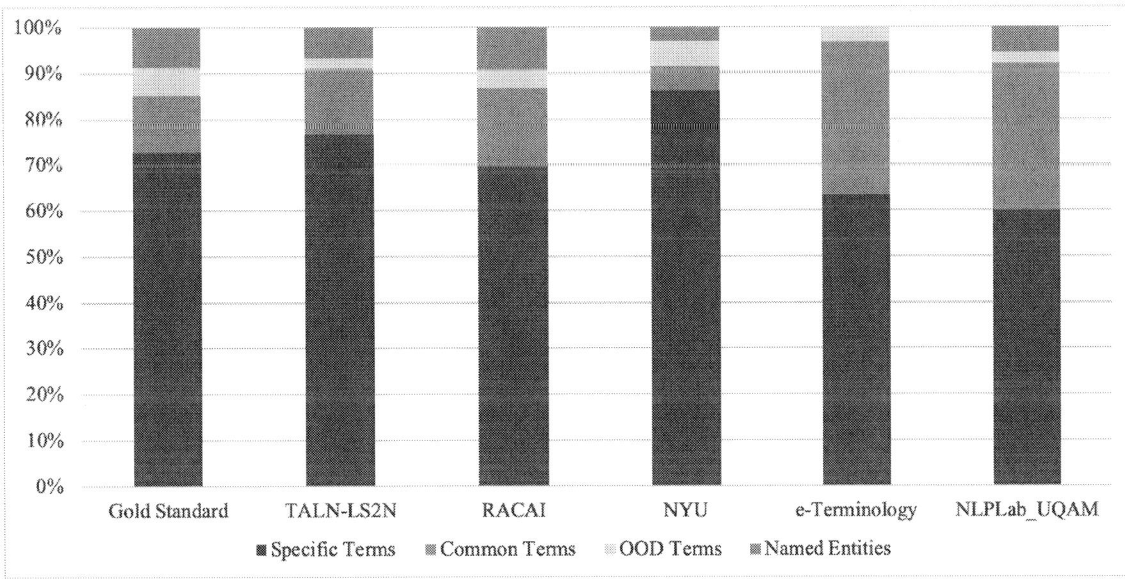

Figure 1: Proportion of Specific, Common, and OOD Terms, and Named Entities in the gold standard versus the true positives extracted by each team (averaged over all languages if teams participated in multiple tracks).

may be part of the explanation for their high scores, and, in the case of TALN-LS2N's system, may be related to their reliance on the training data.

A preference for Common Terms or Specific Terms can already give an indication of the system performance for rare terms, but we can also look directly at the recall of terms for various frequencies, as shown in Figure 2. Here, the recall of all systems for various term frequencies is shown for the English track. Results for the other languages were similar, so will not be discussed separately. The dataset actually contains many hapax terms (which appear only once). In English, when Named Entities are included, there are 1121 (43%) hapax terms, 398 (15%) terms that appear twice, 220 (9%) terms that appear three times, 232 (9%) terms with a frequency between 4 and 5, 259 (10%) terms with a frequency between 5 and 10, 199 (8%) terms with a frequency between 10 and 25, and only 156 (6%) terms that appear more than 25 times. In line with previous findings on the difficulties of ATE, recall is lowest for hapax terms

for all systems, and increases as frequency increases. Of course, e-Terminology has 0% recall for hapax terms due to the frequency cut-off, but the other systems also have difficulties. Notably, TALN-LS2N's system obtains a surprisingly stable recall for various frequencies and a very high recall of 64% for hapax terms. This is likely a consequence of the fact that they use none of the traditional statistical (frequency-related) metrics for ATE. Recall is almost always highest for the most frequent terms, though when looking at these frequent terms in more detail, recall appears to drop again for the most extreme cases (terms appearing over 100 times; not represented separately in Figure 2), presumably because these are more difficult to distinguish from common general language words.

The final analysis concerns term length. Similarly to the analysis for frequency, Figure 3 presents recall for different term lengths per team, using the English data, including Named Entities, as a reference. The majority of gold standard terms are single-word terms (swts) (1170, or 45%),

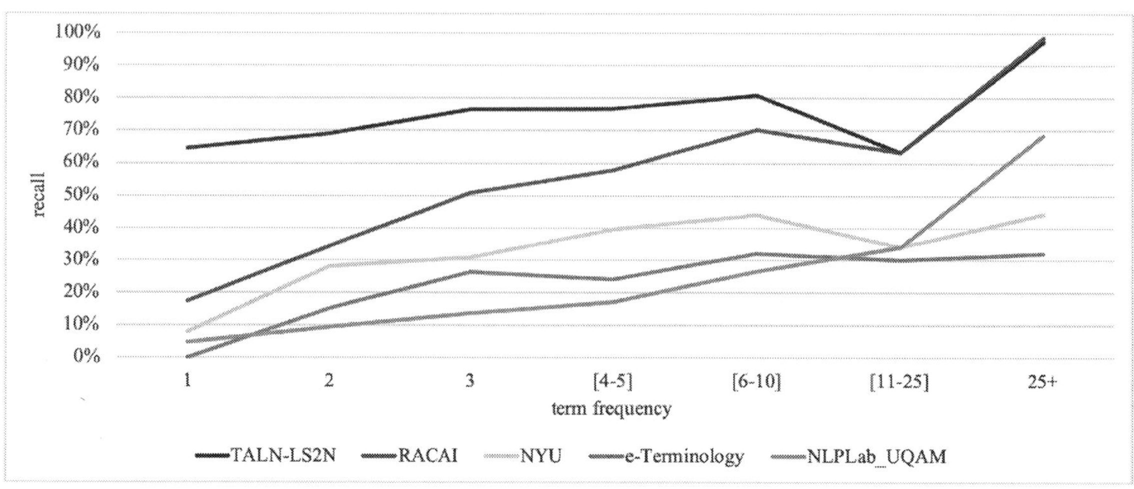

Figure 2: Recall for terms with various frequencies per team in English, including Named Entities

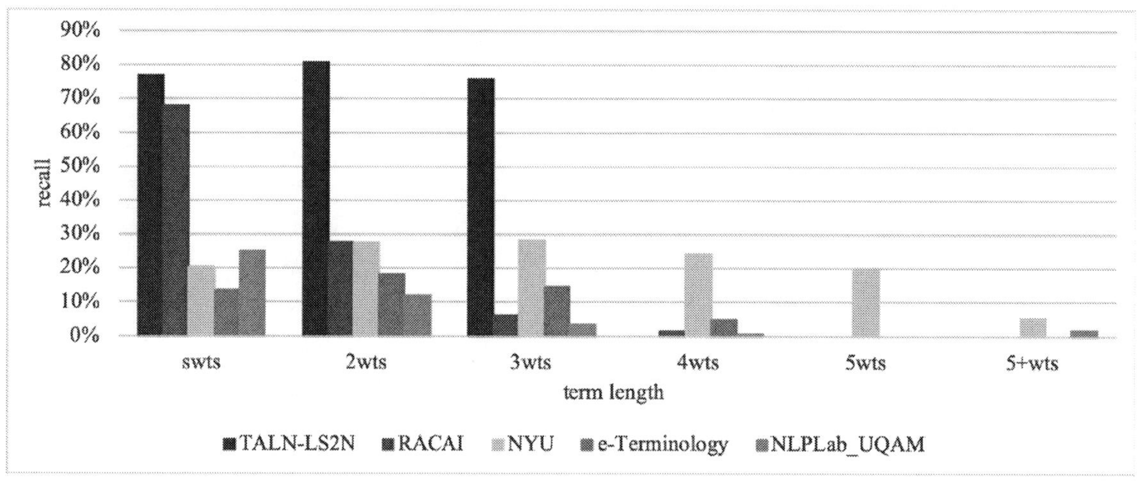

Figure 3: Recall per term length (single-word terms (swts) to terms with over 5 tokens (5+wts) for each team in English, including Named Entities

with frequencies decreasing as term length increases (800 or 31% 2-word terms (2wts), 376 or 15% 3wts, 144 or 6% 4wts, 40 or 2% 5wts, and 55 or 2% terms that are longer than 5 tokens. As can be seen in Figure 3, two out of five teams (RACAI and NLPLab_UQAM) have lower recall for 2wts than for swts, and, overall, recall decreases for terms with more than 3 tokens. TALN-LS2N extracts no terms beyond a length of 3 tokens at all, though this is different for their French system, where recall decreases more gradually with term length. NYU's system has a surprisingly stable performance for different term lengths, especially compared to TALN-LS2N and RACAI.

5. Discussion and Conclusions

Five different teams submitted their results for the TermEval shared task on ATE, based on the ACTER dataset. With the domains of corruption, dressage, and wind energy from the dataset as training data or simply as reference material, the teams either used (and adapted) their existing systems or developed a new methodology for ATE. The domain of heart failure was used as the test set, with three different tracks for English, French and Dutch. The teams were all ranked based on the f1-score they obtained on the test data, with additional evaluations of the types of terms they extracted and recall for different term frequencies and term lengths.

The results show quite a large variation between all methodologies. The highest scores were obtained by a deep learning methodology using BERT as a binary classification model. The second best system does not rely on deep learning and combines pre-trained word embeddings with more classical features for ATE, such as statistical termhood measures. Such results show how there is still a lot of potential for deep learning techniques in the field of ATE, highlighting also the importance of large datasets like ACTER. However, it also illustrates that more traditional methodologies can still lead to state-of-the-art results as well, especially when updated with features like word embeddings.

The more detailed analyses also revealed how the composition of the output of the different systems varies, e.g., including or excluding more Named Entities, and focusing on either the most domain-specific and specialised terms (Specific Terms) or also on more general terms (Common Terms). This is a clear indication of how different applications for ATE may require different methodologies. For instance, translators may be more interested in a system that extracts mostly Specific Terms, since Common Terms may already be part of their general vocabulary.

Checking recall for terms with different frequencies and terms with different lengths confirmed two often-cited weaknesses of ATE: low-frequency terms and long terms are more difficult to extract. However, in each case, there were some systems for which the performance was more stable and less impacted by these factors. The winning deep learning approach achieves a high recall even for hapax terms (64%) and one of the rule-based systems maintains a more or less stable recall for terms up to a length of five tokens.

With these results, we conclude that there remains a lot of room for improvement in the field of ATE, both by trying the latest deep learning methodologies which have been successfully used in other natural language processing tasks, and by updating and combining more traditional methodologies with state-of-the-art features and algorithms. Taking into account the unpredictability of many machine learning approaches and the considerable variety between the potential outputs, as demonstrated in this shared task, it is essential for ATE to be evaluated beyond precision, recall, and f1-scores. To further encourage and facilitate both supervised machine learning approaches and high-quality evaluations on diverse data, the complete AC-TER dataset has been made freely available online (Rigouts Terryn, Ayla and Drouin, Patrick and Hoste, Véronique and Lefever, Els, 2020).

6. Bibliographical References

Amjadian, E., Inkpen, D., Paribakht, T., and Faez, F. (2016). Local-Global Vectors to Improve Unigram Terminology Extraction. In *Proceedings of the 5th International Workshop on Computational Terminology*, pages 2–11, Osaka, Japan.

Azé, J., Roche, M., Kodratoff, Y., and Sebag, M. (2005). Preference Learning in Terminology Extraction: A ROC-based approach. In *Proceeedings of Applied Stochastic Models and Data Analysis*, pages 209–2019, Brest, France. arXiv: cs/0512050.

Bada, M., Eckert, M., Evans, D., Garcia, K., Shipley, K., Sitnikov, D., Baumgartner, W. A., Cohen, K. B., Verspoor, K., Blake, J. A., and Hunter, L. E. (2012). Concept annotation in the CRAFT corpus. *BMC Bioinformatics*, 13:161–180.

Bernier-Colborne, G. and Drouin, P. (2014). Creating a test corpus for term extractors through term annotation. *Terminology*, 20(1):50–73.

Bernier-Colborne, G. (2012). Defining a Gold Standard for the Evaluation of Term Extractors. In *Proceedings of the 8th international conference on Language Resources and Evaluation (LREC)*, Istanbul, Turkey. ELRA.

Billami, M., Camacho-Collados, J., Jacquey, E., and Kister, L. (2014). Annotation sémantique et validation terminologique en texte intégral en SHS. In *Proceedings of TALN 2014*, pages 363–376, Marseille, France.

Bolshakova, E., Loukachevitch, N., and Nokel, M. (2013). Topic Models Can Improve Domain Term Extraction. In David Hutchison, et al., editors, *Advances in Information Retrieval*, volume 7814, pages 684–687. Springer Berlin Heidelberg, Berlin, Heidelberg.

Drouin, P. (2003). Term Extraction Using Non-Technical Corpora as a Point of Leverage. *Terminology*, 9(1):99–115.

Estopà, R. (2001). Les unités de signification spécialisées élargissant l'objet du travail en terminologie. *Terminology*, 7(2):217–237.

Fedorenko, D., Astrakhantsev, N., and Turdakov, D. (2013). Automatic recognition of domain-specific terms: an experimental evaluation. In *Proceedings of the Ninth Spring Researcher's Colloquium on Database and Information Systems*, volume 26, pages 15–23, Kazan, Russia.

Foo, J. and Merkel, M. (2010). Using machine learning to perform automatic term recognition. In *Proceedings of the LREC 2010 Workshop on Methods for automatic acquisition of Language Resources and their evaluation methods*, pages 49–54, Valetta, Malta. ELRA.

Gao, Y. and Yuan, Y. (2019). Feature-Less End-to-End Nested Term Extraction. *arXiv:1908.05426 [cs, stat]*, August. arXiv: 1908.05426.

Hätty, A. and Schulte im Walde, S. (2018a). Fine-Grained Termhood Prediction for German Compound Terms Using Neural Networks. In *Proceedings of the Joint Workshop on,Linguistic Annotation, Multiword Expressions and Constructions (LAW-MWE-CxG-2018)*, pages 62–73, Sante Fe, New Mexico, USA.

Hätty, A. and Schulte im Walde, S. (2018b). A Laypeople Study on Terminology Identification across Domains and Task Definitions. In *Proceedings of NAACL-HLT 2018*, pages 321–326, New Orleans, USA. ACL.

Hazem, A., Bouhandi, M., Boudin, F., and Daille, B. (2020). Termeval 2020: Taln-ls2n system for automatic term extraction. In *Proceedings of CompuTerm 2020*.

Judea, A., Schütze, H., and Brügmann, S. (2014). Unsupervised training set generation for automatic acquisition of technical terminology in patents. In *Proceedings of COLING 2014, the 25th international conference on computational linguistics: Technical Papers*, pages 290–300, Dublin, Ireland.

Kageura, K. and Marshman, E. (2019). Terminology Extraction and Management. In O'Hagan, Minako, editor, *The Routledge Handbook of Translation and Technology*.

Kageura, K. and Umino, B. (1996). Methods of automatic term recognition. *Terminology*, 3(2):259–289.

Kessler, R., Béchet, N., and Berio, G. (2019). Extraction of terminology in the field of construction. In *Proceedings of the First International Conference on Digital Data Processing (DDP)*, pages 22–26, London, UK. IEEE.

Kim, J.-D., Ohta, T., Tateisi, Y., and Tsujii, J. (2003). GE-

NIA corpus - a semantically annotated corpus for bio-textmining. *Bioinformatics*, 19(1):180–182.

Kosa, V., Chaves-Fraga, D., Dobrovolskyi, H., and Ermolayev, V. (2020). Optimized Term Extraction Method Based on Computing Merged Partial C-Values. In *Information and Communication Technologies in Education, Research, and Industrial Applications. ICTERI 2019*, volume 1175 of *Communications in Computer and INformation Science*, pages 24–49. Springer International Publishing, Cham.

Kucza, M., Niehues, J., Zenkel, T., Waibel, A., and Stüker, S. (2018). Term Extraction via Neural Sequence Labeling a Comparative Evaluation of Strategies Using Recurrent Neural Networks. In *Interspeech 2018*, pages 2072–2076, Hyderabad, India, September. ISCA.

Loginova, E., Gojun, A., Blancafort, H., Guégan, M., Gornostay, T., and Heid, U. (2012). Reference Lists for the Evaluation of Term Extraction Tools. In *Proceedings of the 10th International Congress on Terminology and Knowledge Engineering*, Madrid, Spain. ACL.

Loukachevitch, N. (2012). Automatic Term Recognition Needs Multiple Evidence. In *Proceedings of LREC 2012*, pages 2401–2407, Istanbul, Turkey. ELRA.

Macken, L., Lefever, E., and Hoste, V. (2013). TExSIS: Bilingual Terminology Extraction from Parallel Corpora Using Chunk-based Alignment. *Terminology*, 19(1):1–30.

Meyers, A. L., He, Y., Glass, Z., Ortega, J., Liao, S., Grieve-Smith, A., Grishman, R., and Babko-Malaya, O. (2018). The Termolator: Terminology Recognition Based on Chunking, Statistical and Search-Based Scores. *Frontiers in Research Metrics and Analytics*, 3.

Oliver, A. and Vazquez, M. (2015). TBXTools: A Free, Fast and Flexible Tool for Automatic Terminology Extraction. In *Proceedings of Recent Advances in Natural Language Processing*, pages 473–479, Hissar, Bulgaria.

Oliver, A. and Vàzquez, M. (2020). Termeval 2020: Using tsr filtering method to improve automatic term extraction. In *Proceedings of CompuTerm 2020*.

Pais, V. and Ion, R. (2020). Termeval 2020: Racai's automatic term extraction system. In *Proceedings of CompuTerm 2020*.

Pollak, S., Repar, A., Martinc, M., and Podpečan, V. (2019). Karst Exploration: Extracting Terms and Definitions from Karst Domain Corpus. In *Proceedings of eLex 2019*, pages 934–956, Sintra, Portugal.

Qasemizadeh, B. and Handschuh, S. (2014). Investigating Context Parameters in Technology Term Recognition. In *Proceedings of SADAATL 2014*, pages 1–10, Dublin, Ireland.

Qasemizadeh, B. and Schumann, A.-K. (2016). The ACL RD-TEC 2.0: A Language Resource for Evaluating Term Extraction and Entity Recognition Methods. In *Proceedings of LREC 2016*, pages 1862–1868, Portorož, Slovenia. ELRA.

Ramisch, C., Villavicencio, A., and Boitet, C. (2010). Multiword Expressions in the wild? The mwetoolkit comes in handy. In *Coling 2010: Demonstration Volume*, pages 57–60, Beijing, China.

Rigouts Terryn, A., Drouin, P., Hoste, V., and Lefever, E. (2019a). Analysing the Impact of Supervised Machine Learning on Automatic Term Extraction: HAMLET vs TermoStat. In *Proceedings of RANLP 2019*, Varna, Bulgaria.

Rigouts Terryn, A., Hoste, V., and Lefever, E. (2019b). In No Uncertain Terms: A Dataset for Monolingual and Multilingual Automatic Term Extraction from Comparable Corpora. *Language Resources and Evaluation*, pages 1–34.

Schumann, A.-K. and Fischer, S. (2016). Compasses, Magnets, Water Microscopes. In *Proceedings of LREC 2016*, pages 3578–3584, Portorož, Slovenia. ELRA.

Shah, S., Sarath, S., and Shreedhar, R. (2019). Similarity Driven Unsupervised Learning for Materials Science Terminology Extraction. *Computación y Sistemas*, 23(3):1005–1013.

Stenetorp, P., Topić, G., Pyysalo, S., Ohta, T., Kim, J.-D., and Tsujii, J. (2011). BioNLP Shared Task 2011: Supporting Resources. In *Proceedings of BioNLP Shared Task 2011 Workshop*.

TermITH, P. (2014). Annotation sémantique et terminologique avec la plateforme SMARTIES.

Vivaldi, J. and Rodríguez, H. (2001). Improving term extraction by combining different techniques. *Terminology*, 7(1):31–48, December.

Vàzquez, M. and Oliver, A. (2018). Improving term candidates selection using terminological tokens. *Terminology*, 24(1):122–147, May.

Wang, R., Liu, W., and McDonald, C. (2016). Featureless Domain-Specic Term Extraction with Minimal Labelled Data. In *Proceedings of Australasian Language Technology Association Workshop*, pages 103–112, Melbourne, Australia.

Zhang, Z., Petrak, J., and Maynard, D. (2018). Adapted TextRank for Term Extraction: A Generic Method of Improving Automatic Term Extraction Algorithms. *ACM Transactions on Knowledge Discovery from Data*, 12(5):1–7.

Šajatović, A., Buljan, M., Šnajder, J., and Bašić, B. D. (2019). Evaluating Automatic Term Extraction Methods on Individual Documents. In *Proceedings of the Joint Workshop on Multiword Expressions and WordNet (MWE-WN 2019)*, pages 149–154, Florence, Italy. ACL.

7. Language Resource References

Rigouts Terryn, Ayla and Drouin, Patrick and Hoste, Véronique and Lefever, Els. (2020). *Annotated Corpora for Term Extraction Research (ACTER)*. Ghent University, 1.2.

Proceedings of the 6th International Workshop on Computational Terminology (COMPUTERM 2020), pages 95–100
Language Resources and Evaluation Conference (LREC 2020), Marseille, 11–16 May 2020
© European Language Resources Association (ELRA), licensed under CC-BY-NC

TermEval 2020: TALN-LS2N System for Automatic Term Extraction

Amir Hazem, Mérième Bouhandi, Florian Boudin, and Béatrice Daille

LS2N - UMR CNRS 6004, Université de Nantes, France

{amir.hazem,merieme.bouhandi,florian.boudin,beatrice.daille}@ls2n.fr

Abstract

Automatic terminology extraction is a notoriously difficult task aiming to ease effort demanded to manually identify terms in domain-specific corpora by automatically providing a ranked list of candidate terms. The main ways that addressed this task can be ranged in four main categories: (i) rule-based approaches, (ii) feature-based approaches, (iii) context-based approaches, and (iv) hybrid approaches. For this first TermEval shared task, we explore a feature-based approach, and a deep neural network multitask approach -BERT- that we fine-tune for term extraction. We show that BERT models (RoBERTa for English and CamemBERT for French) outperform other systems for French and English languages.

Keywords: Terminology extraction, Feature-based, BERT.

1. Introduction

Automatic terminology extraction (ATE) is a very challenging task beneficial to a broad range of natural language processing applications, including machine translation, bilingual lexicon induction, thesauri construction (Lin, 1998; Wu and Zhou, 2003; van der Plas and Tiedemann, 2006; Hagiwara, 2008; Andrade et al., 2013; Rigouts Terryn et al., 2019), to cite a few.

Traditionally, this task is conducted by a terminologist, but hand-operated exploration, indexation, and maintenance of domain-specific corpora and terminologies is a costly enterprise. The automatization aims to ease effort demanded to manually identify terms in domain-specific corpora by automatically providing a ranked list of candidate terms.

Despite being a well-established research domain for decades, NLP methods still fail to meet human standards, and ATE is still considered an unsolved problem with considerable room for improvement. If it is generally admitted that terms are single words or multiword expressions representing domain-specific concepts and that terminologies are the body of terms used with a particular domain, the lack of annotated data and agreement between researchers make ATE evaluation very difficult (Terryn et al., 2018). In order to gather researchers around a common evaluation scheme, TermEval shared task (Rigouts Terryn et al., 2019) offers a unified framework aiming a better ATE's comprehension and analysis [1]. The shared task provides four data sets: Corruption, dressage, wind energy and heart failure; in three languages: English, French and Dutch.

With the advance of neural network language models and following the current trend and excellent results obtained by transformer architecture on other NLP tasks, we have decided to experiment and compare two classification methods, one feature-based and the BERT-based. We show that BERT models (RoBERTa for English and CamemBERT for French) outperform other systems for French and English languages. Also, the feature-based approach shows competitive results.

2. Task Description

The shared task provides four data sets. Three of them are dedicated to the training phase: corruption, dressage and wind energy, and one to the test phase: heart failure. All the corpora are provided in three languages: English, French and Dutch. The data sets are described in detail in (Rigouts Terryn et al., 2019). Five teams have participated in the TermEval shared task. All teams submitted results for English, three submitted for French and two for Dutch. We submitted results for the French and English data sets. The Precision, recall, and F1-score were calculated twice: once including and once excluding Named Entities.

3. Proposed System

We present in this section the two experimented approaches during the training phase that is: (i) the feature-based and, (ii) the BERT-based approaches. For the test phase, the submitted results are those of BERT approach only. However, we also report the obtained results of the feature-based approach for comparison.

3.1. Feature-based Approach

3.1.1. Feature Extraction

Classical methods for extracting terms from corpora often consist of three major steps: the first one uses some linguistic filtering, the second one consists of describing the candidates through different features in order to give them a weight indicating the degree of confidence that they are indeed a term, and the third is more of a selection phase. As for the first step, we know that, often, the first requirement is for a term to be a noun phrase, and our main morphosyntactic pattern is defined (primarily by observing recurrent patterns in the given reference lists of terms): a noun or nouns (or proper nouns), which might be preceded or followed by adjectives (vertical axis wind turbine), or of-genitives (United States of America). These patterns are then passed to spaCy's rule-matching engine[2] to extract a list of candidate terms. Once our candidate terms are extracted, we processed to the second step, and we assign to

---

[1] https://termeval.ugent.be/

[2] https://spacy.io/

each one of them linguistic, stylistic, statistic, and distributional descriptors that might help us get insights as to the nature of terms (Table 1). In this work, beyond the common statistical descriptors, we wanted to focus on different measures of specificity and termhood, since we know that a term is much more common and essential in a specialized corpus than it is in a general domain corpus. Termhood is defined by (Kageura and Umino, 1996) as "the degree to which a linguistic unit is related to domain-specific context":

- Measures of specificity and termhood

  - Specificity ($Specificity$): $Specificity(a) = 2 \cdot \frac{f_D(a) \times f_G(a)}{f_D(a) + f_G(a)}$ with a the term, $f_D(a)$ the term frequency in the specialized corpus and $f_G(a)$ its out-of-domain frequency.

  - Term's relation to Context (W_{rel}): $W_{rel}(a) = (0.5 + ((WL \cdot \frac{TF(a)}{MaxTF}) + PL)) + (0.5 + ((WR \cdot \frac{TF(a)}{MaxTF}) + PR))$ with $TF(a)$ the term frequency in the document, $MaxTF$ the frequency of the most frequent word, WL (or $[WR]$) is the ratio between the number of different words that co-occur with the candidate term (on the left [right] side) and the total number of words that it co-occurs with. PL (or $[PR]$) is the ratio between the number of different words that co-occur with the candidate term (on the left [right] side) and the $MaxTF$. W_{rel} measures the singularity of the term a in the corpus and quantifies the extent to which a term resembles the characteristics of a stopword. The more a candidate word co-occurs with different words, the more likely it is to be unimportant in the document.

  - Cvalue ($Cval$): $Cval(a) = log_2|a| \cdot (f(a) - \frac{1}{P(T_a)} \sum_{n \in T_a} f(n))$ with $f(a)$ the frequency of term a, $|a|$ the number of words in a, T_a is the set of extracted candidate terms that contain a, $P(T_a)$ is the total number of longer candidate terms that contain a.

  - Termhood (TH): $W(a) = \frac{f_a^2}{n} \cdot \sum_1^n (log \frac{f_{n,D}}{N_D} - \frac{f_{n,R}}{N_R})$ with f_a^2 the absolute frequency of the word in the domain-specific corpus, n the number of words in a, $\frac{f_{n,D}}{N_D}$ the frequency of each constituent of the term in the domain-specific corpus ($\frac{f_{n,R}}{N_R}$ for the general domain) relative of the size of the corpora (in tokens).

As for the last step, classification is conducted to select the terms using these features.

3.1.2. Classification

Boosting is a classification method that consists of iteratively learning several classifiers whose individual weights are corrected as they go along to better predict difficult values. The classifiers are then weighted according to their performance and aggregated iteratively. We use the XGBoost model (eXtreme Gradient Boosting) (Chen and Guestrin, 2016), and we feed it our feature vectors after being normalized using $sklearn^3$ standard scaler, which transforms an x value into a $z = \frac{x-u}{s}$ value, with u being

---

^{3}https://scikit-learn.org/stable/

Feature	Reference
First letter is a capital letter	-
Number of words	-
Length of term in characters	-
Number of stopwords	-
Relevance (how many other candidates contain this term)	-
Position of the first occurrence	(Aquino et al., 2014)
Spread	(Hasan and Ng, 2014)
TF, IDF, TF-IDF	(Jones, 2004)
Relative frequency (RF, in and out-of-domain)	-
Sum of subparts' RF (in and out-of-domain)	-
Specificity (harmonic mean of RF in-domain and RF out-domain)	-
Cvalue	(Vu et al., 2008)
Z-Score	(Aquino et al., 2014)
Term's relation to context	(Campos et al., 2018)
Termhood	(Vintar, 2010)

Table 1: Summary Table of Features

the mean of the x and s its standard deviation. However, these features can be more or less essential to characterize our terms. After several tests, we have empirically determined that only the elements that correlate at more than a certain threshold (mean correlation) with our target class are retained for classification (bolded in 1).

3.2. BERT

BERT has proven to be efficient in many downstream NLP tasks (Devlin et al., 2018) including next sentence prediction, question answering and named entity recognition (NER). It can also be used for feature extraction or classification. Prior to the emergence of transformer-based architectures like BERT, several deep learning architectures for terminology extraction have been proposed. Wang et al. (2016) introduce a weakly-supervised classification-based approach. Amjadian et al. (2016) leverage local and global embeddings to encapsulate the meaning and behavior of the term for the classification step, although they only work with unigram terms.

We must note that exploring these architectures is not the focus of this work; we mainly want to observe how BERT-based models can be used for ATE and how they perform in comparison to more traditional feature-based methods. In order to do that, we use different versions of BERT as a binary classifier for term prediction.

For English, we use RoBERTa (Liu et al., 2019), which is a model built based on BERT but modifies key hyperparameters in the original BERT model, eliminating its next-sentence pretraining objective and training the model with much larger mini-batches and more substantial learning rates, leading to more solid downstream task performance. For French, we use CamemBERT (Martin et al., 2019), the French version of the BERT model. For both languages, we

	English																	
	NES									ANN								
Tools	Corp			Equi			Wind			Corp			Equi			Wind		
	P	R	F1	P	R	F1	P	R	F1	P	R	F1	P	R	F1	P	R	F1
Patterns	2.42	**76.2**	5.60	6.60	68.4	11.7	1.50	76.1	2.40	2.60	**61.5**	5.10	6.80	50.2	10.7	1.20	55.8	2.20
Features	**40.6**	16.4	23.7	**38.7**	19.4	25.5	**51.1**	10.9	17.2	**39.4**	17.6	24.4	**38.7**	19.1	25.4	**51.2**	10.8	17.4
	P	R	F1	P	R	F1	P	R	F1	P	R	F1	P	R	F1	P	R	F1
BERT3	27.1	41.4	32.8	28.4	82.0	**42.2**	22.2	81.1	**34.8**	18.4	35.6	24.2	20.5	80.6	**32.7**	16.0	82.4	**26.9**
BERT4	28.5	38.9	32.9	26.5	**85.0**	40.4	21.3	83.8	33.9	17.8	30.7	22.5	19.1	**83.5**	31.1	15.4	85.6	26.2
BERT5	25.5	42.9	32.0	27.3	80.5	40.8	19.9	**93.5**	32.8	16.7	35.7	22.8	19.4	78.1	31.1	14.7	90.5	25.4
BERT6	25.6	57.6	**35.5**	27.6	84.3	41.6	16.9	89.9	28.5	18.7	53.4	**27.7**	19.8	82.6	32.0	12.4	**93.0**	22.0
	French																	
	NES									ANN								
Tools	Corp			Equi			Wind			Corp			Equi			Wind		
	P	R	F1	P	R	F1	P	R	F1	P	R	F1	P	R	F1	P	R	F1
Patterns	3.08	**74.6**	5.93	5.26	67.9	9.76	1.69	77.2	3.31	3.69	**72.8**	7.08	6.75	71.3	12.3	2.09	76.3	4.08
Features	30.9	25.1	27.7	**54.3**	11.5	19.6	**46.4**	16.4	24.2	**31.5**	25.9	28.4	**54.3**	11.5	19.1	**45.4**	16.4	**24.1**
	P	R	F1	P	R	F1	P	R	F1	P	R	F1	P	R	F1	P	R	F1
BERT3	41.5	23.1	29.6	25.8	61.7	**36.4**	18.2	58.9	27.8	23.2	15.9	18.9	19.8	58.1	**29.5**	13.6	55.5	21.9
BERT4	27.9	48.5	35.4	24.8	63.0	35.6	17.9	67.4	**28.2**	20.8	44.9	28.4	18.9	59.1	28.7	13.7	64.8	22.6
BERT5	30.1	57.2	39.5	20.1	71.2	31.4	11.3	76.9	19.8	23.1	54.4	32.5	15.7	68.6	25.6	8.89	75.2	15.9
BERT6	**36.7**	48.4	**41.7**	9.08	**78.1**	16.2	9.11	**82.5**	16.4	26.6	43.5	**33.1**	7.27	**76.8**	13.2	7.21	**81.8**	13.2

Table 2: Terminology extraction scores (%) obtained on the training data sets. BERT3 for instance, stands for BERT using ngrams of length 3 for training.

will use pre-trained models, and both of them are fine-tuned during the classification. The general objectives BERT is trained on gives the model an innate sentence classification capability. The main idea is to associate each term with its context. Hence, by analogy to the next sentence prediction, the first sentence given to BERT is the one which contains the term, and the sentence to predict is the term itself. For training, we feed the model with all the context/term pairs that appear in the corpus as positive examples. The negative examples are generated randomly. Given the following sentence: *"this is the first global instrument in the fight against corruption"*, *corruption* is annotated as a positive example (term) and a randomly chosen word or n-gram, *global* for instance, is annotated as a negative example. It is important to highlight the fact that the negative examples are all the n-grams that do not appear in the training evaluation term list. Also, the number of negative examples is equal to the number of positive ones.

4. Experiments and Results

Hand-engineering features is a challenging assignment, even more so for a task as challenging as extracting terms from domain-specific corpora and finding features to capture the right characteristics for each term and stay relevant with any corpora in hand. We can observe, from our results (table 2), that we often fail to find a good trade-off between recall and precision. As a matter of fact, with features as strict as these, we often find ourselves with correct precision and quite a weak recall.

4.1. BERT Settings

For the fine-tuning phase of BERT, we used the simpletransformers [4] library and its default parameters setting. For English, we used RoBERTa with n-gram size of four while for French, we used CamemBERT with n-gram size of five.

4.2. Experiments on the Training Data Sets

We started with the hypothesis that the features of a term noun phrase must be different from the features of a non term noun phrase and that the features that characterize these terms must be valid from one corpus to the other. However, we can clearly see that the main problem encountered with the feature-based method is that the features learned by the model are hardly transferable from one corpus to another, as the notion of the relevance of each candidate term changes from one application area to another, and from one domain to another. Hard-coded features learned on one corpus do not transfer well to another during classification, since not only are the texts and domains vary greatly, but even the range of the values for the noun phrases features in the different corpora can vary enormously (see figures 1, 2, 3). Going for a feature-less method seems to be a nice direction to explore (table 4). Our experiments with BERT, even if they were somewhat successful, were a bit abrupt, since we consider all the n-

[4] https://github.com/ThilinaRajapakse/simpletransformers

grams as potential candidates, without prior filtering. We end up, after classification, with false positives in our list, such as phrases beginning or ending with pronouns or conjunctions. One of the reasons that pushed us first to test this configuration without prior noun phrases filtering was our fear of losing potential positive candidates (we can in table 4 see that recall post-filtering is average). Future work will incorporate syntactic information into this BERT process in order to get better precision.

4.3. Results of the Test Set

| | English | | | | | |
| | NES | | | ANN | | |
	P	R	F1	P	R	F1
TALN-LS2N	34.78	**70.87**	**46.66**	32.58	**72.68**	**44.99**
RACAI	42.40	40.27	41.31	38.57	40.11	39.33
NYU	**43.46**	23.64	30.62	**42.18**	25.12	31.48
e-Termino	34.43	14.20	20.10	34.43	15.54	21.42
NLPLab	21.45	15.59	18.06	20.06	15.97	17.78
	French					
	NES			ANN		
	P	R	F1	P	R	F1
TALN-LS2N	**45.17**	**51.55**	**48.15**	**41.88**	**50.88**	**45.94**
e-Termino	36.33	13.50	19.68	36.33	14.37	20.59
NLPLab	16.07	11.18	13.19	15.12	11.20	12.87

Table 3: Official results on the heart failure test set(%).

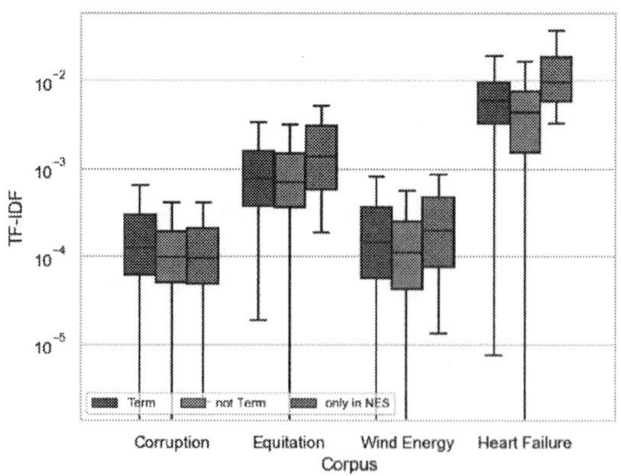

Figure 1: Range of the TFIDF values on all the corpora for English

The results on the test set are consistent with the results on the training corpora. The same patterns can be observed, and results on the test set are in the same range. Based on the F1-score, our approach represented by TALN-LS2N using BERT obtained the best results of the competition. However, we see that in terms of precision, the NYU team obtained the best results for English. Overall, feature-based and BERT-based approaches exhibit similar performance on the French test set while for English, BERT is more accurate. Further experiments are certainly needed to improve

| | English | | | | | |
| | NES | | | ANN | | |
	P	R	F1	P	R	F1
Patterns	11.8	77.3	20.5	12.9	77.1	22.1
Features	**39.4**	29.2	33.6	**39.6**	29.4	33.7
	P	R	F1	P	R	F1
BERT3	34.0	69.9	**45.7**	31.5	70.9	**43.6**
BERT4	31.7	78.3	45.2	29.3	79.1	42.7
BERT5	26.9	**83.7**	40.8	24.9	**84.6**	38.4
BERT6	30.8	77.7	44.1	28.3	78.3	41.6
	French					
	NES			ANN		
	P	R	F1	P	R	F1
Patterns	16.9	65.3	25.8	17.9	65.1	27.8
Features	**48.9**	53.4	**50.9**	**48.9**	53.3	**50.9**
	P	R	F1	P	R	F1
BERT3	41.3	58.5	48.4	38.5	58.0	46.3
BERT4	40.2	66.9	50.3	37.7	66.8	48.2
BERT5	34.3	73.1	46.7	32.2	73.2	44.7
BERT6	24.3	**76.3**	36.9	22.9	**76.4**	35.2

Table 4: Results on the heart failure test set(%) using BERT with different ngram's size. BERT3 for instance, stands for BERT using ngrams of length 3 for training.

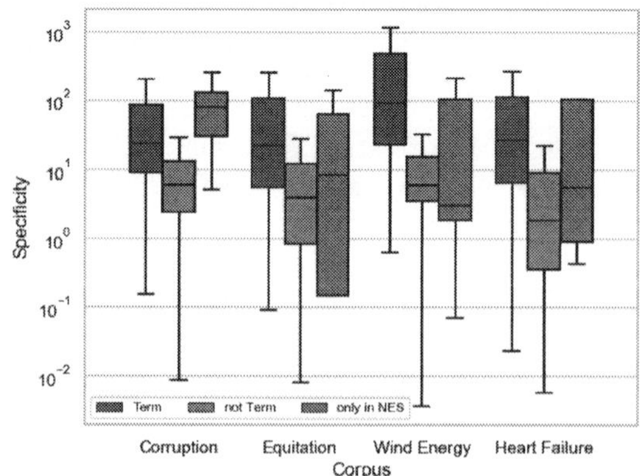

Figure 2: Range of the Specificity values on all the corpora for English

both methods. However, the capability of BERT (certainly thanks to its attention mechanism) to learn hidden features suggests less effort is needed compared to the feature-based approach, which requires more efforts in the design of the features. Also, the n-gram size used in BERT was fixed empirically based on the development data sets. Further anal-

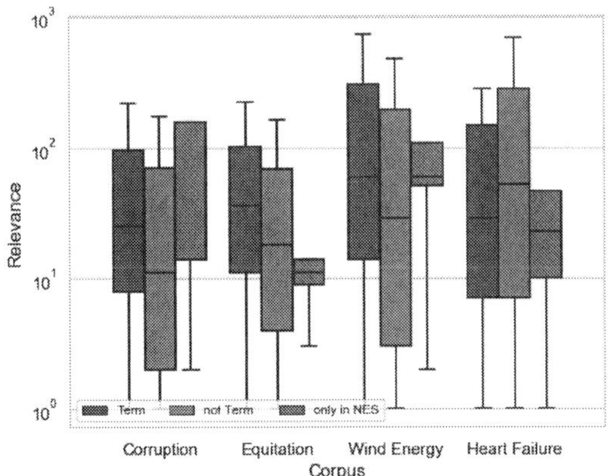

Figure 3: Range of the Relevance values on all the corpora for English

ysis is needed to make our approach n-gram independent for better term length coverage. Indeed, we limited our system outputs to 4-grams for English and 5-grams for French, which did not allow the extraction of longer terms. Finally, recent work has shown several improvements of BERT such as StructBERT (Wang et al., 2020) and T5 (Raffel et al., 2019). These recent state-of-the-art approaches can, in the future, be used to further improve the results of ATE.

5. Conclusion

Term extraction has been a very active field of research for many decades. Methods based solely on linguistic analysis and patterns have given way to new statistical, machine, and deep learning methods. We conducted several experiments using classical hand-engineered features-based methods in order to find the best way to extract terms in several specialized domains. These models that combine linguistic, statistical and distributional descriptors suggest that the relation between test and training corpora are of central importance. Moreover, we have seen that it is only natural for the very notion of termhood in different domains to be more pragmatic than theoretical. We then proposed a BERT-based classification approach that outperformed classical methods on this shared task. This contribution is setting a new, simple and strong baseline for terminology extraction. However, the overall results of this task are average at best, and much room is left for improvement.

6. Bibliographical References

Amjadian, E., Inkpen, D., Paribakht, T., and Faez, F. (2016). Local-global vectors to improve unigram terminology extraction. In *Proceedings of the 5th International Workshop on Computational Terminology (Computerm2016)*, pages 2–11, Osaka, Japan, December. The COLING 2016 Organizing Committee.

Andrade, D., Tsuchida, M., Onishi, T., and Ishikawa, K. (2013). Synonym acquisition using bilingual comparable corpora. In *International Joint Conference on Natural Language Processing (IJCNLP'13)*, Nagoya, Japan.

Aquino, G., Hasperué, W., and Lanzarini, L. (2014). Keyword extraction using auto-associative neural networks.

Campos, R., Mangaravite, V., Pasquali, A., Jorge, A. M., Nunes, C., and Jatowt, A. (2018). A text feature based automatic keyword extraction method for single documents. In Gabriella Pasi, et al., editors, *Advances in Information Retrieval*, pages 684–691, Cham. Springer International Publishing.

Chen, T. and Guestrin, C. (2016). Xgboost: A scalable tree boosting system. *CoRR*, abs/1603.02754.

Devlin, J., Chang, M.-W., Lee, K., and Toutanova, K. (2018). Bert: Pre-training of deep bidirectional transformers for language understanding. *arXiv preprint arXiv:1810.04805*.

Hagiwara, M. (2008). A supervised learning approach to automatic synonym identification based on distributional features. In *Proceedings of the ACL-08: HLT Student Research Workshop*, pages 1–6, Columbus, Ohio, June. Association for Computational Linguistics.

Hasan, K. S. and Ng, V. (2014). Automatic keyphrase extraction: A survey of the state of the art. In *Proceedings of the 52nd Annual Meeting of the Association for Computational Linguistics (Volume 1: Long Papers)*, pages 1262–1273, Baltimore, Maryland, June. Association for Computational Linguistics.

Jones, K. S. (2004). A statistical interpretation of term specificity and its application in retrieval. *Journal of Documentation*, 60(5):493–502.

Kageura, K. and Umino, B. (1996). Methods of automatic term recognition: A review. *Terminology. International Journal of Theoretical and Applied Issues in Specialized Communication*, 3(2):259–289.

Lin, D. (1998). Automatic retrieval and clustering of similar words. In *Proceedings of the 36th Annual Meeting of the Association for Computational Linguistics and 17th International Conference on Computational Linguistics - Volume 2*, ACL '98, pages 768–774, Stroudsburg, PA, USA. Association for Computational Linguistics.

Liu, Y., Ott, M., Goyal, N., Du, J., Joshi, M., Chen, D., Levy, O., Lewis, M., Zettlemoyer, L., and Stoyanov, V. (2019). Roberta: A robustly optimized bert pretraining approach. *arXiv preprint arXiv:1907.11692*.

Martin, L., Muller, B., Ortiz Suárez, P. J., Dupont, Y., Romary, L., Villemonte de la Clergerie, É., Seddah, D., and Sagot, B. (2019). CamemBERT: a Tasty French Language Model. *arXiv e-prints*, page arXiv:1911.03894, Nov.

Raffel, C., Shazeer, N., Roberts, A., Lee, K., Narang, S., Matena, M., Zhou, Y., Li, W., and Liu, P. J. (2019). Exploring the limits of transfer learning with a unified text-to-text transformer. *arXiv e-prints*.

Rigouts Terryn, A., Hoste, V., and Lefever, E. (2019). In no uncertain terms: a dataset for monolingual and multilingual automatic term extraction from comparable corpora. In *Language Resources and Evaluation*.

Terryn, A. R., Hoste, V., and Lefever, E. (2018). A Gold Standard for Multilingual Automatic Term Extraction from Comparable Corpora: Term Structure and Translation Equivalents. In *Proceedings of the Eleventh International Conference on Language Resources and Evaluation (LREC 2018)*, Miyazaki, Japan, May 7-12, 2018.

European Language Resources Association (ELRA).

van der Plas, L. and Tiedemann, J. (2006). Finding synonyms using automatic word alignment and measures of distributional similarity. In *21st International Conference on Computational Linguistics and 44th Annual Meeting of the Association for Computational Linguistics ACL'06*, Sydney, Australia.

Vintar, S. (2010). Bilingual term recognition revisited: The bag-of-equivalents term alignment approach and its evaluation. *Terminology. International Journal of Theoretical and Applied Issues in Specialized Communication*, 16(2):141–158.

Vu, T., Aw, A., and Zhang, M. (2008). Term extraction through unithood and termhood unification. In *IJCNLP*.

Wang, R., Liu, W., and McDonald, C. (2016). Featureless domain-specific term extraction with minimal labelled data. In *Proceedings of the Australasian Language Technology Association Workshop 2016*, pages 103–112, Melbourne, Australia, December.

Wang, W., Bi, B., Yan, M., Wu, C., Xia, J., Bao, Z., Peng, L., and Si, L. (2020). Structbert: Incorporating language structures into pre-training for deep language understanding. In *International Conference on Learning Representations*.

Wu, H. and Zhou, M. (2003). Optimizing synonym extraction using monolingual and bilingual resources. In *In Proceedings of the second international workshop on Paraphrasing*, page 72.

Proceedings of the 6th International Workshop on Computational Terminology (COMPUTERM 2020), pages 101–105
Language Resources and Evaluation Conference (LREC 2020), Marseille, 11–16 May 2020
© European Language Resources Association (ELRA), licensed under CC-BY-NC

TermEval 2020: RACAI's automatic term extraction system

Vasile Păiş, Radu Ion
Research Institute for Artificial Intelligence "Mihai Drăgănescu", Romanian Academy
CASA ACADEMIEI, 13 "Calea 13 Septembrie", Bucharest 050711, ROMANIA
{vasile, radu}@racai.ro

Abstract

This paper describes RACAI's automatic term extraction system, which participated in the TermEval 2020 shared task on English monolingual term extraction. We discuss the system architecture, some of the challenges that we faced as well as present our results in the English competition.

Keywords: automatic term extraction, ATE, natural language processing

1. Introduction

Automatic term extraction, also known as ATE, is a well-known task within the domain of natural language processing. Given a text (this can be either a fragment or an entire corpus), an automatic term extractor system will produce a list of terms (single or multiword expressions) characteristic for the domain of text.

Felber, in the "Terminology Manual" (Felber, 1984), defines a term as "any conventional symbol representing a concept defined in a subject field". Nevertheless, considering current practice in natural language processing tasks, it is not always possible to give a general definition applicable for the workings of a term extractor. One question is whether or not to include named entities as part of the identified terms. This problem is also raised by the organizers of the TermEval 2020 shared task, each system being evaluated twice, once including and once excluding named entities[1]. Furthermore, since named entity recognizers can be trained on many classes (such as diseases or chemicals for example), another potential question is what kinds of entities (if any) can be included as part of the identified terms. However, an agreement must be made that all identified terms must be specific to the domain of the analyzed text, regardless of inclusion or not of named entities. For example, in the shared task's provided training dataset, the named entity "United States Dressage Federation" is included as a term in the "equestrian" section.

The present paper presents our attempt at constructing an automatic term extraction system in the context of the TermEval 2020 shared task on monolingual term extraction (Rigouts Terryn et al., 2020). We start by presenting related research, then continue with the description of our system and finally present concluding remarks.

2. Related work

The usefulness of the term identification process is both in its own use, such as creation of document indices, and as a pre-processing step in other more advanced processes, such as machine translation. Furthermore, the output produced by an automatic system can be manually validated by a human user in order to remove irrelevant terms.

Traditional approaches for ATE (Kageura, 1998) make use of statistical features such as word frequency or "termhood" (degree of relatedness of a proposed term to the domain) metrics. Additionally, information such as part of speech can be used to further filter candidate terms. Term formalization attempts can be identified in the literature as early as e.g. 1996, when Frantzi and Ananiadou (1996) defined C-value as a basic measure of termhood, a principle we have also used in one of our algorithms. In this section, we will briefly mention the inner workings of some existing term extraction algorithms that we used in our term extraction system. For a detailed coverage of this rather vast sub-domain of NLP, the reader is referred to e.g. Pazienza et al. (2005) or the more recent Firoozeh et al. (2019).

TextRank (Mihalcea and Tarau, 2004) is a term extraction algorithm using a graph representation of the text in which each word is a node and an edge is created between words collocated within a certain window of words. Based on the number of links to each node a score is computed similar to the PageRank algorithm (Brin and Page, 1998). Further filtering is performed based on the part of speech of the words. The graph is created based on single words. However, as the last step of the algorithm a reconstruction of multi-word terms is performed if multiple single word terms are collocated in the sentence.

RAKE, an acronym for Rapid Automatic Keyword Extraction (Rose et al., 2010), combines graph measures such as the degree (number of connected edges) with statistical measures such as word frequency. Furthermore, RAKE uses a strategy similar to TextRank for combining single words that occur together at least twice into a multi-word term. An interesting idea deriving from the RAKE paper is the importance of the stop words list used. In this context, it is mentioned that FOX (Fox, 1989) stop list produces an increase in the F1 score for the RAKE algorithm. An improvement over the initial RAKE algorithm is described in Gupta et al. (2016).

Campos et al. (2020) present YAKE, which makes use of statistical features. According to their analysis[2] it is comparable or even better in some cases to previous state-of-the-art methods. In the HAMLET system (Rigouts Terryn et al., 2019) a number of 152 features are computed on each candidate term and a binary decision tree classifier is trained. Candidates are determined based on their part of speech, but the patterns of occurrence are determined automatically based on training data.

---

[1] https://termeval.ugent.be/task-evaluation/

[2] https://github.com/LIAAD/yake

3. Dataset and basic processing

The dataset proposed for the TermEval task is described in detail in the task paper (Rigouts Terryn et al., 2020). However, several aspects must be mentioned. It is comprised of 4 domains: wind energy ('wind'), corruption ('corp'), horse dressage ('equi') and heart failure ('hf'). The first 3 domains were provided with annotations for training purposes, while the heart failure domain was used for testing. All the domains were made available in English, French and Dutch.

For the purposes of our experiments, we focused on the English version of the corpus. However, we tried to keep our algorithms independent of the actual language being used. Towards this end, we used only resources normally available for many languages, such as annotations and stop words, and did not create any rules or patterns specific to the English language.

One of the primary processing operations was to annotate the corpus with part-of-speech and lemma information. For this purpose, we used Stanford CoreNLP (Manning et al., 2014). Furthermore, we precomputed statistical indicators based on the corpus, such as n-gram frequency, document frequency and letters used (in some cases terms contained non-English letters). Statistics were computed for both the corpus and the provided training annotations.

Unfortunately, the corpus is not balanced with respect to the different domains. Therefore, some statistical indicators may be less meaningful. For example, the corruption part of the corpus contains 12 annotated texts with an additional 12 texts provided without annotations. However, the equestrianism part contains 34 annotated text files and 55 unannotated documents. Furthermore, the evaluation section on heart failure contains 190 files. This seems to suggest that indicators like document frequency (the number of documents containing a certain word/expression) may be more meaningful for certain sections and less meaningful for others.

More statistics regarding the English domains of the corpus are presented in Table 1.

	equi	corp	wind	hf
Annotated files	34	12	5	190
Unannotated files	55	12	33	-
Unique lowercase tokens	6854	7958	21591	6092
Terms (without NE)	1155	927	1091	2361
Terms (with NE)	1575	1174	1534	2585

Table 1: Statistics regarding the English sections of the corpus

One of the characteristics specific only to the wind energy section of the corpus is the presence of mathematical formulas in some of the files. We could not identify an easy way to automatically remove them and did not want to manually perform this action. For example, "CP" is considered a term and it also appears in some formulas. Furthermore, there are lines of text presumably between formulas which look similar to a formula, like "CP ,max CT CTr" or full lines of text containing embedded formulas. Even more, the term "PCO2", indicated in the gold annotations, seems to only appear inside a formula ("PCO2 = TCO2 − HCO2 PCO2"). Therefore, in order to avoid removal of potentially useful portions of text, the files were used as they were provided.

Given these discrepancies between the different domain sub-corpora, it was our assumption, from the beginning, that different algorithms will obtain different results on each of the domains. Therefore, we started first by analyzing the results provided by known algorithms on the training parts of the corpus. These results are presented in Tables 2, 3, 4 and are compared against the provided annotations with named entities included. In these tables, the algorithm with the best F1 score in each section is marked in bold. The "1W" specification besides an algorithm denotes the score for single word terms.

In accordance with our previous observation, because of the imbalances between the different sections of the corpus, from Table 2 it can easily be seen that most of the algorithms perform better on the "equi" section and worse on the other sections. In some cases, there are even extreme differences. For example, the YAKE implementation gives on multi-word expressions an F1 score of 22.3 on the "equi" section and only 5.94 on the "wind" section. This is improved for single word expressions with 12% on the "equi" section and less then 3% for the other sections.

	P%	R%	F1%
TFIDF 1W	27.80	26.70	27.24
TFIDF	10.63	19.30	13.71
RAKE 1W	20.43	69.23	31.55
RAKE	15.39	65.97	24.95
YAKE 1W	39.31	31.00	34.66
YAKE	18.39	28.32	22.30
TRANK 1W	**29.21**	**42.76**	**34.71**
TRANK	26.86	25.27	26.04

Table 2: Precision, Recall, F1 measures for tested algorithms on the "equi" section

	P%	R%	F1%
TFIDF 1W	16.02	27.29	20.19
TFIDF	7.81	18.65	11.01
RAKE 1W	**16.80**	**75.30**	**27.47**
RAKE	12.95	65.08	21.60
YAKE 1W	30.94	8.57	13.42
YAKE	11.81	9.88	10.76
TRANK 1W	17.67	39.24	24.37
TRANK	17.05	18.40	17.70

Table 3: Precision, Recall, F1 measures for tested algorithms on the "corp" section

	P%	R%	F1%
TFIDF 1W	17.30	19.96	18.54
TFIDF	13.18	11.60	12.34
RAKE 1W	13.62	58.13	22.07
RAKE	**13.90**	**63.17**	**22.79**
YAKE 1W	64.29	3.18	6.06
YAKE	12.37	3.91	5.94
TRANK 1W	14.57	34.81	20.54
TRANK	14.11	13.62	13.86

Table 4: Precision, Recall, F1 measures for tested algorithms on the "wind" section

4. System Architecture

Looking at the above tables, two observations can be made: a) no single system performs best on all three sections; b) systems tend to balance precision and recall, but in extreme cases they prefer either precision (for example the YAKE method in "corp" and "wind" sections) or recall (for example the RAKE method).

A first idea that we explored was to implement a voting mechanism between the systems. However, the results presented only slight improvements. Without a complete and in-depth analysis, we concluded that each system was good at identifying certain terms (based on their pattern of occurrence) but performing badly for other terms. Therefore, we decided to extend the basic system and implement additional algorithms that would try to complement and extend the previous ones, by using new methods and finally use the same voting mechanism.

The first algorithm, PLEARN (from "pattern learn") is trying to identify patterns based on statistics computed on the train set annotations and their appearance in context. We used the following features: letters accepted in annotations (for example there is no term using ","), stop words accepted at start or end of a term (for example there is no term starting or ending with "and"), stop words accepted inside multi word terms, stop words accepted before or after a term (for example "and" usually is not contained within a term but rather it separates two distinct terms, thus appearing before or after a term), suffixes of words other than stop words present in terms (usually we tend to find nouns as terms, but we tried not to impose this condition, thus we only checked the suffixes of words).

For the purpose of the algorithm, all information was extracted automatically from the training set and no manual conditions or word lists were created. One immediate problem with the algorithm is that the training set did not provide the actual position of the term. Therefore, if the same word or multi-word expression was used both as term and as a non-term then the feature extraction part was not able to identify this case. Nevertheless, the algorithm was able to produce the good recall that we were expecting, presented in Table 5.

	P%	R%	F1%
Equi 1W	21.28	87.56	34.24
Equi	7.96	86.22	14.57
Corp 1W	15.61	91.43	26.66
Corp	4.85	89.86	9.19
Wind 1W	13.37	89.93	23.28
Wind	5.53	88.33	10.41

Table 5: Precision, Recall, F1 measures for the PLEARN algorithm on the training parts of the corpus

A second algorithm used a clustering approach, thus we'll refer to it as "CLUS" for the purposes of this paper. In this case we worked under the assumption that terms belonging to a particular domain will tend to cluster together because they will be related in meaning. In order to model this relation, we represented the words using word embeddings and used the cosine distance. For the clustering algorithm, we implemented a DBSCAN algorithm (Ester et al., 1996).

The input for the clustering algorithm was composed of the terms identified by the PLEARN algorithm. From these terms we kept only the single word terms. Furthermore, we decided to use an approach similar to the one used in TextRank to compose at the end multi-word terms based on the colocation of single word terms. This last operation was done in a post-processing step.

For the word embedding representation we considered necessary to use a model trained on a large enough corpus to allow for words to be used in different domains, including those of interest for this work. Therefore, we decided to use a word embeddings model trained on the Open American National Corpus (Ide, 2008). Furthermore, due to the relatively short time available for the task participation, we decided to use a pre-trained model[3]. Results are given in Table 6.

This algorithm already has a much better F1 score for single word terms then all the other algorithms tested. In the case of the "wind" section the F1 score is almost double (45.02%) then the best previous result (22.79%).

	P%	R%	F1%
Equi 1W	42.37	48.98	45.44
Equi	32.58	33.97	33.26
Corp 1W	44.14	28.49	34.62
Corp	36.46	12.27	18.36
Wind 1W	40.71	50.35	45.02
Wind	36.45	21.58	27.11

Table 6: Precision, Recall, F1 measures for the CLUS algorithm on the training parts of the corpus

Since the CLUS algorithm works on single word terms and only in the post-processing step combines them to create multi-word terms, we decided to work on a third algorithm that would work directly with multi-word expression candidates.

The third (and last) algorithm that we developed is called WEMBF (word embeddings filtered) and, as its name implies, uses the word embeddings vector representation of words to measure the termhood of each word. The algorithm executes the following steps:

1) Tokenizes and POS tags all text files of the specified domain of the corpus, using the NLTK Python library (Bird et al., 2009);

2) Extracts all NPs from the domain sub-corpus, using simple prenominal-nominal patterns, including all prepositional phrases headed by the preposition 'of', which are almost always attached to the previous NP. Furthermore, it deletes any determiners that start NPs and removes URLs, emails, numbers and other entities considered to be irrelevant for the term extraction task;

3) For each content word (i.e. nouns, adjectives, adverbs and verbs) of each NP, computes a cosine distance between two word embeddings vectors. The first vector is obtained from training on a "general"-domain corpus containing news, literature, sports, etc., being careful *not to include* texts from the domain of interest. The second vector is obtained from training only on the domain of interest (e.g. 'wind');

---

[3] https://data.world/jaredfern/oanc word embeddings

4) Score each NP by averaging the previously computed cosine distance of its member content words.

Step 4 of the WEMBF algorithm gives us a preliminary term list on the assumption that the larger the cosine distance of the general and domain word embeddings vectors is, the more likely is that the word is a term in the domain of interest. However, the obtained list contains too many NPs which makes it perform poorly in terms of precision. Thus, we decided to remove some term NPs from this initial list, using the following filters:

a) Only keep NPs which appear (are embedded) in other NPs from the preliminary term list (Frantzi and Ananiadou, 1996). The number of occurrences (in other NPs) is kept for each surviving NP to be rescored later;

b) Remove all single-word terms that appear as head nouns in other NPs on the assumption that if they can be modified, they are too general to be kept as terms.

The termhood score of each NP in the final list is modified by multiplying the following indicators: the original score of the NP, the number of words in the NP, the number of NPs in which this NP appeared.

Thus, if an NP has more words, it appeared in many other NPs and its average cosine distance (between the general domain and the domain of interest) of its member content words is higher, the NP is more likely to be a term.

Results of the WEMBF term extraction algorithm are given in Table 8.

	P%	R%	F1%
Equi 1W	30.48	41.06	34.99
Equi	32.83	31.49	32.15
Corp 1W	15.42	52.79	23.86
Corp	16.50	36.80	22.78
Wind 1W	7.72	52.65	13.47
Wind	8.97	38.72	14.56

Table 8. Precision, Recall, F1 measures for the WEMBF algorithm on the training parts of the corpus

The WEMBF algorithm has a performance similar to the PLEARN algorithm for single words, even though with a more balanced precision and recall, but better performance for multi-word terms.

The final step in our approach was to construct an ensemble module that takes the annotations from different algorithms and combines them together via a voting scheme. This is presented schematically in Figure 1.

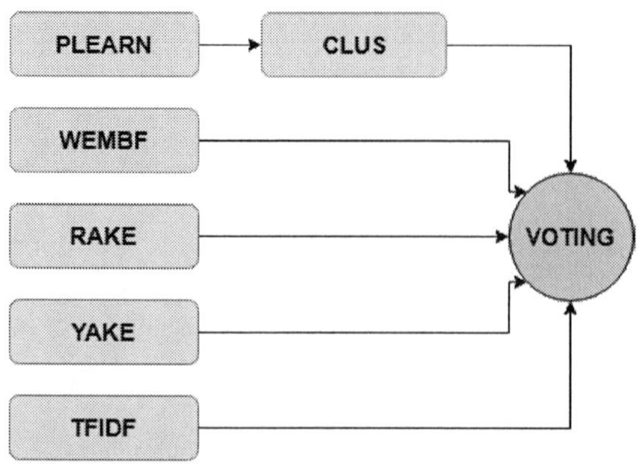

Figure 1. RACAI's term extraction system architecture that participated in TermEval 2020

Each algorithm is fed into the voting module, having one vote for the final result. An exception is in the case of PLEARN and CLUS algorithms which are linked together and thus constitute a single vote.

5. System evaluation

Once the test set annotations were released, we were able to evaluate our system, including all the other algorithms on the final data. When comparing this information with results based on the different training sections, we must keep in mind the peculiarities of each section of the corpus, as presented in Table 1 above. Evaluation results on the "heart failure" section are presented in Table 9.

Our CLUS algorithm performed best on the single word terms giving an F1 score of 53.48 with balanced precision and recall. Furthermore, the PLEARN algorithm produced the best recall, which was to be expected since it was designed especially for this purpose. However, the final algorithm with the combination of all of them did perform better on the multi-word terms, this being reflected in the final F1 score.

	P%	R%	F1%
TFIDF 1W	23.22	24.27	23.74
TFIDF	12.57	15.67	13.95
RAKE 1W	29.79	58.29	39.43
RAKE	19.48	58.88	29.27
YAKE 1W	28.93	62.22	39.50
YAKE	11.11	54.89	18.47
TRANK 1W	32.72	42.39	36.93
TRANK	28.93	22.28	25.17
PLEARN 1W	24.53	90.94	38.64
PLEARN	6.45	87.12	12.02
CLUS 1W	**49.11**	**58.72**	**53.48**
CLUS	41.17	35.82	38.31
WEMBF 1W	38.32	32.82	35.36
WEMBF	38.98	20.74	27.07
FINAL 1W	42.20	67.95	52.06
FINAL	42.40	40.27	41.31

Table 9. Precision, Recall, F1 measures of different algorithms on the evaluation set ("heart failure").

6. Conclusions and future work

This paper presented our system proposal[4] for the TermEval 2020 shared task. We started by investigating the performance of existing algorithms. Then went on and created three new algorithms: PLEARN, CLUS and WEMBF as described in section 4. Finally, we constructed an ensemble module, based on voting, which combined the results of all the algorithms in order to produce the final results. Evaluation on the "heart failure" dataset is presented in Table 9 above.

The approach behind the ACTER dataset, of building a term annotated corpus in multiple languages is very interesting and it was extremely helpful for building our automatic term extractor system. It is our hope that this or

---

[4] https://github.com/racai-ai/TermEval2020

a similar approach could be used for Romanian language as well. In this context, we envisage extending our term extractor to support Romanian language and further include it in the RELATE platform (Păiş et al., 2019) dedicated to processing Romanian language.

We managed to successfully use pre-trained word embeddings on a large corpus for our CLUS algorithm. This proves that transfer learning is a possibility that should be explored also in the field of term extraction. Therefore, amongst our future work we'll try to use the same approach for the Romanian language, by using pre-trained word embeddings (Păiş and Tufiş, 2018) on the Reference Corpus of Contemporary Romanian Language (CoRoLa) (Mititelu et al., 2018).

7. Acknowledgements

Part of this work was conducted in the context of the ReTeRom project. Part of this work was conducted in the context of the Marcell project.

8. Bibliographical References

Bird, S., Klein, E. and Loper, E. (2009) Natural Language Processing with Python --- Analyzing Text with the Natural Language Toolkit. O'Reilly Media; available online at http://www.nltk.org/book_1ed/.

Brin, S. and Page, L. (1998). The anatomy of a large-scale hypertextual Web search engine. *Computer Networks and ISDN Systems*, 30(1–7).

Campos, R., Mangaravite, V., Pasquali, A., Jatowt, A., Jorge, A., Nunes, C. and Jatowt, A. (2020). YAKE! Keyword Extraction from Single Documents using Multiple Local Features. In *Information Sciences Journal*. Elsevier, Vol 509, pp 257-289.

Ester, M., Kriegel, H. P., Sander, J. and Xu, X. (1996). A density-based algorithm for discovering clusters in large spatial databases with noise. In *Proceedings of the Second International Conference on Knowledge Discovery and Data Mining (KDD-96)*,pp 226-231.

Felber, H. (1984). Terminology Manual. Paris: International Information Centre for Terminology.

Firoozeh, N., Nazarenko, A., Alizon, F. and Daille, B. (2019). Keyword extraction: Issues and methods. Natural Language Engineering, pages 1-33, Cambridge University Press.

Fox, C. (1989). A stop list for general text. *ACM SIGIR Forum*, vol. 24, pp. 19–21. ACM, New York, USA.

Frantzi, K. T. and Ananiadou, Sophia. (1996) Extracting Nested Collocations. In Proceedings of the 16th conference on Computational Linguistics - Volume 1, pages 41—46, Association for Computational Linguistics.

Gupta, S., Mittal, N., & Kumar, A. (2016). Rake-pmi automated keyphrase extraction: An unsupervised approach for automated extraction of keyphrases. In *Proceedings of the International Conference on Informatics and Analytics,* pp. 1-6.

Ide, N. (2008). The American National Corpus: Then, Now, and Tomorrow. In Michael Haugh, Kate Burridge, Jean Mulder and Pam Peters (eds.), *Selected Proceedings of the 2008 HCSNet Workshop on Designing the Australian National Corpus: Mustering Languages*, Cascadilla Proceedings Project, Sommerville, MA.

Kageura, K.; Umino, B. (1998). Methods of automatic term recognition. Terminology. 3(2):259-289.

Manning, C.D., Surdeanu, M., Bauer, J., Finkel, J., Bethard, S.J. and McClosky, D. (2014). The Stanford CoreNLP Natural Language Processing Toolkit. In *Proceedings of the 52nd Annual Meeting of the Association for Computational Linguistics: System Demonstrations*, pp. 55-60.

Mihalcea, R., Tarau, P. (2004). TextRank: Bringing Order into Text. In *Proceedings of the 2004 Conference on Empirical Methods in Natural Language Processing EMNLP 2004*, pp 404-411.

Mititelu, B.V., Tufiş, D. and Irimia, E. (2018). The Reference Corpus of Contemporary Romanian Language (CoRoLa). In *Proceedings of the 11th Language Resources and Evaluation Conference – LREC'18*, Miyazaki, Japan, European Language Resources Association (ELRA).

Pazienza M.T., Pennacchiotti M. and Zanzotto F.M. (2005). Terminology Extraction: An Analysis of Linguistic and Statistical Approaches. In: Sirmakessis S. (eds) Knowledge Mining. Studies in Fuzziness and Soft Computing, vol 185. Springer, Berlin, Heidelberg

Păiş, V., Tufiş, D. (2018). Computing distributed representations of words using the COROLA corpus. In *Proceedings of the Romanian Academy*, Series A, Volume 19, Number 2/2018, pp. 403–409.

Păiş, V., Tufiş, D. and Ion, R. (2019). Integration of Romanian NLP tools into the RELATE platform. In *Proceedings of the International Conference on Linguistic Resources and Tools for Processing Romanian Language – CONSILR 2019*, pages 181-192.

Rigouts Terryn, A., Drouin, P., Hoste, V., & Lefever, E. (2020). TermEval 2020: Shared Task on Automatic Term Extraction Using the Annotated Corpora for Term Extraction Research (ACTER) Dataset. In *Proceedings of CompuTerm 2020*.

Rigouts Terryn, A., Drouin, P., Hoste, V., & Lefever, E. (2019). Analysing the Impact of Supervised Machine Learning on Automatic Term Extraction: HAMLET vs TermoStat. In *Proceedings of Recent Advances in Natural Language Processing – RANLP 2019*, pages 1012–1021, Varna, Bulgaria, Sep 2–4, 2019.

Rose, S., Engel, D., Cramer, N., & Cowley, W. (2010). Automatic keyword extraction from individual documents. *Text mining: applications and theory*, 1, 1-20.

Sparck Jones, K. (1972). A statistical interpretation of term specificity and its application in retrieval. Journal of Documentation, 28:11-21.

Proceedings of the 6th International Workshop on Computational Terminology (COMPUTERM 2020), pages 106–113
Language Resources and Evaluation Conference (LREC 2020), Marseille, 11–16 May 2020

TermEval 2020: Using TSR Filtering Method to Improve Automatic Term Extraction

Antoni Oliver, Mercè Vàzquez
Universitat Oberta de Catalunya
Barcelona (Spain)
aoliverg, mvazquezga@uoc.edu

Abstract

The identification of terms from domain-specific corpora using computational methods is a highly time-consuming task because terms have to be validated by specialists. In order to improve term candidate selection, we have developed the Token Slot Recognition (TSR) method, a filtering strategy based on terminological tokens which is used to rank extracted term candidates from domain-specific corpora. We have implemented this filtering strategy in TBXTools. In this paper we present the system we have used in the TermEval 2020 shared task on monolingual term extraction. We also present the evaluation results for the system for English, French and Dutch and for two corpora: corruption and heart failure. For English and French we have used a linguistic methodology based on POS patterns, and for Dutch we have used a statistical methodology based on n-grams calculation and filtering with stop-words. For all languages, TSR (*Token Slot Recognition*) filtering method has been applied. We have obtained competitive results, but there is still room for improvement of the system.

Keywords: Automatic Terminology Extraction, TSR, Token Slot Recognition

1. Introduction

Automatic Term Extraction (ATE) has been considered a relevant Natural Language Processing task involving terminology since the early 1980s, due to its accurate terminology construction that can improve a wide range of tasks, such as ontology learning, computer-assisted translation or information retrieval. However, automatic term extraction methods implemented up to now usually involve extracting a large list of term candidates that has to be manually selected by specialists (Bourigault et al., 2001; Vivaldi and Rodríguez, 2001), a highly time-consuming activity and a repetitive task that poses the risk of being unsystematic, and very costly in economic terms (Loukachevitch, 2012; Conrado et al., 2013; Vasiljevs et al., 2014).

In order to achieve a more accurate term candidate selection, we implemented the Token Slot Recognition (TSR) method, a filtering strategy based on terminological tokens used to rank extracted term candidates from domain-specific corpora. The TSR filtering method has been implemented in TBXTools, a term extraction tool, and can be used both with statistical and linguistic term extraction (Oliver and Vàzquez, 2015).

The main goal of this paper is to determine whether the TSR filtering method could provide an accurate term candidate's selection from the Annotated Corpora for Term Extraction Research (ACTER) Dataset (Rigouts Terryn et al., 2019), provided by the organizers of the TermEval 2020 shared task on monolingual term extraction (Rigouts Terryn et al., 2020). The TSR filtering method is based on reference terms to provide a precise term candidate selection.

This paper is structured as follows: in Section 2, the background of automatic term extraction is described. In Sections 3 and 4, the TSR filtering method and the TBXTools are described. In Section 5, the experimental part is presented. In section 6 the discussion about the obtained results is presented. The paper is concluded with some final remarks and ideas for future research.

2. Automatic terminology extraction

Under the generic name of *Automatic Terminology Extraction* (ATE) we can find a series of techniques and algorithms for the detection of terms in corpora. ATE programs provide a list of term candidates, that is, a set of words or group of words with high probability of being terms. Results of the ATE programs should be revised by human specialists. The methods for ATE can be classified in two main groups: (Pazienza et al., 2005):

- Statistical methods: term extraction is performed based on statistical properties (Salton et al., 1975) and usually implies the calculation of n-grams of words and filtering them with a list of stop-words. Although the most common and easiest to implement statistical property is the term candidate frequency, a long set of statistical measures and other approaches have been developed for term candidate scoring and ranking (Evert and Krenn, 2001; Vàzquez and Oliver, 2013; Astrakhantsev et al., 2015).

- Linguistic methods (Bourigault, 1992): term extraction is performed based on linguistic properties. Most of the systems use a set of predefined morphosyntactic patterns (Evans and Zhai, 1996). After term candidates are extracted using the patterns, a set of statistical measures, the simplest of them being the frequency, are also used to rank the candidates (Daille et al., 1994).

Most of the systems may be considered as hybrid, as they use both approaches in a higher or lesser extent (Earl, 1970). A recent study indicates that the hybrid approaches are the most relevant, and the strategies that use noun identification, compound terms and TF-IDF metrics are the most significant (Valaski and Malucelli, 2015).

In the last few years a semantic and contextual information is used to improve term extraction systems. The first one involves using lexical semantic categories from an external lexical source of the corpus, such as WordNet (Miller, 1995). The second one involves extracting the semantic categories of the words from the same corpus through contextual elements that refer to the syntactic-semantic combination of words (Velardi et al., 2001). Recently, external semantic resources are also used for building ontologies in the medical domain (Bouslimi et al., 2016).

As already mentioned, with any of these methods we are able to detect a set of term candidates, that is, units with a high chance of being real terms. After the automatic procedure, manual revision must be performed in order to select the real terms from the list of term candidates.

3. Token Slot Recognition filtering method

To get a more accurate term candidate selection from specialized corpora, we implemented the Token Slot Recognition (TSR) method (Vàzquez and Oliver, 2018), a filtering strategy which uses terminological units to rank extracted term candidates from domain-specific corpora.

The algorithm is based on the concept of *terminological token* (a token or word of a term) to filter out term candidates. Thus, an unigram term is formed by a token that can be the first token of a term (FT) or the last token of a term (LT) depending on the language, a bigram term is formed by FT LT, a trigram term is formed by FT MT LT (where MT is the middle token of a term), and a tetragram term is formed by FT MT1 MT2 LT. In general, an n-gram term is formed by FT MT1 [..] MTn-2 LT. For example: for English, a unigram term like "rate" can be considered an LT unit as it can also be part of a bigram term like "interest rate". However, a term like "interest" can be considered either an LT unit, such as "vested interest", or an FT, like "interest rate".

The algorithm reads the terminological tokens from a list of already known terms and stores them taking into account its position in the terminological unit (first, middle, last). As a list of already known terms a terminological database for the language and subject can be used. If no terminological database is available, a first terminology extraction without TSR filtering can be performed to create a small set of terms to use for TSR filtering. TSR filtering can be performed iteratively to enrich the set of already known terms to use in the next TSR filtering process. Thus, the TSR method filters term candidates by taking

into account their tokens. To do so, two filtering variants are designed: *strict* and *flexible* filtering. In strict TSR filtering, a term candidate will be kept only if all the tokens are present in the corresponding position. In flexible TSR filtering, a term candidate will be kept if any of the tokens is present in the corresponding position.

The algorithm performs this filtering process recursively, that is, by enlarging the list of terminological tokens with the new selected term candidates. In strict mode this is not possible, because all the validated candidates are formed with already known terminological tokens. With flexible filtering it is possible to extract new terminological units, as the candidates are validated if they have a terminological unit in any position. Furthermore, we designed a *combined TSR filtering* variant. In combined TSR filtering, strict filtering is first used and is then followed by flexible filtering.

Using flexible and combined TSR filtering variants the term candidates are processed in each iteration in descending order of frequency. If a term candidate is not filtered out, this is stored in the output stack following that order. Since the process is recursive in these filtering strategies, the term candidates filtered out in the previous iteration are processed again in descending order of frequency in the following iterations. The process is repeated until no new terminological tokens are detected.

4. TBXTools, a term extraction tool

TBXTools (Oliver and Vàzquez, 2015) is a Python class that provides methods to perform a set of terminology extraction and management tasks. Using this class, Python programs performing state-of-the art terminology extraction tasks can be written with few lines of code. A completely new version of TBXTools have been developed. The old version stored most of the data in memory and this provoked memory problems when working with large corpora. The new version of TBXTools uses a SQLite database to store all the data of a given terminology extraction project, allowing us to work with very big corpora in standard computers with no memory restrictions. Using this database we can open again a project, and we can continue to work in the project.

To use TBXTools a Python3 interpreter[1] should be installed on the computer. As the interpreter is available for most operating systems, TBXTools can be used in Linux, Windows and Mac.

A sample script to perform statistical terminology extraction over the corpus *corpus.txt*, using bigrams and trigrams, and filtering with stopwords (*stop-eng.txt*) is shown below. Term candidates are stored in *candidates.txt*.

```python
from TBXTools import *
e=TBXTools()
e.create_project("project.sqlite","eng")
e.load_sl_corpus("corpus.txt")
e.ngram_calculation(nmin=2,nmax=3)
e.load_sl_stopwords("stop-eng.txt")
e.statistical_term_extraction()
e.save_term_candidates("candidates.txt")
```

The use of TBXTools is very easy but some minimal knowledge of Python is required. In the near future a graphical user interface providing the main functionalities will be developed.

TBXTools holds a free licence (GNU GPL) and can be downloaded from its Sourceforge page[2].

5. Experimental part

5.1. Methodology

We have participated in the TermEval 2020 shared task on monolingual term extraction in order to provide an accurate term candidate's selection in three languages (English, French and Dutch) and two domain-specific corpora (Corruption and Heart failure) using the ACTER Dataset.

We report in the sections below the results we have obtained for the Corruption corpora, a manually created corpora with the help of the Dutch DGT of the European Commission; and Heart failure corpora, a manually collected corpora based on a corpus of titles (Hoste et al., 2019). Both corpora are part of the ACTER Dataset.

Two different strategies have been used:

- For English and French corpora: linguistic strategy

- For Dutch corpora: statistical strategy

For all the strategies and language pairs a TSR filtering method has been performed. To use TSR filtering a reference terminological glossary should be used. The IATE[3] database has been used in the experiments. We have downloaded the TBX file and used the *IATExtract.jar* program provided to get a subset for the subjects LAW and HEALTH for the three working languages. Then, for each language we have selected the *full form* terms with a *confidence score* of 3 or higher. In Table 1 the number of terms for each reference glossary can be observed.

The linguistic strategy has been performed in the following steps. In Figure 2 the scripts used for each step are shown:

- Corpus tagging has been performed using Freeling (Padró and Stanilovsky, 2012) through its Python API.

[2]https://sourceforge.net/projects/
tbxtools/

[3]https://iate.europa.eu/

Glossary	Terms
LAW eng	16,055
LAW fra	15,566
LAW nld	14,860
HEALTH eng	29,463
HEALTH fra	29,051
HEALTH nld	28,825

Table 1: Number of terms in the reference glossaries

```
228  |#|NN
112  |#|JJ  |#|NN
40   |#|JJ #||NNS
36   |#|NN  |#|IN  |#|NN
32   |#|NN  |#|NN
```

Figure 1: Example of automatically learnt patterns.

- Automatic learning of POS patterns: Using the tagged corpus and the list of reference terms, a set of POS patterns are automatically learnt. TBXTools can provide a list of learnt patterns along with its frequency, that is, the number of terms that can be detected with the given POS pattern. In Figure 1 an example of the learnt patterns is shown. These patterns are manually revised and some of them are dropped. To decide whether to accept or reject a pattern we take into account its frequency and the examples of extracted terms that can be retrieved using TBXTools. In Table 2 the number of automatically learnt and accepted patterns are shown.

- Linguistic terminology extraction and TSR filtering: the terminology extraction is performed using the tagged corpus and the accepted POS patterns. An additional step of filtering using stop-words and a step of nested terms detection are performed. For English a list of 399 stop-words is used and for French a list of 352 stop-words. As a last step, a combined TSR filtering using the IATE reference terms is performed. As a result, a list of term candidates is obtained.

The script for statistical automatic terminology extraction performed for Dutch can be observed in Figure 3:

- N-gram calculation (with *n* from 1 to 5) and filtering wit stop-words.

- Case normalization.

- Nested terms detection.

- Dropping some term candidates using a rejection regular expressions list. This list usually includes combinations of .+ (any character) \w+ (combinations of word characters, that is [a-zA-Z0-9_], \W+ (combinations of non word characters) and [0-9]+ (numbers). Each element of the regular expression will be matched against each component of the given n-gram. For example, the regular expression .+ \W+

would reject any bigram with the second element containing one or more non-word characters.

- TSR filtering.

Lang.	Subject	Learnt	Accepted
eng	LAW	62	45
fra	LAW	76	58
eng	HEALTH	41	23
fra	HEALTH	88	77

Table 2: Number of learnt and accepted POS patterns.

5.2. Results and evaluation

The number of term candidates obtained for each language and corpus are shown in Table 3. The evaluation of the results has been performed using the term list provided by the organizers of the task. As no detection of named entities is done in our scripts, the sets of terms including named entities are used. In Table 4 the number of tokens of each corpus along with the number of terms are shown.

Corpus	eng	fra	nld
Corruption	1,001	740	358
Heart failure	1,066	900	744

Table 3: Number of term candidates

Corpus	lang	tokens	terms
Corruption	eng	45,218	1,174
Corruption	fra	50,403	1,217
Corruption	nld	47,288	1,295
Heart failure	eng	45,665	2,585
Heart failure	fra	46,626	2,423
Heart failure	nld	47,734	2,257

Table 4: Number of tokens and terms

As the TSR filtering method aims to filter and resort term candidates with a high likelihood to be terms in the top positions, for each corpus and language, we show the evaluation results for subsets of the list of candidates: the top 100, 200, 500 and 1,000 (when the number of candidates is higher than 1,000). The last row of the Table of results shows the overall values.

In Table 6 the evaluation values for the Corruption corpus for English are shown. As we can observe, best values of precision are achieved for the top positions: 37% of precision for the top 100 candidates, whereas we achieve 26.4% for the overall set (position 1001). But values of recall and F_1 show that top candidates results are very low, because we are getting fewer candidates than the current

number of terms in the corpus. To illustrate this benefits of using TSR filtering, in Table 5 we offer results of term candidates extraction without filtering for the corruption English corpus.

Position	Precision	Recall	F1
100	0.23	0.02	0.036
200	0.205	0.035	0.06
300	0.207	0.053	0.084
400	0.21	0.072	0.107
500	0.21	0.089	0.125
600	0.22	0.112	0.149
700	0.22	0.131	0.164
800	0.212	0.145	0.172
1000	0.2	0.17	0.184
2395	**0.151**	**0.307**	**0.202**

Table 5: Evaluation results: Corruption English with no TSR filtering

Position	Precision	Recall	F1
100	0.37	0.032	0.058
200	0.36	0.061	0.105
500	0.336	0.143	0.201
1000	0.264	0.225	0.243
1001	**0.264**	**0.225**	**0.243**

Table 6: Evaluation results: Corruption English

Results for the Corruption corpus for French have a similar behaviour (see Table 7), but we tend to get lower precision but higher recall for all the evaluation positions. The overall results for French achieves lower precision but higher recall, yielding to almost exact F_1 value.

Position	Precision	Recall	F1
100	0.28	0.023	0.043
200	0.285	0.047	0.08
500	0.298	0.122	0.174
1000	0.252	0.207	0.227
1633	**0.214**	**0.287**	**0.245**

Table 7: Evaluation results: Corruption French

The situation is different for Corruption corpus in Dutch (see Table 8), where we achieve worse values both of precision (11.5%) and recall (3,2%), yielding to a very low value of F_1 (0.05). It may suggest that the statistical methodology doesn't work well for this language.

In Tables 9, 10 and 11 we can observe the values for the Heart failure corpus. These values are the one that have been compared with other participants in the shared task. In general, if we compare the results for the Corruption corpus and the Heart failure corpus we observe a higher

Corpus tagging:

```
from TBXTools import *
extractor=TBXTools() extractor.create_project("ACTER-corruption-ling-eng.sqlite","eng",overwrite=True)
extractor.load_sl_corpus("corpus-en.txt")
extractor.start_freeling_api("en")
extractor.tag_freeling_api()
extractor.save_sl_tagged_corpus("corpus-tagged-en.txt")
```

Automatic learning of POS patterns

```
from TBXTools import *
extractor=TBXTools()
extractor.create_project("learnpatterns.sqlite","eng",overwrite=True)
extractor.load_sl_tagged_corpus("corpus-tagged-en.txt")
extractor.load_evaluation_terms("IATE-LAW-eng.txt",nmin=1,nmax=5)
extractor.tagged_ngram_calculation(nmin=1,nmax=5,minfreq=1)
extractor.learn_linguistic_patterns("learnt-patterns-eng.txt",representativity=100)
```

Linguistic terminology extraction and TSR filtering:

```
from TBXTools import *
extractor=TBXTools()
extractor.create_project("linguistic-tsr.sqlite","eng",overwrite=True)
extractor.load_sl_tagged_corpus("corpus-tagged-en.txt")
extractor.load_linguistic_patterns("clean-patterns-eng.txt")
extractor.tagged_ngram_calculation(nmin=1,nmax=5,minfreq=2)
extractor.load_sl_stopwords("stop-eng.txt")
extractor.linguistic_term_extraction(minfreq=2)
extractor.nest_normalization(verbose=False)
extractor.tsr("IATE-LAW-eng.txt",type="combined",max_iterations=100)
extractor.save_term_candidates("candidates-linguistic-tsr-eng.txt",minfreq=2,show_measure=True)
```

Figure 2: Steps and scripts for linguistic terminology extraction

```
from TBXTools import *
extractor=TBXTools() extractor.create_project("statistical-tsr-nld.sqlite","nld",overwrite=True)
extractor.load_sl_corpus("corpus-nl.txt")
extractor.ngram_calculation(nmin=1,nmax=5,minfreq=2)
extractor.load_sl_stopwords("stop-nld.txt")
extractor.load_sl_exclusion_regexps("regexps.txt")
extractor.statistical_term_extraction(minfreq=2)
extractor.case_normalization(verbose=True)
extractor.nest_normalization(verbose=True)
extractor.regexp_exclusion()
extractor.tsr("IATE-HEALTH-nld.txt",type="combined",max_iterations=100)
extractor.save_term_candidates("candidates-tsr-nld.txt",minfreq=2,show_measure=True)
```

Figure 3: Script for statistical terminology extraction

precision value for Heart failure (for example 34.3% vs. 26.4% for English), but lower values of recall (for example 14.2% vs. 22.5% for English).

As regards Heart failure corpus the best values of precision are obtained for French, but the best values for recall are obtained for English. The values of F_1 for English and French are again almost identical.

With regard to Heart failure corpus the worse results

Position	Precision	Recall	F1
100	0.08	0.006	0.011
200	0.15	0.023	0.04
300	0.12	0.028	0.045
358	**0.115**	**0.032**	**0.05**

Table 8: Evaluation results: Corruption Dutch

are obtained again for Dutch, but results are much better than results obtained from Corruption corpus (29% vs. 11.5% of precision and 9.6% vs. 3.2% of recall).

Position	Precision	Recall	F1
100	0.35	0.014	0.026
200	0.435	0.034	0.062
500	0.43	0.083	0.139
1000	0.347	0.134	0.194
1066	**0.343**	**0.142**	**0.2**

Table 9: Evaluation results: Heart failure English

Position	Precision	Recall	F1
100	0.37	0.015	0.029
200	0.375	0.031	0.057
500	0.384	0.079	0.131
900	**0.363**	**0.135**	**0.197**

Table 10: Evaluation results: Heart failure French

Position	Precision	Recall	F1
100	0.44	0.019	0.037
200	0.385	0.034	0.063
500	0.352	0.078	0.128
744	**0.29**	**0.096**	**0.144**

Table 11: Evaluation results: Heart failure Dutch

The difference in the results between languages can be explained by the different strategies used. For English and French corpora we have used linguistic terminology extraction obtaining better results. Results for English and French are comparable, and the differences between them can be produced by different factors: the precision of the tagger for each language, the number of POS tags in the tagset for each language, French having a higher number of tags. This fact can make the revision of the automatically learnt patterns more difficult.

The different results obtained for the two corpora, Corruption and Heart failure, can be due to several factors. Although the size of the corpora for every subject and every language is almost equal, the number of different terms in Heart failure is higher. For example, for English the Corruption corpus has 45,218 tokens and 1,174 terms, whereas the Heart failure corpus has almost the same number of tokens (45,665) but more than twice number of terms (2,585). The IATE reference terms used for the Token Slot Recognition filtering for Heart failure is almost twice the number of terms used for Corruption (see Table 1).

6. Discussion

The experimental results confirm that the combined TSR filtering method we have implemented to identify terms from Corruption and Heart failure domain-specific corpora is productive in terms of precision than recall for all three languages. As for Corruption domain the best results are obtained for English and as for Heart failure the best results are obtained for French. To apply the TSR filtering strategy we have use IATE glossaries for law and health. These glossaries are domain-specific, but for broader domains than the corpora. Results obtained could be enhanced using more specific reference glossaries.

The low results obtained for Dutch may be explained by the statistical methodology used. We decided to use statistical terminology extraction because the tagger we use, Freeling, is not available for Dutch. In further experiments we plan to use any available Dutch tagger, as for example TreeTagger[4] (Schmid, 1994) or Frog[5] (Bosch et al., 2007). We will adapt the output of these taggers to the TBXTools format for tagged corpora and perform a linguistic terminology extraction.

7. Conclusions and future work

In the TermEval 2020 shared task on monolingual term extraction we have implemented the combined TSR filtering method using TBXTools in order to extract the highest number of terms from Corruption and Heart failure corpora from the ACTER Dataset. This methodology uses tokens from already known terms, in this case from IATE glossaries, to search term candidates containing some tokens related to the subject of the corpora. The process is iterative and the list of terminological tokens can be enriched in each iteration, allowing the discovery of completely new terms.

The results obtained from the shared task can confirm that the combined TSR filtering method is suitable for term candidates extraction in any domain-specific corpora. Moreover, the TSR filtering method results would have been better if the reference terms had been more closely associated with the subject corpora.

---

[4] https://www.cis.uni-muenchen.de/~schmid/tools/TreeTagger/

[5] https://languagemachines.github.io/frog/

As a future work, we plan to test the TSR filtering method with larger corpora and in other languages and domains.

8.   References

Astrakhantsev, N. A., Fedorenko, D. G., and Turdakov, D. Y. (2015). Methods for automatic term recognition in domain-specific text collections: A survey. *Programming and Computer Software*, 41(6):336–349.

Bosch, A. v. d., Busser, B., Canisius, S., and Daelemans, W. (2007). An efficient memory-based morphosyntactic tagger and parser for dutch. *LOT Occasional Series*, 7:191–206.

Bourigault, D., Jacquemin, C., and L'Homme, M.-C. (2001). Introduction. In *Recent Advances in Computational Terminology*, page iix–xviii, Amsterdam, The Netherlands. John Benjamins.

Bourigault, D. (1992). Surface grammatical analysis for the extraction of terminological noun phrases. In *Proceedings of the 14th Conference on Computational Linguistics - Volume 3*, COLING '92, pages 977–981, Stroudsburg, PA, USA. Association for Computational Linguistics.

Bouslimi, R., Akaichi, J., Gaith Ayadi, M., and Hedhli, H. (2016). A medical collaboration network for medical image analysis. In *Network Modeling Analysis in Health Informatics and Bioinformatics*, 5, pages 1–11.

Conrado, M. S., Pardo, T., and Rezende, S. O. (2013). Exploration of a rich feature set for automatic term extraction. In *Advances in Artificial Intelligence and Its Applications*, Lecture Notes in Computer Science, page 342–354, Berlin, Heidelberg. Springer.

Daille, B., Gaussier, E., and Langé, J.-M. (1994). Towards automatic extraction of monolingual and bilingual terminology. In *Proceedings of the 15th Conference on Computational Linguistics - Volume 1*, COLING '94, pages 515–521, Stroudsburg, PA, USA. Association for Computational Linguistics.

Earl, L. L. (1970). Experiments in automatic extracting and indexing. *Information Storage and Retrieval*, 6(4):313 – 330.

Evans, D. A. and Zhai, C. (1996). Noun-phrase analysis in unrestricted text for information retrieval. In *Proceedings of the 34th Annual Meeting on Association for Computational Linguistics*, ACL '96, pages 17–24, Stroudsburg, PA, USA. Association for Computational Linguistics.

Evert, S. and Krenn, B. (2001). Methods for the qualitative evaluation of lexical association measures. In *Proceedings of the 39th Annual Meeting on Association for Computational Linguistics*, page 188–195. AWERProcedia Information Technology Computer.

Hoste, V., Vanopstal, K., Rigouts Terryn, A., and Lefever, E. (2019). The trade-off between quantity and quality. comparing a large web corpus and a small focused corpus for medical terminology extraction. In *Across Languages and Cultures*, pages 197–211.

Loukachevitch, N. V. (2012). Automatic term recognition needs multiple evidence. In *Proceedings of the 8th International Conference on Language Resources and Evaluation (LREC 2012)*, page 2401–2407.

Miller, G. A. (1995). Wordnet: a lexical database for english. In *Communications of the ACM*, 38, page 39–41.

Oliver, A. and Vàzquez, M. (2015). Tbxtools: a free, fast and flexible tool for automatic terminology extraction. In *Proceedings of the International Conference Recent Advances in Natural Language Processing*, pages 473–479.

Oliver, A. and Vàzquez, M. (2015). TBXTools: A free, fast and flexible tool for automatic terminology extraction. In *Proceedings of Recent Advances in Natural Language Processing (RANLP-2015)*, pages 473–479.

Padró, L. and Stanilovsky, E. (2012). Freeling 3.0: Towards wider multilinguality. In *Proceedings of the Language Resources and Evaluation Conference (LREC 2012)*, Istanbul, Turkey, May. ELRA.

Pazienza, M. T., Pennacchiotti, M., and Zanzotto, F. M. (2005). Terminology extraction: an analysis of linguistic and statistical approaches. In *Knowledge mining*, pages 255–279. Springer.

Rigouts Terryn, A., Hoste, V., and Lefever, E. (2019). No uncertain terms: A dataset for monolingual and multilingual automatic term extraction from comparable corpora. *Language Resources and Evaluation*.

Rigouts Terryn, A., Drouin, P., Hoste, V., and Lefever, E. (2020). Termeval 2020: Shared task on automatic term extraction using the annotated corpora for term extraction research (acter) dataset. In *Proceedings of Computational Terminology CompuTerm 2020*, COMPUTERM 2020, pages 1–4, Paris, France. European Language Resources Association.

Salton, G., Yang, C.-S., and Yu, C. T. (1975). A theory of term importance in automatic text analysis. *Journal of the American society for Information Science*, 26(1):33–44.

Schmid, H. (1994). Probabilistic part-of-speech tagging using decision trees. In *Proceedings of International Conference on New Methods in Language Processing, Manchester, UK*.

Valaski, J., R. S. and Malucelli, A. (2015). Approaches and strategies to extract relevant terms: How are they being applied? In *Proceedings of the International Conference on Artificial Intelligence (ICAI 2015)*, page 478–484, San Diego, USA. The Steering Committee of the World Congress in Computer Science, Computer Engineering and Applied Computing (WorldComp).

Vasiljevs, A., Pinnis, M., and Gornostay, T. (2014). Service model for semi-automatic generation of multilingual terminology resources. In *Proceedings of the Terminology and Knowledge Engineering Conference*, page 67–76.

Velardi, P., Missikoff, M., and Basili, R. (2001). Identification of relevant terms to support the construction of domain ontologies. In *Proceedings of the Workshop on Human Language Technology and Knowledge Management*, pages 1–8, Morristown, USA. Association for

Computational Linguistics.

Vivaldi, J. and Rodríguez, H. (2001). Improving term extraction by combining different techniques. In *Terminology. International Journal of Theoretical and Applied Issues in Specialized Communication*, page 31–48, Amsterdam, The Netherlands. John Benjamins.

Vàzquez, M. and Oliver, A. (2013). Improving term candidate validation using ranking metrics. In *Proceedings of the 3rd World Conference on Information Technology (WCIT-2012)*, page 1348–1359. AWERProcedia Information Technology Computer.

Vàzquez, M. and Oliver, A. (2018). Improving term candidates selection using terminological tokens. In *Terminology. International Journal of Theoretical and Applied Issues in Specialized Communication*, pages 122–147, Amsterdam, The Netherlands. John Benjamins.